Preservation of Electronic Information

Preservation of Electronic Information

Editor

R.C. Ganguly

ISHA

ISHA BOOKS

Delhi-110009

Preservation of Electronic Information

ISBN: 81-8205-430-3

Published in 2007 in India by
ISHA Books
B-63, 1st Floor, New Gupta Colony,
Near DDA Market,
Delhi-110009
Phone: 9212142040
ishabooks@hotmail.com

Laser Type Setting by: Rudra Computer Graphics, Delhi
Printed at: Salasar Imaging System, Delhi

Preface

We are living in an age where information explosion and information technology are the lifelines which run the world. Advances in information processing storage and communication technologies have completely revolutionised the way information is accessed, and offer innumerable media in this regard. Libraries which were once the cornerstone of all scholarly endeavour are now existing in a digital format, without walls, and equip themselves with various technologies in the age of the internet and other multimedia.

Electronic media, though undoubtedly the most preferred form of collecting information today, presents numerous challenges which hardly show any signs of relenting. Outdated word processor files, old database formats and technology which renders itself redundant after every 18 months, has meant that information which is stored digitally is being lost rapidly due to a confluence of the above mentioned factors. Already, thousands of megabytes of information have been lost owing to the contradictory nature of technology, and unless a perfect, final form of technology is invented which safeguards the information in the most enviable manner possible, there is hardly hope of finding any other solution.

The present book explores at length the various upheavals and changes in the use of libraries as they move from print to electronic and digital matter, and how their preservation in this manner presents daunting challenges. Earlier, print preservation used to be a problem due to the damage caused to books because of age, and now the challenge is that of preserving digital information. The present book expounds, in an erudite manner, the trends, techniques and devices that are in place to handle the situation, and detailed critical insights into the future of this arena have also been include. With its comprehensive content, the book should prove to be an enlightening one for students and faculty working in libraries.

Editor

Contents

1 Introduction

In the paper era, libraries subscribed to and maintained collections of many periodicals, and collections were highly redundant. Libraries invested in a range of activities intended to maintain the usability of what they collected: binding materials in protective enclosures, repairing damage, housing collections securely and in environments designed to prolong the life span of paper, and reformatting deteriorated materials through photocopying or microfilming. With the exception of microfilm masters, the copies of journals being saved for future generations were the same copies being read by the library's current users.

While in research libraries operations were always planned with one eye on the indefinite future, the actions that preserved materials for future generations also served to maintain them for current use. The new world of Web-delivered periodicals is different. While libraries continue to subscribe to periodicals as they migrate to digital form (subscriptions to electronic journals number in the thousands today in most academic libraries), the service model has changed fundamentally.

Libraries no longer receive and store materials locally, and subscriptions no longer provide copies but a license to access.

This change has profound implications for the archiving and preservation of periodicals because it removes two key attributes of the current system:

— maintenance of copies of periodicals primarily for users of future generations; and

— redundancy of copies, which ensures that accidents, theft, conscious destruction, or changes in policy or priority at any given institution do not result in the complete loss of the published record.

Digital materials are surprisingly fragile. They depend for their continued viability upon technologies that undergo rapid and continual change. All digital materials require rendering software to be useful, and they are generally created in formats specific to a given rendering environment. In the world of paper, many valuable research resources have been saved passively: acquired by individuals or organisations, stored in little-visited recesses, and still viable decades later. That will not happen with the digital equivalents. There is no digital equivalent to that decades-old pile of Life or National Geographic magazines in the basement or attic. Changes in computing technology will ensure that over relatively short periods of time, both the media and the technical format of old digital materials will become unusable.

Keeping digital resources for use by future generations will require conscious effort and continual investment. In the new world of digital periodicals, copies of materials are often held by a single institution, and the investments required to maintain their long-term viability must be made by that institution, which presumably owns them. Factors such as changes in the economic viability of materials, the high cost of a technical migration, a new market focus, company failure, or a reduction in available resources all cause worry about whether such continuing investments will be made. Without such investments, materials will be lost. Such concerns have led libraries to cling to paper copies, when available, even while they provide electronic versions of the same material for the daily use of their readers. This duplicate cost will obviously be problematic over time, and the issue of how to archive and preserve Web-based periodicals is widely felt to have reached a critical state. Digital periodicals are surprisingly complex given the seeming simplicity of their paper antecedents, and the level of complexity is growing.

The content of digital periodicals comes in a wide variety of technical formats, varying not just among publications, but within a single title or article. The core content of most periodicals is text. The text of a periodical or periodical article, however, can be created and maintained in a number of ways.

Some current periodicals are composed of digital pictures of printed pages (frequently, these are then embedded in portable document format [PDF] wrappers for delivery and viewing in the Web environment). More commonly, text is encoded in one of several ways. Some simple publications encode the output of word-processing programs in hypertext markup language (HTML) for Web viewing. HTML provides a rather simplified level of content "markup," primarily oriented toward good visual presentation in today's Web browsers. More sophisticated publications, particularly those thought by their creators to be of lasting interest, are frequently encoded in standard generalised markup language (SGML) or extensible markup language (XML), both of which support much more detailed labelling of components of a textual document than HTML does. However, SGML and XML are enormously flexible, and different publishers use highly varied markup schemes (e.g., document type definition [DTD] schemas).

Software to render text marked up in this way must be sensitive to the specific scheme used in the text being displayed. A critical issue with computerised text is the character set used to represent the letters, ideographs, or other components. Standardisation in the encoding of text components has progressed enormously in recent years, particularly with the development and adoption of Unicode by an increasing range of technology providers. Text for most contemporary languages can be fully encoded in Unicode. However, textual documents contain more than letters and words, and many of the specialised symbols used in periodicals do not have standard digital representations, or evolving standards are not yet widely implemented for them. These include:

— mathematical symbols

— chemical formulas

— archaic scripts or ideographs, such as Egyptian or Mayan hieroglyphs

— musical notations

Publications containing such extended characters or notations today use a variety of conventions for storage, and rendering software must be sensitive to these conventions when preparing text for Web display. Periodicals contain more than simple text. Visual materials such as photographs and drawings are extremely common and can be encoded in different technical formats. Increasingly, sound and video clips are found in periodical publications, again in a variety of technical formats.

Advertisements represent particular difficulties for archiving and preservation. In paper periodicals, advertisements were usually tied inextricably to specific issues. With Web publications, although most periodical content is relatively static once published, advertisements seen in a particular context can change from minute to minute or from day to day. Advertisements can be selectively displayed for specific audiences or national communities (varying in language or in response to legal restrictions, such as those for drug advertisements). Advertisements are often delivered from a different source than the periodical itself and in fast-changing, proprietary, and challenging technical formats that try to stay on the cutting edge.

Advertisements represent a rich source for historical research, and their preservation will be of interest. However, archiving and preserving advertisements will pose a significant challenge. There are other new types of periodical content that raise technical issues. Increasingly, scholarly articles are accompanied by "supplementary materials"-files containing detailed research data, further explication of the article information, or demonstrations of points made in the article. These files contain many types of information (statistical data, instrumentation data, computer models, visualisations, spreadsheets, digital images, sound, or video) and come in a wide range of formats, usually dependent on whatever technical tools the author is using at a given moment.

Journal editors and publishers frequently exercise no control over these formats, accepting whatever the author chooses to deposit. More than any other instance of periodical content, these supplementary materials introduce a rapidly growing and essentially unbounded flow of new technical formats that will pose significant difficulties for long-term preservation.

Because digital periodicals are composed of many pieces, frequently in differing technical formats, some form of relationship information is required to map the pieces into a coherent form for delivery to a user. This relationship information can take many forms: "container" formats (such as PDF) that hold explicit or implicit relationships, XML documents, metadata databases, and static HTML documents. Practices for what data are recorded and how they are structured vary enormously and are primarily based on the current rendering and delivery applications a publication uses. One other type of periodical content warrants note. A particular strength of the Web is its ability to link distributed pieces of content, a power as frequently used in digital periodicals as in other types of Web objects.

Such linkages come in many forms: some links are to other content in the publisher's delivery system, where both the link and its target are under the control of the same organisation; others are to independent sources. The latter can be of the casual reference sort; other links to separate systems, however, are integral to the publication.

Some links are standard URLs, providing static addresses for specific objects on specific computers. Other links point instead to intermediary systems, capable of finding the current location(s) of the pointed-to object. In archiving digital periodicals, it will be important to determine the best way to handle links and the level of responsibility an archive has for maintaining the ability to find independent linked-to objects referenced in archived periodicals.

The Open Archival Information System (OAIS) reference mode is a powerful abstract model for digital archiving that has informed much contemporary thinking and practice. OAIS defines roles for three players in archiving: creators, archive operators, and end users. In the case of digital periodicals, "creator" is not a sufficient term, because many players are involved in digital content creation, formatting, distribution, and ownership. A scholarly journal, for instance, can involve any or all of the following:

— author(s)
— copyright owner(s) of the included material (e.g., photographs, drawings)
— scholarly society that owns the journal
— publisher responsible for peer review, editing, layout, etc.
— distributor(s) providing online access to the title
— aggregator(s) that includes an article in an online compilation

At least some of these players have a role in "deposit." It may be useful to distinguish among players who have the rights, the motivation, and the appropriate technical manifestation to deposit materials and to cooperate in archiving. The deposit of materials into an archive involves questions of ownership and rights: who is legally positioned to provide content to an archive and to negotiate appropriate licenses, if required, for archiving? Because digital periodicals are composed of many separately created pieces, the issue of ownership can be complex.

Authors can vary from scholars (who generally, but not always, turn over all copyrights to the periodical owner) to publisher's employees to freelance writers and illustrators. Individual articles can contain separately owned objects, whose owner's rights also vary. The interests of different possible deposit agents vary with the nature of the content, intended audience, and business model associated with specific materials.

Some players' concerns are purely short-term. The economic value of some products falls quickly following publication, and the audience served has little interest in anything but today's information. Such players are unlikely to want to invest in archiving or preservation of their content, but they may also have little concern if others want to do so. Other players may believe that their publications have enduring economic value and may therefore be enormously concerned about independent archives holding copies of their content and, if archiving is permitted, about the terms and conditions of access to archived content.

Still others, such as scholarly societies and original authors, may want to have their materials preserved and may be willing to invest in that preservation. A number of middlemen are often involved between the owner and the user of periodical content. In the scholarly journal example, the publisher, distributors, and aggregators all play the role of middleman. Each middleman has its own systems, and copies of periodical content contained in each system can vary on the basis of the particular nature and function of those systems.

A key consideration in archiving periodical content is the location of an appropriate archival copy: in many cases, the most appropriate copy for archiving may be held by someone other than the owner. There is an increasing belief that archiving needs to be the responsibility of institutions for which it is a core mission, rather than an ancillary operation of an organisation whose central interest lies elsewhere.

Digital archiving will be a technically and organisationally challenging task, and it is unlikely that a large number of institutions will have the motivation, skill, or resources to undertake the long-term archiving of digital periodicals. The great majority of periodical subscribers and readers will, over time, probably rely on a few institutions to provide storage and preservation of periodical content. Archives are likely to differ in focus.

The organisation of archiving activity across institutions involves the following important issues. Each archive must clearly delineate the bounds of its archiving activity. Different institutions may define their scope of responsibility in different terms: by topic, by source of publication (publisher, distributor), by designating selected individually important titles, or by defining samples to be taken across specific literatures. Some level of redundancy is desirable, particularly for titles of potential historical importance.

Both the selection of content for archiving and the specifics of archiving and preservation practice are sensitive to the particular user community for which archiving is being done. Different user communities have different requirements as to what is saved, how it is organised and accessed, the technical formats available from the archive, and the technical and support services available from an archive.

A key observation of the OAIS model is that archiving activity needs to be designed with an understanding of the specified community being served. Relationship to depositors: An archive does not automatically have the right to copy and store the publications of any given owner. In some cases, archiving activity may fall under the blanket of copyright deposit. But even then, unless the conditions of archiving are clearly specified in copyright legislation, the owner of archived material may legitimately require a specific license covering the terms of archiving.

Given the large number of publishers and owners of digital periodical content, the transactional cost of negotiating archiving agreements will have to be minimised. Among the elements that will help are community agreement on archiving parameters and conventionalised licenses for archiving. Archiving will come at a noticeable cost. A key issue in the relationship among archives, owners, and users will be the distribution of costs. Some of the major cost elements involved, arranged roughly in order of occurrence, are as follows:

— notification/identification of content to be archived

— creation of an archival version of content

— creation of archiving metadata

— storage, monitoring, and management of the archival collection

— preservation of archived content

— service to users

The OAIS model suggests that archiving is done to meet the needs of a specified user community. User communities vary not only with the nature of publications but also with the passage of time. While some periodical content continue to be used primarily as originally intended, other kinds of uses become common over time.

The historian of science or the analyst of trends uses material in ways that are different from those of the original audience of a publication. Trigger events vary from owner to owner and from publication to publication. It is interesting to note the contrasting business models in today's periodical environment that are likely to influence a time-based trigger event. Some publishers charge significant subscription fees for current issues but offer free access to back files. Others, including some newspapers and magazines, provide free access to current issues but charge for access to back files. Still other business models may yet emerge.

Unsettled Archiving

All society's progress—perhaps even its ultimate survival—rests on whether science continues to develop. Scientists will discover the cures for disease, hunger, global warming, and other threats to humanity by building on research conducted to date, but only if that research continues to be available to them. Beyond altruism in supporting science and human progress, publishers have another reason to archive. The changes in distribution and the fiscal uncertainties of electronic publishing make it especially important to capitalise on potential derivative—and collaborative—products. Archiving provides the fodder for that kind of product development.

In the long term, archiving should yield both societal and financial rewards. In the short term, however, both librarians and publishers confront financial challenges. Librarians are in a bind because they face demands for more and more services, while their purchasing power has declined. For publishers, costs are escalating for traditional supplier services and new technology costs are appearing and recurring, yet publishers' constituents are less willing or able to pay increased fees for both traditional and new products. We should be concerned about who does archiving and how, because in the last few years we have experienced technical difficulties in accessing data that were stored electronically as recently as the 1970s.

With the emergence of completely electronic publications, the function of archiving, once the sole province of the library, is receiving increased attention from others in the scholarly communication process. We have a bits-versus-atoms issue —publishing in the ether versus publishing on paper.

Information in electronic formats forces publishers and authors to focus on creating the same stability for future access to those digital bits as we have had for the physical page. Scholarly publishers want to calm authors' concerns about future generations' inability to read their work because of technical obsolence. Thus, the publisher must devise methods not just to produce information and knowledge but to preserve it in a form that can be used in the future. As Negroponte pointed out, "media will become digitally driven by the combined forces of convenience, economic imperative, and deregulation.

Archiving is the systematic development and retention of information preserved to assure that people will have access to it at any point in the future. Librarians, who traditionally have been the keepers of archives, consider integrity, accuracy, and predictability the most important attributes of archiving. The functions of preservation and access are essential components of knowledge development, because we build our knowledge base incrementally from the work of those who came before us. The need to maintain an unbroken record of science is such a key scientific principle that hardly anyone questions the need for archiving. Instead, in the 1990s, as roles have changed and the issues surrounding archiving have become more complex, several questions have arisen. What should be saved? Who will be responsible for archiving? How can it be accomplished?

How can archiving be financed? Archivists attempting to preserve paper face natural threats such as light, moisture, and heat; organic threats such as rodents and insects; and chemical threats such as acid content, air pollution, and plastic. Ironically, the threats to preservation seem to have increased with the advent of the digital age. Not only are electronic products vulnerable to the same enemies that threaten paper, they face new problems. The most serious of these is obsolescence.

Data degradation is a concern, as is the ease with which a document can be changed, either deliberately or by accident, is an issue as well. Human carelessness and maliciousness, always threats to preservation of a document, may be even more dangerous for electronic products. How can we be certain which is the authentic version? There are no standards yet in place for maintaining digital information or for recording the incremental changes that are inserted because the technology enables the delivery of fluid documents. Collection managers noted that top-level administrators often do not understand the strain that digital collections place on their resources or the need for standards, planning, infrastructure, and models of best practices. The actual substance of the content may be no different from a print product, although the presentation may be very different if it includes video, animation, 3-D, and so forth.

For a print product, the context, or provenance, is apparent in the container: the book, journal, or reference work. Provenance is not as clear for electronic products. Because digital information is so fluid—so easily changed without evidence—authentication is particularly important. Librarians have long made archival decisions based on criteria such as usage, quality, and substantiation. Publishers can develop a similar set of criteria to accept or reject material for an archive.

Saving multiple versions of the same basic document only confuses readers. Many ephemeral documents, such as informal publications or the contents of electronic bulletin boards, may not warrant saving. The problem is that someone must make decisions, and recognising the material that will have long-term value is extraordinarily difficult. Determining what should be retained requires intellectual judgment from a broad perspective. Unfortunately, many archiving decisions in history were made from a narrower viewpoint. For digital information, accessibility in terms of hardware and software is another criterion. Although the word systematic is often used in conjunction with archiving, there are no national or international standards or agreements by discipline for how material slated for preservation should be selected. In the end, happenstance may play more of a part in determining what is preserved than we would like to think.

Popularity and ongoing use are almost always guarantors that works will be preserved. For those materials that are sought after, the redundancy that is essential to assure survival occurs naturally as multiple copies are made and kept. Traditionally, libraries have borne responsibility for archiving; in fact, the term research library is often used synonymously with archives. Publishers, authors, and the community at large have looked to libraries to maintain the entire corpus of our knowledge. While scientific knowledge grew rapidly, particularly in the 40-plus years after Sputnik in 1957, library resources declined.

At the same time, the growth of digital information exacerbated the demands on libraries. At the end of the 20th century, publishers must assume some of the burden of maintaining archives.

There are significant advantages to the publisher who takes on the role of archivist. For example, at a point when many authors and some librarians are questioning the value the publisher brings to the business, assuring perpetual access is a strong reinforcement of the added value the publisher provides. A commitment to ongoing access signals a clear commitment to the discipline the publisher serves and to the individuals in that discipline. There are other business reasons for archiving as well.

Developing an archive of materials that can be put together in various ways for derivative products makes it possible to reach different market segments with a different combination of the same information, perhaps in different medium. That is not to say that taking on the responsibilities of archiving is either inexpensive or profitable, just that some returns are possible. Solutions for the unsettled state of archiving will involve not just technology, but legal and social change. And there are many hurdles to leap, including lack of standardisation and resolution of ownership issues. The technology solutions are likely to be the easiest, and social change the most difficult.

Authors of scholarly articles are motivated by many compelling reasons: claim to discovery, tenure, promotion, and peer recognition. They also want their work to join the larger corpus of knowledge within a discipline, to become a part of history. Contribution to scholarship has become a standard for the career quest of the academic researcher, and to some extent for those toiling in industry and government.

Every scholar predicates his or her own line of inquiry on an awareness of previous research. That awareness can come only from access to a well-preserved archive of subject literature. The archive of a scholarly discipline constitutes a larger knowledge base -- an unbroken record of research upon which successive generations can build. How well the record of scholarship will be preserved depends on resolving some critical issues. Historically, at least in the United States, the archive for any discrete subdiscipline could be found in the library of record designated by mutual agreement among the members of the Research Libraries Group.

With the economic and physical constraints of the last few decades weighing heavily on libraries, it can no longer be assumed that those institutions will accept the burden of archiving all information in all media, and be responsible for migrating it from technology to technology over the years. One clear advantage of archiving information in well-tagged, platform-independent formats is the potential for creating derivative products.

Publishers, faced with the increased financial risks associated with electronic publishing and archiving, need to obtain all rights in all media to protect their opportunities to obtain a return on their investment. They believe it is essential that they control the distribution of a product to avoid wholesale copying and piracy that impinges on their revenues. They also want to protect the value they add in bringing the product to market.

The publishers' added value traditionally starts with gathering and selection; continues with editing, production, marketing, and dissemination; and is completed with rights and permissions. Authors, on the other hand, are increasingly reluctant to sign over their ownership to publishers. The litany heard in various forums has been that the university finances the research, the author invests time and intellectual capital, and the publisher reaps the reward.

Publishers traditionally have been leery of any free distribution that might encroach on their sales; however, many are now sanctioning more distribution by authors. Because publisher policies vary widely at this point, it is likely to be some time before a clear standard evolves. And how that standard affects the economics of publishing may not be evident for even longer. When libraries began to purchase electronic products, they found that they were buying access to information that would be theirs only as long as they continued to subscribe. If they discontinued the subscription, they could no longer make even the old information, for which they had paid, available to their patrons. Clearly, they lost the ability to serve as an archive.

As publishers and librarians have negotiated site licenses and debated the issues, there has been movement to establish a standard for maintaining access to the information previously obtained when subscriptions lapse. The impact of the Digital Millennium Copyright Act and Copyright Term Extension, both passed in 1998, will be felt throughout scholarly communication. Scholars in different disciplines have specific idiosyncrasies, and most products have some unique features. However, consumers do have general expectations for all digital products that include the following:

— greater functionality
— more rapid delivery
— more value for cost
— cross-publisher databases
— streamlined licensing agreements
— ability to identify fragments of content
— clear understanding of any limitations.

As new technologies become more commonplace, customer expectations rise exponentially. Customers want high quality information, and they want it cheap and fast. The information that now comes quickly from the action of a few keystrokes in the past would have taken travel to a library and minutes, if not hours, of searching. Along with speed, however, we must consider quality. The age-old production triangle of time, quality, and cost does not change across media.

To produce a timely, peer-reviewed, high-quality publication—whether the container is wood pulp or plastic—will still demand attention to process and, therefore, a price that reflects the cost of that process. With the "information wants to be free" attitude that prevails on the Internet, distributing a scholarly journal's content electronically becomes more than a technological challenge for today's access and tomorrow's archive, it is a financially dubious prospect. That financial uncertainty is underlined by the differently evolving acceptance of electronic publishing in different disciplines.

Indeed, market research must be done discipline by discipline. What is acceptable to a historical scholar may not satisfy an entomologist, or a civil engineer, or a cardiologist. Moreover, the acceptance of electronic publishing may depend on the age of the customer, even within the discipline. Many proponents of e-journals feel secure in their opinions that the archival component will be of little interest to future scholars. If today's researchers are any measure, then at least for disciplines based on historical records, that will not be the case.

As technology for electronic communication evolved through the 1970s, 1980s, and early 1990s, we imagined that it would solve all our communications problems. Paper shortages, postal strikes, bulging bookshelves, and escalating costs would recede from our memories. Technology is changing so rapidly that it is no longer possible for anyone to keep up. Specialists can have in-depth knowledge of only very narrow fields, whereas generalists can hope only to recognise terminology when it comes into popular use and perhaps recall that they knew specific advances were under way. Computer obsolescence occurs with frightening speed. A two-year-old computer is nearly an antique. To maintain archives and develop new systems, publishers and librarians are finding that they need to upgrade equipment regularly.

And each upgrade, whether it is just a component or an entirely new system, introduces the need for training and an allowance for a learning curve, both of which are expensive. In addition, software and hardware do not always follow the same development cycles. The need for regular upgrades in equipment and software has a major impact on planning for preservation and access to information in years to come. To assure that future readers will be able to obtain the information, archivists—whether they are publishers, librarians, or others—must plan to migrate the data to a new medium on a regular basis. Archivists have a variety of options when they are considering formats for preservation.

Some of these formats are very new, and others, such as microform, have been in existence for decades. Microform is a medium (microfilm or microfiche) that stores large amounts of print information in a condensed format. Microform is most often used to archive newspapers, magazines, and journals. Libraries collect microforms to conserve space most especially for rarely used serials. Microform also provides a means to acquire a copy of out-of-print publications (for example, back issues of journals); some documents are produced only on microfiche or microfilm for distribution. All archiving institutions, such as national, state, and local archives, historical societies, libraries, and museums, rely on microforms to preserve their print collections.

Portable Document Format (PDF), a derivative of Adobe's PostScript page description language, allows publishers to produce electronic documents with all the original formats, fonts, and page layout. Often producers of documents delivered on the Web will offer versions in both Hypertext Markup Language (HTML) and PDF to satisfy the consumer's desire for the look and feel of a printed page. PDF was created to facilitate the exchange of information between computer systems, and was based on the assumption that the sender would want the receiver to see the document exactly as it was created.

Some publishers have used it for archiving to assure that they can continue to deliver the same document no matter where it is printed. Although PDF files can be linked and searched, PDF does not offer the robust structuring capacity of Standardised General Markup Language

(SGML).The most efficient way to assure that migration can occur is to use portable, platform-independent formats such as SGML. Because SGML-tagged information can be used in any medium, SGML greatly enhances the potential for long-term access. Kasdorf described several advantages to SGML: it offers powerful and flexible structuring capabilities; it can capture and organise metadata; and it is a hedge against technological change.

In addition, SGML can be parsed; that is, software can automatically verify that all the coding is correct. Publishers incorporate SGML at different stages in the publication process. Some apply it in the editing phase, asking editors to tag the document. Some have added it to the composition phase, and still others tag materials for electronic products after the paper product has been printed. Authors and some publishers have suggested that Hypertext Markup Language (HTML), which is much simpler to use, is a suitable substitute.

HTML has been extremely successful when used to define headers and other parts of documents designed for delivery on the World Wide Web. However, its simplicity makes it less useful for complex materials such as journals and books. Extensible Markup Language (XML) is somewhat of a cross between HTML and SGML—less complex and flexible than SGML, but more structured than HTML. SGML is an International Standards Organisation standard (ISO 8879, adopted in 1986), and there is also a standard (ISO 12083) for DTDs. However, most publishers have treated DTDs almost as "house style," creating a unique DTD for their own journal program, and some have created new DTDs for individual journals. As we move more and more toward journal databases, the lack of standardisation in identifying items such as references may create some complexities in linking and assembling databases.

Information Management

As keepers of archives assemble more and more information in digital form, the management of the data becomes an increasingly complex task. These digital archives can be large data warehouses that contain information from a variety of publications or databases, in addition to all of the business, marketing, and promotional data.

Managing this storehouse of information requires that we have a way to know what is in it and how the information is defined. This need leads to metadata, or data about data. There are three types of metadata:

— Operations-level metadata, which define the structure of the information in the original format

— Warehouse-level metadata, which define how the data are interpreted when they are integrated into the warehouse

— Business-level metadata, which link the warehouse data to business applications.

The operations-level metadata might contain the title, the author, and other information specifically related to the original content. Warehouse-level data might include when permissions were received or when the content was updated. Business-level data could include the various forms in which the content has been published. If an organisation does not plan carefully, the administration of its warehouse can consume time that should be spent on product development and delivery.

In describing how to build an effective data warehouse, Sigal issued a strong call for standardising the equipment you use in your own operation to avoid incompatibilities and project failure, as well as cost overruns. Storage capacity for very large amounts of digital information has become less of a concern as the costs of storage have decreased dramatically.

Nonetheless it is still an issue. Materials that may be used infrequently can be stored most efficiently offline, usually on tape. If multiple copies are not retained, failure in any part of the system could result in loss or corruption of digital information. Redundancy involves having multiple copies in multiple storage units. A lack of redundancy for all archived materials is an ongoing concern for librarians. In US, the National Register of Microform Masters (NRMM) reports on materials held in microform depositories.

These materials have publication dates primarily from the late 19th and early 20th centuries; in addition, 16 percent were published before 1850, some as early as the 13th century. Over 40 percent of the microforms are in languages other than English, primarily Western European. The "National Register of Microform Masters is itself a landmark in library cooperation," noted Reed-Scott. The National Digital Library Program began on May 1, 1995 when Librarian of Congress James Billington signed the National Digital Library Federation Agreement with the Commission on Preservation and Access and 14 other research libraries and archives. NDLP builds on the experience of two earlier projects, the Optical Disk Pilot Project and the American Memory project. The American Memory project, the primary precursor to NDLP, emphasized digitising "the nation's memory." The Library's development of an SGML scheme is particularly noteworthy as it serves NDLP for historical texts and documents and conforms to the Text Encoding Initiative, an international standards effort.

Basically NDLP will convert into digital form, from the Library of Congress's print and non-print material holdings, a core of primary source material that reflects American history and culture. In addition to reaching a much broader audience, NDLP affords the opportunity for the Library along with other agencies and organisations to mount research and development projects directed to real problems of indexing, managing, presenting, and storing such diverse collections. Microfilming is the most accepted preservation method for textual materials, and photographic reproduction is used for pictorial materials. But as digital techniques are applied, the question arises of whether to add enhancements to facilitate access to the content, and there is the challenge to develop general principles guiding decisions for enhancements.

Other challenges include the establishment of naming schemes, the fact that uniformity of description is not practical, the question of where descriptive information should be stored, and the issue of how to design the groupings of digital objects. In addition, NDLP must provide navigational tools to support access. NDLP's solution for navigational tools is the development of "finding aids" or documents used in searching to locate pertinent materials in the collection.

NDLP has the same concern with access and use of a collection that every library does. Following are the challenges to building an effective Digital Library:

— Develop improved technology for digitising analog materials.

— Design search and retrieval tools that compensate for abbreviated or incomplete cataloging or descriptive information.

— Design tools that facilitate the enhancement of cataloging or descriptive information by incorporating the contributions of users.

— Establish protocols and standards to facilitate the assembly of distributed digital libraries.

— Address legal concerns associated with access, copying, and dissemination of physical and digital materials.

— Integrate access to both digital and physical materials.

— Develop approaches that can present heterogeneous resources in a coherent way.

— Make the National Digital Library useful to different communities of users and for different purposes.

— Provide more efficient and more flexible tools for transforming digital content to suit the needs of end-users.

— Develop economic models for the support of the National Digital Library.

At the 1998 annual conference of the American Library Association, UMI announced its plan to create the largest digital collection of printed works in the world. For their "Digital Vault Initiative" they will completely convert all of their vast microform holdings to electronic format.

Fifteenth century literature, 19th century newspapers, and current business magazines are just some of the items in the collection of 5.5-billion page images, all stored in three temperature-controlled vaults at the company's headquarters in Ann Arbor. UMI built the original vault in 1965 to protect the integrity of the collection, and followed it with a second and a third structure.

Bell & Howell Learning and Information (formerly UMI) expects that it will take several years to scan all of the holdings into a digital format. The work of putting old documents into the Digital Vault Initiative will run parallel to the annual addition of 37 million images of current information. Bell & Howell intends that its online archive will provide "greater, richer depth of content than any other online resource." Library patrons will have access through their online service, ProQuest Direct, to entire documents—with illustrations and photographs with context provided by adjacent stories and advertisements.

The roles are shifting, and publishers are increasingly expected to preserve their own content. Librarians, still leery about how adequately publishers will perform the role, are nonetheless relinquishing some of the responsibility. They have no choice when they do not own the information, as is the case for many electronic products. Even when the access versus ownership issue is resolved, the sheer volume of information to be preserved and the cost of archiving will lead to shared responsibilities.

Canonical Formats

Assume that we can define a canonical form for a class of digital objects that, to some extent, captures the essential characteristics of that type of object in a highly determined fashion. This form may be quite bulky and not necessarily reasonable for storing, transmitting, or manipulating objects. It's an idealised form of the object, without regard to efficiencies. In addition, specific representations of the object may be richer than the canonical form. There may be a hierarchy of canonical forms, some of which are capable of representing much more detail or richer semantics than others. All the actual formats used for storing an object of a given type must be translatable to the canonical form. It is also critical that, while there may be multiple ways to represent a specific object of a given type in a working storage format, all of them should translate to the identical bit stream in the canonical form. Popular working storage formats may include lists of parameters that are not order-dependent. A canonical form must enforce a specific ordering on these parameters. Similarly, a given storage format may incorporate default values for unspecified parameters. The canonical format should be identical whether these defaults' values are obtained by omitting parameters or by explicitly specifying the parameters in question and their default values. There is a long history of buggy software that includes irrelevant data with a stored version of a digital object.

The most common cause of this is the inclusion of uninitialised fields in the stored form of the object, which just pick up whatever data happens to be in memory at the time. Recently, Microsoft issued a set of updates to Word 98 because this program was including random information as part of Word documents, creating a serious security exposure. But from the archival perspective, this problem meant that if you saved the identical document from Microsoft Word on two different occasions, you would produce two different sets of sequences of bits.

Canonical formats can provide a method of compensating for these kinds of software problems. This irrelevant data isn't part of the canonical format, and would be removed during canonicalisation. Because most storage formats are intended to be used stand-alone, they usually include some minimal level of fields for mandatory and/or optional metadata associated with the object. These fields are another source of problems and can be omitted from the canonical format, and thus discarded as part of canonicalisation.

Many different representations of an object in a given storage format may produce the same canonical form. And translating back from the canonical form to a given storage format may not produce a bit-equivalent object.

It is worth noting that some current standards are creating a very complex environment for canonicalisation. For example, UNICODE, which is the underlying character set for a growing number of current storage standards, allows multiple bit streams to represent the same stream of logical characters.

Canonicalisation also helps to make precise what is important about a class of objects. For example, comments are ignored in most programming languages and in most markup schemes. Yet a document with comments is a different set of bits than a document with the comments deleted. The definition of the canonical form will make it very clear whether the comments matter, and this will be represented in authenticity and referential integrity metadata for the object since that metadata will include the name of the canonicalisation algorithm. By signing a canonical form, authors can make implied statements about what they view as the minimal, essential version of the work in question.

As a byproduct, canonicalisation helps define the space available for steagonographic constructs such as watermarks that can be used within a given storage or interchange format without damaging the integrity of the object. This is precisely the set of bits that are irrelevant in translation to the canonical form. Canonicalisation is valuable in notary or registry relationships. In order to register an object with a notary or register, the typical transaction is to pass a hash of the object to the service, which then signs the hash and returns the signed hash to the registrant as a receipt.

2

Information Highways and Services

The information highway is the convergence of computer and communication technologies. Not surprisingly, given its complex array of components and transformative power, perceptions of what constitutes the information highway differ, often according to vested interests. Academics, for example, tend to think of the information highway and the Internet as synonymous. Some use the term 'information highway' as a catch-all to describe the technological revolution, the transformative process that is sweeping most of the globe. For others, the words 'information highway' identify the individual technological innovations that affect our everyday life: most prominently, the Internet, interactive television and electronic banking.

Yet others view it as a massive infrastructure, constituting a 'seamless and transparent network of networks' capable of transmitting a full range of interactive, audio, video, and data services. No matter which component is emphasized, the phenomenon of the information highway is massive, transformative and inevitable, given the enabling power of the technologies involved.

Although the 'information highway' initiative was given its name in the United States, the phenomenon was recognised simultaneously in many places in the world.

Developmental stages differ, however. Singapore was one of the first countries worldwide to perceive and capitalise upon the economic benefits to be gained from the development of an IT-based infrastructure. The incentives were strong: upon achieving self-rule in 1959, Singapore was saddled with severe poverty and chronic unemployment of its poorly educated population. From 1965 Singapore switched to a development strategy of export production, first in the industrial and manufacturing sector and then in technological diversification, a strategy which met with exceptional success. This remarkable result of high-tech leading to information highway development can be attributed to the activist policies of the government in creating macro-economic stability (low inflation, positive real interest rates, sound fiscal management) and above all a liberal foreign trade environment.

Europe, in the early stages of forming itself as a world trading block, had reasons similar to Singapore's to seize upon the economic opportunities provided by the emerging information technologies. Seeking to bolster private sector growth, it did this particularly in terms of research and development. From the mid-1980s, the European Strategic Programme for Research in Information Technology (ESPRIT) has been a remarkable source of R&D funding. Convinced that information technology would be a large factor not only in the successful formation of the European Union itself but also in its effectiveness in global trade, the European Commission established the first ESPRIT programme with the aim of strengthening an already growing information technology industry. The overall objective is to contribute to the healthy growth of the information infrastructure so as to improve the competitiveness of all industry in Europe, not just the IT industry, and to help enhance the quality of life. Outlining plans for the Common European Information Area, it provided the impetus for the establishment at the 1993 Brussels Summit of a group of prominent persons to prepare a report on the information society with concrete recommendations for action.

Although this High-Level Group on the Information Society, chaired by Martin Bangemann, was not charged to advise on the information highway *per se*, nearly all of the recommendations of the subsequent report relate to its development. Overriding the specific recommendations of the Bangemann Report concerning competition rules, protection of intellectual property, interconnection, interoperability and other information highway issues is the urge for the European Union 'to put its faith in market mechanisms as the motive power to carry us into the Information Age'.

The Group also proposed an action plan of concrete initiatives based on a partnership between the private and public sectors to carry Europe forward into the information society. The Bangeman Report, presented at the Corfu Summit, gave way in July 1994 to a European Commission Action Plan (1994) which urged activity in the following four areas: the required regulatory and legal framework for trans-European networks; basic services and content applications; social, societal and cultural aspects; and the promotion of the Information Society. Within the European Union itself, several member countries have undertaken their own initiatives regarding national information highway development and related policies. France, in fact, can rightly be called the pre-information highway 'pioneer' with the development of Minitel by France Telecom in the early 1980s.

Minitel, now an integral part of daily life for French people, both at home and at work, currently offers a wide range of electronic directories including the International Minitel Directory covering over 200 million telephone subscribers in Europe (Belgium, Germany, Portugal, Spain, Switzerland) and the United States. In addition to its directories, popular Minitel electronic services have expanded to include banking, transport information, mail-order selling, tourist information, weather reports, classified advertisements, radio and television information, and various business services. With over fourteen years of online service experience, France Telecom made its approximately 25,000 Minitel services available on the Internet in May 1996 and is moving into multimedia applications.

The United States, meanwhile, was the first government to call for action and advice focused specifically on the information highway. An Information Infrastructure Task Force (IITF) was established by the White House Office of Science and Technology Policy and by the National Economic Council as part of the NII Agenda for Action initiative. The Council was established by Executive Order 12864 in September 1993 to advise the IITF. Major issues for the Council were: the appropriate roles of the private and public sectors in NII development; a vision for the evolution of the NII and its public and commercial applications; the impact of current and proposed regulatory regimes on the evolution of the NII; privacy, security and copyright issues; national strategies for maximising interconnection and interpretability of communications networks; and universal access.

In April 1994 the Council organised itself into three MegaProject Working Groups to explore: the vision and goals for the information superhighway; access to the superhighway; and intellectual property, privacy and security issues. The purpose of the MegaProjects was to frame discussion and draft recommendations to facilitate the full Council's ability to reach consensus in these areas. The Council met across the United States from February 1994 to the end of 1995, receiving voluminous public comment. In March 1995 it published its emerging framework, an articulation of basic principles, the first of which addressed five areas: universal access and service, privacy and security, intellectual property, education and lifelong learning, and electronic commerce.

The Council concluded that the most efficient way to develop the information highway ('super-highway') in the United States was through community effort. Its KickStart Initiatives document offered guidelines for achieving universal access by connecting the nation's schools, libraries and community centres. In Canada, the Final Report of the Information Highway Advisory Council (IHAC), produced in September 1995, addresses many of the issues mandated to the United States Council. It also echoes to a large extent the policy stance recommended by the Bangemann Report. Established by the Minister of Industry Canada in May 1994, with McGill University Professor David Johnston as Chair, IHAC was a high-level group of twenty-nine Canadians from the private sector (telecommunication, cable television, computer and networking technologies), government, education, and other interested groups such as consumers, labour and libraries.

IHAC was charged to advise the Canadian Government specifically on fifteen issues, including competitiveness, culture, access to learning, and research and development. The Council's deliberations were guided by three objectives: to create jobs through innovation and investment in Canada; to reinforce Canadian sovereignty and cultural identity; and to ensure universal access at reasonable cost. The Council also established five principles: an interconnected and interoperable network of networks; collaborative public-and private-sector development; competition in facilities, products and services; privacy protection and network security; and lifelong learning as a key design element of the information highway.

In Asia, despite recent progress in China, the Republic of Korea, Malaysia and Thailand, no country compares with frontrunner Singapore in information highway development. However, it is also important to note the progress of Japan. Despite its history as one of the most 'informatised' societies of the world, Japan was in fact slower than the United States to progress toward formalising its information highway development. This was due partly to the proliferation of government departments and other agencies which claimed responsibility, including the Ministry of International Trade and Industry (MITI), the Ministry of Posts and Telecommunications (MPT), Nippon Telephone and Telegraph (NTT), numerous cable television companies, telecommunication equipment suppliers and media owners.

In June 1993 the Information Industry Subcommittee of MITI's Industrial Structure Council published a report on improving the social infrastructure for the information society. Later in 1993 NTT announced its grand plan, at a cost of US$400 billion, to install optical fibre throughout Japan by the year 2015. Also in 1993 the MPT was framing new regulatory policies for infrastructure development. A new vision for an advanced information society, with Japan taking the lead in Asia in the multimedia industry, was announced in September 1994 by Prime Minister Murayama's Advanced Information and Telecommunications Society Promotion Headquarters. In recent years the ministerial meetings and conferences of the G-7 member countries have provided a focal point for global information highway development by the industrialised nations.

The Organisation's programmes in this area are designed to assist all Member States to respond to the new challenges of the information society. More particularly, they aim to ensure that all sectors of society benefit from the potential of information and communication technologies to support development processes. At the centre of the challenges posed by the emerging information society is the concept of universal access and how a 'right to communicate' will evolve in an increasingly digital world. Access in this context involves not only physical availability and cost, but also ensuring that the user can benefit from the services concerned, with a minimum level of 'digital literacy'. In the increasingly competitive and commercial world of information and communication, the risks of excluding disadvantaged populations are substantial, both within and among societies as well as among developed and developing countries. An important facet of the 'right to communicate' concerns access to telematics facilities at affordable cost by the 'intellectual' sectors - education, science, culture, media, libraries and archives - which have a crucial role to play in the development of national information infrastructures. Another important issue is the maintenance of linguistic and cultural diversity in the information society.

Technology-induced globalisation is seen by many as a threat to local customs, values and beliefs, as exemplified by the fact that, today, a large majority of the data on the Internet is in English. Increased access to interconnected networks and databases raises major ethical and legal issues. These include:

— privacy of information and the right of individuals to check data pertaining to themselves;

— regulation for the content of information circulating through information highways; computer piracy and other informatics crimes; and

— copyright, where efforts are required to extend legitimate intellectual property protection while maintaining access to information.

At the twenty-eighth session of the UNESCO General Conference, a joint meeting of the Programme Commissions discussed the 'educational, scientific and cultural challenges of the new communication and information technologies'. The General Conference also adopted 28C/ Resolution VII.15, which stressed the societal problems of information technologies and potential dangers of information highways to developing nations. UNESCO has undertaken a wide range of activities which may be described under three headings: Overall societal impact, at the global level, of new information and communication technologies. Co-operative links have been established with the International Telecommunications Union (ITU) and other IGOs and NGOs; and various meetings have been or are being organised: Copyright in the Information Society; Education and Informatics; and Ethical, Legal and Societal Aspects of Digital Information.

In 1994, in the framework of their Joint Programme on Promotion of Telematics for Development, ITU and UNESCO completed a study entitled The Right to Communicate - At What Price: Economic Constraints to the Effective Use of Telecommunications in Education, Science, Culture and in the Circulation of Information. This defined a new strategy for ensuring access to modern telematics facilities at affordable cost for users in UNESCO's fields of competence in the developing countries. More recently, a United Nations system-wide, Special Initiative on Africa was launched 'Harnessing Information Technology for Development' - for which ECA, the World Bank, UNESCO, the ITU and UNCTAD are identified as the lead agencies. A large number of projects are under way, in many areas related to new information technologies and information highways.

Examples are the linking of African countries to the Internet, improved access to telematics services in the Caribbean, the application of electronic information technologies to distance education, safeguarding Internet use by journalists and the media, and the Memory of the World Programme. Libraries are also a source of economic development information for our knowledge-based society and for small businesses or others seeking success. In Arizona, people looking for information to write a resume, start a new business, or to nurture their small business, turn to the Economic Development Information Centres (EDIC) in libraries. EDIC libraries have helped people obtain patents, test the potential of markets through demographic information, and helped small businesses find suppliers. Many libraries have legal collections and most state or university libraries have extensive law libraries that serve members of the public as well as all of you. People who need access to the Internet, or basic computer instruction, come to their community library.

And, children begin reading with their parents, go on to story hours, through Internet exploration, college or employment searches and through career skill set changes and elder care information-all at their local library. We are the only public institution that provides life-long service that changes as individuals change. The role of libraries in the digital age, rather than being usurped as many predicted, has been expanded. Libraries provide content through digital collections and perform editorial functions-insuring the information gathered is authoritative, accurate, and authentic. We work with all aspects of the digital divide-the haves and the have nots, the can and the can nots, and the will and the will nots-providing not just access and assistance, but training and mediation. It is not enough to have a computer or connectivity-you have to know how to use it, and want to use it, to be successful in online research.

Public policy, including legislation attempting to protect our economic and security interests in the digital world, has evoked profound disagreement between publishers, some technology corporations and the education community. The resulting discussions have left some fearing that libraries may be unable to provide services necessary to economic growth and life-long learning. Some proposed "downstream" database legislation would replace footnotes with royalty checks-creating even more of a have not population. Information has a life cycle that must be nurtured and respected. Libraries are the heart of a community. They are the only public meeting space open to all without institutional barriers of authority, cost, age, or other restrictions.

They provide a safe physical place for the community to exchange ideas; serving as the information commons of the 21 century. Libraries have always been places where everyone in a community can find common ground. Libraries provide no-cost access for the public to all types of information in a variety of formats and media. They are the institution most concerned with providing a level playing field for all to participate. Libraries invest their resources for you to have access to information. That includes not only making the material physically or electronically available, but also providing services that make the available material meaningful. These services include basic computer instruction, literacy classes, and reference services, or mediation, to help people identify the most useful material in an avalanche of information. The need to provide internet access and these related services is a growing portion of the traditional library role of providing access to the information that people need to live fulfilling and productive lives-or to participate as informed voters in the governance of our nation. "The library is central to our free society. It is a critical element in the free exchange of information at the heart of our democracy."

Libraries provide opportunities and tools for life-long learning. Public libraries serve as the research library for the University of Life. In today's economic culture, continuously learning new skill sets is a prerequisite for economic viability and is frequently not possible within the traditional educational system.

Twenty-first century learners are self-directed and actively pursue new knowledge on an individual basis. Their community libraries serve as both a source of materials and as a resource to help them identify the materials and services that best meet their needs. Such a society must become a learning society in which all people share in the opportunities to increase skills, knowledge, understanding, and the capacity to reflect on and adapt to change. Learning across a lifetime, supported throughout our communities, is increasingly essential to a healthy and productive society. Much of the education and research and development activities which fuel our economy and define our culture are possible because of the legal doctrines of fair use and first sale, and the research assumption of permanence of information through the public domain. Fair use means being able to refer to earlier research, to build on it, and in turn to provide new information for others to build on and use. First sale allows libraries to share materials between institutions (inter-library loan) and to allow you to borrow material to use and return for others to use. Libraries believe that fair use is essential for the learning enterprise.

Fair use is a lawful use of copyrighted material without prior permission from the copyright holder. It means that, for example, a student can photocopy a journal article for research without checking with the publisher first and could refer to that article in a subsequent paper with a footnote. At the same time, licensors of digital works worry about the vulnerability of these technology-based products to unlawful multiple use, and therefore loss of distribution control resulting in a reduced profit. The US Constitution Clause 8 states that Congress shall have power "To promote the progress of science and useful arts, by securing for limited times to authors and inventors the exclusive right to their respective writings and discoveries." Our patent and copyright laws are based on that clause. Congressional authority was intended to be constrained by the concept of originality; the purpose of promoting science and the useful arts; and to operate within limited periods of time.

Historically, copyrighted works have been sold and the purchaser received a right of use over a particular physical copy of that work, while the creator retained the copyright, or the rights to the intellectual property. The owner of a physical copy is free to sell, loan, or discard that copy. In the digital environment, the created work is licensed not purchased. The licensee of a copy might not be free to transfer, or share that copy if the license prohibits such actions. Librarians are concerned that current legislative activity seeking to foster the market place for digital information may result in limiting activities legally a part of the promotion of research. Activities such as fair use, and first sale under gird our educational and research and development efforts. Section 107 of the Copyright Act provides that "the fair use of a copyrighted work, including such use by reproduction in copies....for purposes such as criticism, comment, news reporting, teaching (including multiple copies for classroom use), scholarship, or research, is not an infringement of copyright." The "first sale" doctrine, embodied in Section 109 of the Copyright Act, limits the copyright holder's "distribution right" by providing that once the owner authorises the release of lawfully made copies of a work, those copies may in turn be passed along to others by sale, rental, loan, gift, or other transfer. It is this provision that allows libraries to lend books without infringing the copyright.

The Digital Millennium Copyright Act of 1998 (DMCA) legally implemented United States treaty obligations under the World Intellectual Property Organisation actions seeking to facilitate worldwide electronic commerce, communication, research development and education. Congress deemed the language of the US Copyright Act, previously updated in 1976, insufficient for information activities in the digital age. The enactment of the DMCA began what must remain an ongoing evaluation of the tension between creators and users of information in the technologically changing information environment. Currently, the library community believes that fundamental rights of fair use and first sale have not received adequate consideration.

The seeming inability of the library community to convince the US Copyright Office of the potential negative impact of certain provisions of the DMCA on public research may have long lasting and problematic repercussions. At the most basic level, the contention is that the DMCA and licensing practices may deny lawful library research support activities such as interlibrary loan, the creation of preservation copies, off-site accessibility, long-term availability of works and the use of digital information donated or gifted to the library. There is a fundamental lack of agreement whether or not such activities are lawful under the current Section 109 language (with its lack of specificity) or whether "digital first sale" language should be adopted. Among sections of particular concern are those quoted below-excerpted from the Executive Summary of the Digital Millennium Copyright Act Section 104 Report.

Section 109(a) and the First Sale Doctrine The common law roots of the first sale doctrine allowed the owner of a particular copy of a work to dispose of that copy. This judicial doctrine was grounded in the common-law principle that restraints on the alienation of tangible property are to be avoided in the absence of clear congressional intent to abrogate this principle. This doctrine appears in section 109 of the Copyright Act of 1976. Section 109(a) specified that this notwithstanding a copyright owner's exclusive distribution right under section 106 the owner of a particular copy or phonorecord that was lawfully made under title 17 is entitled to sell or further dispose of the possession of that copy or phonorecord. Section 117 Computer Program Exemptions Section 117 of the Copyright Act of 1976 was enacted in the Computer Software Copyright Amendments of 1980 in response to the recommendations of the National Commission on New Technological Uses of copyrighted Works' (CONTU).

Section 117 permits the owner of a copy of a computer program to make an additional copy of the program for purely archival purposes if all archival copies are destroyed in the event that continued possession of the computer program should cease to be rightful, or where the making of such a copy is an essential step in the utilisation of the computer program in conjunction with a machine and that it is used in no other manner. There were concerns raised about the potential adverse effects of sections 1201 and 1202 [of the DMCA] on the traditional concepts of first sale, fair use, and the archival and preservation exemptions. It was argued that these prohibitions are likely to diminish, if not eliminate, otherwise lawful uses. It was asserted that copyright management information may also have the capacity to reveal user information in a manner that would chill legitimate uses of copyrighted works. Another prevalent concern was that licenses are being used increasingly by copyright owners to undermine the first sale doctrine and restrict other user privileges under the copyright law. These commenters argued that this trend is displacing the uniformity of federal copyright law with a wide variation of contract terms that must be evaluated and interpreted.

This poses a particular challenge to large institutions, such as universities and libraries, in determining legal and acceptable use in any given work. A number of commenters argued that federal copyright law should preempt such license terms. Other commenters argued that Congress did not intend copyright law broadly to preempt contract provisions. They argue that the freedom to contract serves the interests on both copyright owners and the public by allowing greater flexibility in determining pricing, terms and conditions of use, and other options. We hope and expect that the marketplace will respond to the various concerns of customers in the library community. However, these issues may require further consideration at some point in the future. Libraries serve a vital function in society, and we will continue to work with the library and publishing communities on ways to ensure the continuation of library functions that are critical to our national interest. The inadvertent pitting of creators of information against users and the champions of users, of information is a sad chapter in our national research agenda.

In US, many states the discussion surrounding the Uniform Computer Information Transactions Act (UCITA) proposed by the National Conference of Commissioners on Uniform State Law (NCCUSL) engages both sides on these issues. It is important to note that non-negotiated licenses are the particular focus of UCITA-not the millions of contracts for online information that libraries and others negotiate with a wide variety of vendors. UCITA recognises that non-negotiated contracts (shrink-wrap and click on licenses) are a reality and seeks to codify these transactions. UCITA offers some benefits and protections in the areas of non-negotiated licenses, but librarians insist that the importance of fair use should be stressed by inclusion directly into the language of the law itself rather than being merely mentioned in the NCCUSL written comments. Under current UCITA language, a library accused of violating fair use of a computer information product because a click-on or shrink wrap license prohibited such legally permissible use, must first prove that in the particular example in question, the fundamental public policy of fair use outweighs the fundamental public policy of right to contract. And, if successful in convincing a court that this is the case, the library must go on to prove that its actions fell within the legal provisions of fair use.

Libraries believe that fair use is a right, not a privilege and is carefully crafted in the law to protect copyright owners. Four factors must be considered for actions to constitute fair use:

1) purpose and character of the use of the copyrighted work,
2) nature of the copyrighted work,
3) amount and substantiality used in comparison to the work as a whole, and
4) effect on the potential market for or value of the work.

Publishers and producers of copyrighted works often believe that fair use is only a defense to misuse or infringement and therefore should be a privilege to be exercised under certain conditions or for particular reimbursements...in other words pay per use-as if one were to pay for each episode watched on a cable television channel. In the born digital world it is easy to remove information from public access, as well as to trace who has used what information. Both have a chilling effect on research and product development. In the aftermath of September 11th, with a heightened concern about the threat of further terrorist attacks, the federal government quickly attempted to increase national security.

Congress passed the USA Patriot Act to strengthen our federal information-gathering network. The Patriot Act widens the scope of information federal law enforcement officials can legally access, as well as widening their means of access. For libraries, whose user information has had the same level of confidentiality protection as educational and medical records, the Patriot Act violates the libraries fundamental value of protecting user privacy. Providing a safe place for the community to exchange ideas is one of the fundamental principles of the library, and is threatened by this new legislation that allows federal investigators to access the content of email on library computers as well as tracking what sites a user visited or what books and materials they used.

And finally, a number of federal agencies responded to September 11th by withdrawing previously accessible information from the public. Some have removed information from their websites, while others have requested through the Government Printing Office (GPO), that information held by Federal Depository libraries be pulled from public access, or destroyed or items on web sites indicated by GPO access tools are no longer available. The GPO has traditionally requested that information be returned or destroyed for inaccuracies, but since 9/11 information on waterways, nuclear sites, and other potential targets have been removed from access through a variety of ways peculiar to the digital environment. While there may be information there that is useful to potential terrorists, the information being removed from public access also has many legitimate public uses.

For every information resource that a library handles-whether book, periodical, video, or electronic product, there is a life cycle that our educational, political, social, and economic communities takes for granted. When information is created, or born, it is eligible for the full legal protection of our copyright laws to provide a fair profit to its creator, producer, or distributor. Historically, in the print environment, as that information piece aged, it went through phases of discounted market value, public use, and finally entered the public domain. That life cycle-information matures, is used, and enters the public domain-is critical to research and the production of a new generation of information.

The preservation of information, whether in hard bound book or digitally born document, is the final step, and carries a significant cost to the preserving institution. There may need to be a repurposing of intellectual property guidelines and laws governing use of information for learning in the digital environment to ensure that we continue to have access to a full, robust life cycle. In the digital environment, information is first at risk because the market place does not plan well for long term capitalisation or investment-especially in the absence of current profit. As libraries and information users seek to translate fair use and first sale principles into the digital information environment and ensure the right to share for research, they may have to learn new ways to coexist with fair profit.

Similarly, creators and distributors of digital information may have to consider alternative business practices to coexist with fair use. The initial access to information may need to be circumscribed, but that information in the digital world must age into the public domain to protect our capacity for new economic opportunities, product development, and reinvestment through use and research. Currently, we lose many digitally born documents when their creators decide they lack sufficient further market value. At this time, libraries often cannot obtain the legal or the technical means to make even one preservation copy. Therefore, in the digital environment, short-term profitability determines the longevity of born digital information that our children might need. Without a preservation copy the information will not exist.

There are at least two challenges to be met. First, the information must acquire permanence-perhaps independent of the electronic environment, perhaps within it-that ensures that it has a chance for a robust long-term existence, and that it exists long enough to pass into the public domain. That permanence must not be constrained by market factors since it is impossible to predict what information will lead to research break-throughs or new products in the future.

There should be no cost access to the public domain irrespective of format-at least through libraries. Recognition and exploration of concepts including current practices, other cost models and issues of long term custody or stewardship could raise the level of debate as we work towards reconciliation between fair use and fair profit. Currently libraries respect and track fair use, pay in advance through higher initial licensing costs for multiple use, and reimburse for use beyond legal fair use guidelines. As institutions, libraries may pay more up front to make information available to multiple users and the doctrine of first sale allows us to share and lend those materials.

Telecommunication Infrastructure

The essence of the information highway revolution lies in the convergence of information processing and telecommunication technologies. This has eroded the traditional distinction in communication between carrier and content, resulting in several profoundly new challenges, not least of which is regulatory turmoil. Clearly, the technological issues related to the development of the information highway infrastructure are complex, the costs are immense, and with convergence the stakes for the major carriers are extremely high.

Whereas the governments of Singapore and others in East Asia have intervened strongly to ensure the benefits of a strong infrastructure for their countries, Western governments have attempted to stimulate private sector development. In the countries of the West, where the private sector is expected to drive information highway development, deregulation currently holds centre stage. There is widespread agreement that the United States has taken the lead, beginning with the break-up of the AT&T monopoly in 1984 and culminating to date in the signing by President Clinton of the Telecommunications Act of 1996.

In one sweep, the new Act ends United States Government regulations that have maintained barriers between local and long-distance telephone services, cable television, broadcasting and wireless services. In the age of digital communications, those regulations have become anachronistic. The microchip is placing all forms of communication - from satellite-television images and long-distance telephone calls to e-mail and World Wide Web pages.

Finland, Sweden and the United Kingdom have already at least partially opened their markets to carrier competition. Fifteen European Union countries together with Switzerland and Norway, face a deadline to do this formally on 1 January 1998. In anticipation, new players are already investing many millions of dollars in networking and building alliances; for example, Olivetti of Italy has a joint venture with Bell Atlantic Corporation, with plans to team up with France Telecom and Deutsche Telekom to challenge the monopoly of Telecom Italia.

Meanwhile, amid fears that the 1998 liberalisation agreement will be a case of 'too little too late', new competitors in Europe will be permitted as of July 1996 to lease telephone lines from cable companies, railways and utilities, bypassing the monopoly of national operators and paving the way for a billion-dollar trans-European backbone network.

Meanwhile, liberalisation of trade in basic telecommunication services is currently being negotiated at the international level through the General Agreement on Trade in Services (GATS). In the midst of all this activity, encouragement of standards becomes a crucial governmental role. The key to an effective and efficient global information highway, for competition as well as for society as a whole, is interoperability.

Most obviously, open (as opposed to proprietary) technical standards are required for the infrastructure, but because of digitisation this infrastructure increasingly includes content as well as the carriers. Accordingly, international content/carrier standards are necessary for digital compression, data transmission protocols, software, consumer equipment, etc.

The development of international standards in such a fast-moving area of activity is not without risks; at best, flexibility is required to avoid the costly mistakes of going down wrong developmental paths, technical myopia and monopolistic pressures.

Library Service Programming

In this century, library users have changed, the information tools available to them have changed and, perhaps most significantly, the way in which users interact with libraries has changed. Service programming at most academic libraries has been impacted by these changes. To effectively serve 21st Century library users, librarians must strongly challenge their current assumptions about patron needs, service programming, and about their own roles as information professionals. Several indicators suggest that a disconnect is developing between libraries and their users. Users are seeking and finding alternate information resources. Remote and around-the-clock access to library services is increasingly the norm. Providing assistance to information seekers at the point of need is increasingly challenging because the point of need is becoming ever more broadly defined.

As fewer patrons avail themselves of traditional desk-based reference service, increasing numbers of users are taking advantage of remote-access library services that are often served with no option to seek librarian help. Librarians must be positioned to deliver services to this new generation of academic library users whose service expectations and use patterns differ markedly from those of their predecessors. Complicating the resolution of these issues is the fact that many students are arriving at libraries quite deficient in information literacy skills. Traditional library service models often lack both flexibility and focus to respond to these circumstances, but librarians can embrace a new view of their role and work toward positive solutions of these issues.

Central to the development of an appropriate response to current circumstances is a change in perspective, a fundamental change in the way librarians view their role as participants in the educational and research process. The traditional content, or object-centered, view of library service posits that librarians are to acquire books and other information resources, and engage in a variety of activities designed to make them available to users. This view is reflected in many traditional measures of libraries- number of journal subscriptions, number of volumes owned, the gate count of patrons. Indicators such as these are viable measures of the library, but they often do not reflect a true measure of library service. In the face of changes such as noted above, this traditional view of library service becomes increasingly difficult to support.

Libraries should strive to view their service mission from the perspective of the patron. A patron-centered view of library service addresses modern patron needs and alternative ways of using the library, and it respects the time-related user needs that have evolved along with remote access and the increasing number of busy non-traditional students who cannot adhere to a traditional schedule. Importantly, a patron-centered view of the library mission suggests that academic library service programming must endeavor to directly impact the specific learning and research outcomes of the student or researcher. Such a focus will lead the librarian into closer alliances with teaching faculty and researchers as courses are developed and research teams are formed. Rather than building collections against broad goals, collections can be developed to optimise impact on a focused set of outcomes that are germane to the interests of particular library clientele groups. Users will benefit as librarians implement programming that reflects a philosophical change from a content view (number of books, type of subject matter addressed) to a competency view (what students will be able to do having utilised library resources).

If librarians choose to adopt this view of service programming, they will be in an excellent position to remain relevant in a changing information environment and embrace a leadership role in making these changes successful. An effective implementation of this approach to library service programming will address changes in user patterns, provide human service at the point of need, and accommodate instruction in the information literacy skills needed to use these resources. In a rapidly developing environment with limited resources, it is also essential that libraries assess programs, ongoing and under development, and continue that assessment to ensure that changes remain effective. In this new environment of changing services and logistics, users have developed different information-seeking habits. This clientele can often best be served by programming a mix of traditional and modern services.

Librarians are, however, truly challenged to assist users in the effective use of electronic resources when the majority of users are beyond reach of the librarians. These remote users may be found both inside and outside of the library. Patrons working in the library, accustomed to doing many tasks online, are increasingly hesitant to approach a librarian for assistance. Students often attempt to confer inconspicuously with neighbors or attempt trial-and-error rather than draw attention to themselves by asking for help. A user may be working in a part of the library remote from the reference staff, or may not want to risk losing access to a workstation while going to a reference desk.

In a survey conducted by a major library systems vendor, students indicated that they would prefer studying at home but "at home there is no one to help". Human assistance may be presented in several forms: the traditional staffed desk service point; consultation by appointment in the office of either the patron or the librarian; or a virtual presence via a chat or online/telephone connection. Information literacy has been defined in several ways, but many agree on the basic definition that library information literacy is the ability to access, evaluate and apply creative thinking in the use of information from a variety of sources. Students arriving at college are often ill-prepared to grapple with the information resources presented by the modern academic library. Compounding the problem is the fact that many students have come to believe.that accessing and using information is simple, a belief supported by commercial marketing practices and popular usage of the Internet. In part because the Internet is so often billed as easy to use, even patrons working in the library hesitate to ask librarians for help. Popular usage may be easy, but effective research usage is not.

Librarians often presume that students have grown up with computers but, in many cases, students arrive at college with no significant training in information literacy as defined herein. Many secondary schools claim to integrate information technology into the curriculum but, in fact, this training is often neither monitored nor evaluated. Only in rare instances have educational standards been established for such skills. Information literacy training can and should be adapted to local needs, and academic libraries and librarians are most often the best choice for developing and delivering such training. Evidence of this is found in US, Association of College and Research Libraries (ACRL) Information Literacy Standards for Higher Education, where student learning is viewed as a joint responsibility of the university and the library. When the library changes the focus of its mission from a content view to a competency view the library can actively contribute to achievement of learning outcomes.

Most libraries will find that constructing a new service model must be done without the benefit of additional staff. While staffing is always a challenge, it can be turned into an opportunity to begin the development of new staffing patterns, a new mix of services, and to develop new roles for existing librarians. Whether or not librarians choose to embrace the fact, new roles have already been created for them. Many libraries are now pursuing initiatives that are deliberately structured to emphasize direct contact between library subject specialists and academic departments. This results in the enhancement of much-needed consultative services, but at the expense of librarian hours available for either traditional desk-based or "virtual" service.

Even proponents of increased library electronics note that traditional services are an.integral part of any future reference service model. Response to the need for traditional interaction between patron and librarian should not, however, be limited to the reference desk. Remote users may need as much, or more, librarian assistance as in-person users. Technology now allows the implementation of virtual reference services, either chat or voice-based, that can be quite effective in extending library resources to distant users. Increasingly, librarians are finding themselves employed as content developers- i.e., contributors to or developers of a variety of information resources served to patrons across the Web, often through a digital library setup. Web tutorials, specialised "non-acquired" databases, and specialised subject assistance Web pages are representative examples.

Librarians should be paying attention not only to improving library-use instructional resources, they should also be improving the user (electronic) interface so that less instruction is necessary. At some point, it becomes necessary to make the transition from operational theory to actual practice. It is hoped that the suggestions outlined here are sufficiently representative to be used in the development of a service model for academic libraries. Changing user habits and the increased use of remote-access information resources have, in some libraries, coincided with the development of a digital library project. This situation can provide the opportunity to experiment with new roles for the librarians while tailoring the mix of services to accommodate user needs and staffing realities.

Digital library projects can create roles for librarians as content developers-those who identify and/or create unique content for incorporation into the digital library. While it is always difficult to find room in the curriculum for library literacy instruction, librarians can be both creative and aggressive in developing alternate means of promoting information literacy. College administrators should recognise the need for this type of instruction in specific areas of their respective curricula and accept librarians as partners in course development or as members of research teams. If local circumstance indicate the need for virtual, or "chat", reference service, an opportunity is presented to re-examine the role of the traditional reference desk, and re-balance the allocation of librarian hours. Chat reference can also serve as an excellent forum in which to develop inter-library partnerships. These suggestions represent only the beginning framework of a service model. Each library must construct a model of tailored service based on local circumstances. In the future, the most effective academic libraries will likely provide a tailored mix of both traditional and new library services, while developing new roles for librarians that focus on information literacy and personal service to both local and remote users.

3

Library Materials Preservation

In general civilized nations want to preserve the written evidence of their history, literature and cultural development in the broadest sense because it promotes in their populations a sense of integration and self-identification. In a few cases, however, the cultural heritage stored in archives or libraries is deliberately jeopardized for political reasons, for example, to wipe out the traditions of ethnic or other social groups.

The main source of risk is that conservation, as part of a political duty to posterity, is neglected and the necessary resources in the way of staff, buildings and technical equipment are not provided. Though part of the cultural heritage, archives, manuscripts and print do not survive on their own; it takes political will to safeguard and protect this cultural inheritance and to ensure that it is constantly supplemented by contemporary documents of lasting value. Like an empty house, property that is not managed and cared for by trained archivists and librarians, and not made accessible to researchers and the public at large, will deteriorate and disappear. For this reason many countries have legislation and regulations governing the protection, conservation and use of archival property.

In many cases, it is also a legal requirement that at least one copy of every book or printed work be kept in an 'archive library'. Both endogenous and exogenous factors threaten the continued existence of archives, manuscripts and print. Endogenous (mostly chemical) sources of damage are intrinsic to the information medium itself, the way it is produced or even the material used to record the text. Exogenous sources are physical phenomena acting on the media or text from outside.

Damage caused by the combined action of endogenous and exogenous factors is by no means rare. Globally, though, there is no doubt that endogenous deterioration is the worst source of damage to paper. The steep increase in paper demand since the mid-nineteenth century and the related growth in industrial paper production called for new technologies and caused a revolution in paper manufacture. Two primary factors affected the quality of paper: acid sizing with a mixture of alum and rosin, and the addition of cheap mechanical wood pulp to rag-based or cellulose fibre pulp. Acid paper or paper containing mechanical wood pulp ages visibly and quickly, goes yellow or brown and becomes fragile and brittle.

Papers containing both acid and mechanical pulp lose their colour within a few decades, become brittle and crumble under the slightest mechanical load. In books and documents affected by endogenous deterioration the decay is gradual but unstoppable. The process can be likened to a fire, smouldering slowly and unnoticed in the storerooms, secretly destroying cultural property.

Acid or mechanical pulp-based papers thus carry within them the seed of their own deterioration, as indeed do many modern information media such as nitrocellulose film.Another endogenous source of damage stems from certain inks, including the deterioration caused by ink erosion. For example, the iron gall ink still in general use in law offices in the nineteenth century, which is wash-proof and, in particular, bleach-proof, causes corrosion aggravated by damp, even eating through strong rag paper and leaving sharply etched holes where previously there were letters or characters.

The degree and rate of endogenous deterioration are greatly affected by exogenous factors such as temperature, humidity and oxidizing or acid-forming gases. If high relative humidity and heat are both present, and the air quality is bad with a high sulphur dioxide content, destructive reactions such as the weakening of the paper are greatly accelerated. In addition, high humidity and temperatures enable fungi, microorganisms and destructive insects to begin their damaging work.

Unfortunately, paper deterioration and its consequences are not the only threat to property held in archives and libraries. Brittle and limp papers, fragile leather and parchment, splits, holes, breaks and deformations in binding are today part of the almost normal picture in the case of many old books and archives. Dirt and discoloration, marks on texts, paper turning yellow or brown and text bleaching, if they go beyond the natural effects of ageing, are alarming warning signs of the creeping decay of cultural property.

A large amount of serious damage, however, is of human origin. Obviously, when cultural property is picked up and handled, human incompetence and thoughtlessness are major causes of damage. The users of archives and the organizers of exhibitions, not to mention many negligent archival and library staff, need to be constantly reminded that the books and archives they deal with are not consumer goods intended to last one or two generations.

In our efforts to use books, manuscripts and archives in the most comfortable and rational manner, we often fail to take the necessary care. Splits, folds, spots of fat, ballpoint pen marks, bleached ink and damaged or deformed book spines are to be deplored, and there is no reason consciously to cause such damage. The same applies to well-meant but unprofessional repairs with adhesive tape which generally do more harm than good.

Lastly the display of archives, manuscripts and printed works in exhibitions also has its dark side. Long periods under the strong lighting and severe mechanical loading required for their attractive presentation, as well as the damage often caused during transportation, leave traces on the exhibits that cannot be removed.The damage already caused - or yet to be caused -by endogenous paper deterioration is on a global scale but, quantitatively, it can be neither calculated nor even estimated.

All properties in archives and libraries since the mid-nineteenth century are susceptible to endogenous paper deterioration. Permanent paper is found to an increasing extent since the 1980s, particularly in North America, Australia and central and northern Europe, but no substantial use is yet being made of it for paperwork, books and other documents of lasting value. Surveys of European and North American archives and libraries suggest that at least 60% of the items stored in public archives are potentially subject to endogenous damage. In the case of 20%, the damage is already evident or so imminent that the items can no longer be used and conservation measures will be needed to save them from final destruction.

These surveys enable certain inferences to be drawn: in countries with hot, moist climates the endogenous deterioration will advance more quickly if the archive and library storerooms are not air-conditioned; and environments with a high toxic gas content also accelerate deterioration. These inferences are supported by reports from libraries and archives all over the world. The poor state of materials is often thought to result from bad storage conditions rather than the inevitable deterioration of acid paper, and endogenous factors due to acid and mechanical pulp are not fully appreciated as the underlying causes of damage. It is even more difficult to reach any general conclusions regarding the amount of damage caused to archives, manuscripts or printed materials by exogenous factors.

This very much depends on the way the materials have been stored over the centuries, armed hostilities and natural disasters, frequency of use and, last but not least, the resources that have been or are to be used for their protection and conservation, or even simply their cleaning. As an illustration, however, some orders of magnitude for the amount of damage can be obtained from one survey carried out in central Europe and including eleven scientific libraries and six state archives.

All over the world efforts are being made to halt the creeping deterioration threatening to destroy a substantial part of our cultural heritage, the written works handed down over the last century and a half. Many national and international organizations are actively working on the conservation of the threatened property.

Today there is no difficulty in producing permanent paper that is free from the factors that have caused paper deterioration in the past, that is, free of acids or acid-generating substances and of mechanical pulp (lignin). Such papers (neutral or slightly alkaline) are made from cellulose fibre; it is also possible to obtain the latter from a non-chlorine bleach process. This kind of cellulose can be derived from lean wood, thinning or chipwood.

As a protection against acid in the environment permanent papers are given a coating of at least 2% calcium carbonate. The international standards for permanent paper are laid down in ISO 9706. Incidentally, the production of such paper is advantageous both economically and environmentally, and is in tune with current paper production trends. Permanent papers should be no more costly than less durable papers of comparable quality. While the use of permanent information media and writing materials is designed to prevent future endogenous deterioration, other preventive measures serve to avoid or limit damage to objects already stored in archives and libraries and even to extend the life of documents affected by endogenous deterioration.

The objective of these preventive measures is to create an environment for the objects under threat in which ageing processes are checked and exogenous sources of damage kept, as far as possible, at a distance. This is achieved by appropriate air-conditioning for the archive and library holdings in secure and properly equipped storerooms, the first rule of thumb being to have everything as cool and dry as possible, and the second to avoid sharp changes in temperature and humidity. Provision should also be made for adequate frequency of air change. Lengthy exposure to light, and in particular daylight or artificial light with a high ultraviolet content, should be avoided.

Keeping both the storeroom and the articles themselves clean is another effective measure. All property, excepting books with their binding intact, needs non-acid protective packing using materials meeting the criteria of ISO 9706. An international standard on the above-mentioned preventive measures is under preparation. Under the heading of preventive measures, of course, must also come effective conservation management which ensures that proper care is taken in the removal and return of books and archives, their transport and in particular their use in reading rooms. Care is also required for items on display: technical and organizational measures must be taken to protect them against damage and wear.

Timely protective filming of endangered archives or manuscripts is one of the most effective and yet most economic measures of all.Restoration of materials in archives and libraries is by no means the preferred objective. The primary aim must be to prevent damage by employing the above preventive measures. But if damaged cultural property has to be repaired it needs to be done professionally. For the restoration of archive and library contents, specialists have, with the help of scientists, drawn up a number of principles designed to retain as far as possible the original substance and appearance, and to avoid clumsy renovation or reconstruction.For historians and literary specialists, and also for researchers in the fields of binding and codices, inconspicuous external and formal marks are significant. They are often the only pointers to an object's origin, its legal validity or specific history, and should not be destroyed or disturbed by the craftsman. Only identical or similar materials to the originals should be used.

The work must be reversible so that the object's state prior to the work can be restored at any time. The object's appearance must be retained. What is done must be recognizable and the restorer must explain fully what has been done and how it has been done. Lastly, the work must be described in writing and if necessary documented by photographic means. With the help of this documentation, future generations of restorers and scientists will be able to reconstruct what has been done with total clarity. To deal with dirt or spots that cannot be removed in this way, paper should be carefully moistened to dissolve the dirt or else washed in the normal way. Restorers do not like to use bleach or other chemicals as solvents.

Water is little short of miraculous for the restoration and conservation of paper. Water cleans, washes out harmful residues and can be used to introduce buffer substances to protect paper from endogenous and exogenous acid attack. Common media like black printing ink and iron gall ink survive wet cleaning without any problem. Other inks, such as Indian ink and stamping inks, have to be fixed before washing. After washing, papers are given fresh strength by sizing and then dried and pressed. Water treatment can be made particularly efficient using a programmable transport system to time the immersion in a treatment bath of large quantities of paper suffering from the same kind of damage.

The moistening of water-sensitive papers such as glassine or papers printed with sensitive inks has to be done under careful control. Only moisture in the form of vapour, not liquid, can be allowed to act on the sensitive object. The wonder-material that produces this effect is the micro-fibre Gore-Tex, well-known in the weatherproof clothing industry. For books and binding, where costly breakdown into individual leaves before treatment is to be avoided, de-acidification under spray is used. In this technique the buffer substance is applied to the paper in a very fine spray. Splits in paper are made good with wheat paste, where necessary using Japanese paper, a very thin and transparent but strong handmade paper.

Holes and damage to edges and elsewhere can also be patched up by hand with wheat paste and torn Japanese or stronger handmade paper, but the more elegant and at the same time more rational technique is leaf casting, in which holes and other defects are made good with fibre deposited from a suspension of pulp in water. Sophisticated equipment is available to the restorer for this technique and gives excellent results. Another efficient method for repairing holes in paper or strengthening brittle or fragile papers is paper-splitting.

With this technique, already in use in the mid-nineteenth century, damaged paper only a fraction of a millimetre thick is split in two so that back and front become two separate leaves. Next a very thin but strong paper is glued in between to form a support. Additives can be included in the adhesive in the form of alkali buffer solutions. In this way the strength of the paper is restored or even increased with no change to the original surface, back or front. The structure of the paper is also unchanged and even watermarks remain visible. Paper-splitting, therefore, has clear advantages over use of lamination or

Japanese paper, which restorers, for good reason, prefer not to employ if at all possible.

The treatment of parchment manuscripts, records or binding is difficult because the reaction of this intrinsically permanent animal skin to moisture and heat is more acute and unpredictable than that of paper which is more homogeneous. Smoothing and stretching distorted parchment, here too using controlled wetting, calls for much experience and patience. When repairing splits or holes in parchment, restorers prefer flexible bonding to gluing over the whole area because old and new parchments behave differently and unpredictably. In such cases sewing techniques are used in which special types of stitching ensure that the repaired parchment can stretch unequally without warping.

Small defects or holes in parchment can be corrected by a method similar to leaf casting, with a parchment fibre suspension. Seals made from beeswax and additives, used to certify the validity of official records and contracts, are frequently dirty, but in many cases small or large fragments also are broken off, possibly as a result of mishandling when in use. The main treatments in seal restoration include the manual replacement of damaged parts with pure beeswax, the repair of damaged edges and the making good of breaks in the impression. Fragile seals are dealt with in a conservation unit where tiny cracks and channels are closed under a vacuum after careful heating.

Finally, the restoration of bindings calls for demanding manual work specific to each repair. A thorough knowledge of the history of binding materials and techniques in use since the Middle Ages is necessary. If the repair is more than a matter of gluing down a loose spine or reconstructing a book clasp that has gone astray, the volume has to be patiently stripped down to its different constituent parts. The cover has to be removed from the book block and the block treated on its own.

The book's condition is carefully noted so that the assembling and binding techniques used centuries ago can be reconstituted with perfect accuracy. The covers are repaired separately. This often involves dealing with valuable old wood boards. Next the book is inserted in the cover and the ribs pinned or glued as decided by the original bookbinder several centuries earlier. The headband is not glued but where necessary it is carefully hand-stitched. This is the point at which restoration inevitably becomes reconstruction.

Given the immeasurable quantity of damaged archives, manuscripts and books, and the high cost of repair, restoration and conservation, methods have to be efficient and, wherever possible, machinery should be used. After more than twenty years of research and development, industrial methods can now be employed to control endogenous paper deterioration. 'Mass de-acidification' allows books and bound volumes of official papers to be treated in large batches.

The alkali-buffer process extends the remaining life of acid paper by a factor of three. However, since mass de-acidification is not so far associated with any increase in strength worthy of the name, it is only suitable for relatively new papers whose strength has not yet suffered any serious diminution. Up to now only one mass conservation method is available for improving paper strength: a wet process that fixes inks, washes out the products of decomposition, provides an alkali buffer and adds a coating of size. Unfortunately this machine method is only suitable for treating individual pages one by one.

In the restoration field, incredible though this may sound, paper splitting is the only mechanized and automated method. The German Library in Leipzig has a machine that copes with the difficult task of paper-splitting, glues in the strengthening paper, presses and dries the page and will soon, it is hoped, also automate sheet separation and trimming. Along with the preservation of originals, the conversion of damaged or endangered documents is another conservation process. The specific nature of archives, manuscripts and unique printed works calls for graphic conversion and not simply a coded transfer of the text.

The graphic conversion of endangered archive or library objects to substitute media for preservation purposes and/or as a permanent replacement for decaying documents requires systems that can ensure an optimum quality of reproduction, long-term durability of the conversion medium and a high level of cost-efficiency. Microfilming has become the most usual method to meet all these criteria. It is a highly economic and at the same time efficient conservation method.

Used at first for preservation purposes, it is a life-extending measure saving endangered books or documents from wear. The originals stay in the optimum climatic conditions of a safe storeroom while the user is provided with photographic reproductions. If this does no more than avoid damage due to use on one single occasion, the cost of microfilming, totalling considerably less than that of restoration and conservation, is already recovered. But in many cases microfilm can also fully take the place of endangered originals.

Microfilm is an economic storage medium that meets not only the high demands of scientific research regarding quality of reproduction but also the strict durability requirements of a conservation strategy. With modern equipment, most of it semiautomatic, large quantities of endangered books or archives can be recorded in black and white or colour in a relatively short time. Copies of these films can be made for users in practically any number. In this way the microfilming of unique historic documents helps not only to protect the originals but also to improve accessibility for researchers or interested members of the public. Microfilming still retains its place despite the appearance of new digital media. Obviously the object of conversion must be to replace problematical information carriers such as brittle paper by more reliable media, not ones that cause yet more problems as time goes by.

Compared with electronic image storage, microfilm, using a technique invented over 150 years ago, offers the advantage that the information in analogue form is continuously accessible to the human eye. In principle microfilm systems are not likely to undergo any basic technical change and are compatible with the new digital systems. Film can be scanned more efficiently than the photographed originals.

So in an information world in which nothing ages as rapidly as hightech systems, microfilm is the ideal upwardly-compatible storage medium for the long term. To that extent microfilming endangered documents is still the right answer. To interrupt microfilming projects and switch to long-term digital storage for conservation purposes would be short-sighted.

Image digitizing of endangered archive material giving maximum quality of reproduction, as required in particular for scientific research, is not yet possible at acceptable cost: the necessarily high storage capacity requirements of such image systems will continue to incur relatively high costs for processing, storage and distribution. The permanent accessibility required cannot be ensured either by digital storage media with their limited life or by the long-term availability of compatible systems on which to view them. The hardware and software components of electronic image storage systems are hardly standardized and could be affected by rapid technological change.

The innovation cycles of the hardware will have a shorter life than those of the optical-electronic storage media, and little heed will be taken of the archival need for long-term technological compatibility between emerging generations of systems. Responsible use of digitized storage must therefore make provision for continuous conversion of machine-readable data to keep abreast of hardware/ software innovation cycles, and for the cost involved in so doing.

These are incomparably higher than the costs of microfilm systems, which require only relatively simple long-term storage facilities and equipment. The high-quality digitization of the huge quantities of data necessary if all materials under threat of deterioration are to be included is, for cost reasons alone, inconceivable. It would also be uneconomic given documents' relatively low frequency of consultation, because they would probably have to be converted several times before there was any demand for them. Users' acceptance of microfilm, or archive and library materials reformatted in other ways, depends mainly on quality of reproduction, readability and representation of halftones and colours, layout and the quality of the accompanying user documentation.

Microfilming is highly developed. High-quality, semiautomatics microfilm cameras and automated developing equipment are available that guarantee results in conformity with the international standards (ISO 6199) which are very comprehensive in this field. Readers and reader-printers are available for rollfilm and microfiches that are very luminous and of high optical quality. The conversion of damaged or endangered archive and library materials can only be an effective conservation measure if the use of microfilm is promoted by the provision of the necessary facilities in libraries and archives. With the economic viability and guaranteed future of microfilm as a storage technique safely secured, however, archive offices and libraries should not reject the digital world.

Effective damage prevention measures need to be taken as early as possible, and the same applies to preservation microfilming, which should be done while the graphic information is still complete. Preventive measures, however, are also an essential preliminary before taking steps to prolong the life of endangered objects or to repair damage that has actually occurred, whatever their cost. The major investment involved is only justifiable if the objects are afterwards kept in an environment contributing to their permanent conservation.

The first decision, whether to keep originals or to convert, is technical. The central consideration is the intrinsic value of the objects as determined by their formal external characteristics, which cannot be retained in image form. Archives, manuscripts and printed works that are intrinsically valuable must in every case by kept in their original form. In other cases graphic conversion is generally a much less costly alternative. The low cost of conversion, particularly in view of the normal shortage of resources and the problem of numbers, argues for filming the maximum quantity possible so that as large as possible a share of resources then can be devoted to the far more costly preservation of intrinsically valuable cultural objects.

4

User Services

Librarians must have knowledge of a wide variety of scholarly and public information sources, and follow trends related to publishing, computers, and the media to effectively oversee the selection and organisation of library materials. They manage staff and develop and direct information programs and systems for the public to ensure information is organised to meet users' needs. Most librarian positions incorporate three aspects of library work: User services; Technical services, and Administrative services.

Even librarians specialising in one of these areas perform other responsibilities. Librarians in user services, such as reference and children's librarians, work with the public to help them find the information they need. This involves analysing users' needs to determine what information is appropriate, and searching for, acquiring, and providing information. It also includes an instructional role, such as showing users how to access information. Librarians commonly help users navigate the Internet, showing them how to most efficiently search for relevant information. Librarians in technical services, such as acquisitions and cataloguing, acquire and prepare materials for use and often do not deal directly with the public.

Librarians in administrative services oversee the management and planning of libraries, negotiate contracts for services, materials, and equipment, supervise library employees, perform public relations and fund-raising duties, prepare budgets, and direct activities to ensure that everything functions properly. In small libraries or information centres, librarians usually handle all aspects of the work. They read book reviews, publishers' announcements, and catalogues to keep up with current literature and other available resources, and select and purchase materials from publishers, wholesalers, and distributors.

Librarians prepare new materials by classifying them by subject matter, and describe books and other library materials so they are easy to find. They supervise assistants who prepare cards, computer records, or other access tools that direct users to resources. In large libraries, librarians often specialise in a single area, such as acquisitions, cataloguing, bibliography, reference, special collections, or administration.

Teamwork is increasingly important to ensure quality service to the public. Librarians also compile lists of books, periodicals, articles, and audiovisual materials on particular subjects; analyse collections; and recommend materials. They collect and organise books, pamphlets, manuscripts, and other materials in a specific field, such as rare books, genealogy, or music.

In addition, they coordinate programmes such as storytelling for children, and literacy skills and book talks for adults; conduct classes; publicise services; provide reference help; write grants; and oversee other administrative matters. Librarians are classified according to the type of library in which they work—public libraries, school library media centres, academic libraries, and special libraries.

Some librarians work with specific groups, such as children, young adults, adults, or the disadvantaged. In school library media centres, librarians help teachers develop curricula, acquire materials for classroom instruction, and sometimes team-teach. Librarians also work in information centres or libraries maintained by government agencies, corporations, law firms, advertising agencies, museums, professional associations, medical centres, hospitals, religious organisations, and research laboratories. They build and arrange an organisation's information resources, which usually are limited to subjects of special interest to the organisation. These special librarians can provide vital information services by preparing abstracts and indexes of current periodicals, organising bibliographies, or analysing background information and preparing reports on areas of particular interest.

A special librarian working for a corporation could provide the sales department with information on competitors or new developments affecting their field. Many libraries have access to remote databases and maintain their own computerised databases. The widespread use of automation in libraries makes database searching skills important to librarians.

Librarians develop and index databases and help train users to develop searching skills for the information they need. Some libraries are forming consortiums with other libraries through electronic mail. This allows patrons to simultaneously submit information requests to several libraries. The Internet also is expanding the amount of available reference information. Librarians must be aware of how to use these resources in order to locate information. Librarians with computer and information systems skills can work as automated systems librarians, planning and operating computer systems, and information science librarians, designing information storage and retrieval systems and developing procedures for collecting, organising, interpreting, and classifying information. These librarians analyse and plan for future information needs. The increased use of automated information systems enables librarians to focus on administrative and budgeting responsibilities, grant writing, and specialised research requests, while delegating more technical and user services responsibilities to technicians.

Increasingly, librarians apply their information management and research skills to arenas outside of libraries—for example, database development, reference tool development, information systems, publishing, Internet coordination, marketing, and training of database users. Entrepreneurial librarians sometimes start their own consulting practices, acting as freelance librarians or information brokers and providing services to other libraries, businesses, or government agencies.

Librarians spend a significant portion of time at their desks or in front of computer terminals; extended work at video display terminals can cause eyestrain and headaches. Assisting users in obtaining information for their jobs, recreational purposes, and other tasks can be challenging and satisfying; at the same time, working with users under deadlines can be demanding and stressful.

Some librarians lift and carry books, and some climb ladders to reach high stacks. Librarians in small organisations sometimes shelve books themselves. Public and college librarians often work weekends and evenings, and have to work some holidays. School librarians usually have the same workday schedule as classroom teachers and similar vacation schedules. Special librarians usually work normal business hours, but in fast-paced industries—such as advertising or legal services—they can work longer hours during peak times. Librarians held about 149,000 jobs in 2000. Most were in school and academic libraries; others were in public and special libraries.

A small number of librarians worked for hospitals and religious organisations. Others worked for governments. A master's degree in Library Science (MLS) is necessary for librarian positions in most public, academic, and special libraries, and in some school libraries.

A librarian working for a law firm may also be a licensed attorney, holding both library science and law degrees. In some jobs, knowledge of a foreign language is needed. State certification requirements for public school librarians vary widely. Most States require school librarians, often called library media specialists, to be certified as teachers and have had courses in library science.

Some States require certification of public librarians employed in municipal, county, or regional library systems. Librarians participate in continuing training once they are on the job to keep abreast of new information systems brought about by changing technology. Experienced librarians can advance to administrative positions, such as department head, library director, or chief information officer. Employment of librarians is expected to grow more slowly than the average for all occupations over the 2000-10 period.

The increasing use of computerised information storage and retrieval systems continues to contribute to slow growth in the demand for librarians. Computerised systems make cataloguing easier, which library technicians now handle. In addition, many libraries are equipped for users to access library computers directly from their homes or offices. These systems allow users to bypass librarians and conduct research on their own. However, librarians are needed to manage staff, help users develop database searching techniques, address complicated reference requests, and define users' needs. Despite expectations of slower-than-average employment growth, the need to replace librarians as they retire will result in numerous additional job openings.

Applicants for librarian jobs in large metropolitan areas, where most graduates prefer to work, usually face competition; those willing to work in rural areas should have better job prospects. Opportunities will be best for librarians outside traditional settings. Non-traditional library settings include information brokers, private corporations, and consulting firms.

Many companies are turning to librarians because of their research and organisational skills, and knowledge of computer databases and library automation systems. Librarians can review vast amounts of information and analyse, evaluate, and organise it according to a company's specific needs. Librarians also are hired by organisations to set up information on the Internet. Librarians working in these settings may be classified as systems analysts, database specialists and trainers, webmasters or web developers, or LAN (local area network) coordinators. Salaries of librarians vary according to the individual's qualifications and the type, size, and location of the library. Librarians play an important role in the transfer of knowledge and ideas by providing people with access to the information they need and want. Jobs requiring similar analytical, organisational, and communicative skills include archivists, curators, and museum technicians; and computer and information scientists, research.

The management aspect of a librarian's work is similar to the work of managers in a variety of business and government settings. School librarians have many duties similar to those of school teachers. Other jobs requiring the computer skills of some librarians include database administrators and computer systems analysts.

Technology Use in Libraries

There is no question that new and revolutionary voice, video and data processing technologies are finding their way into our lives, challenging us and our communities to rethink the way we live and work. The debate over the role these technologies will play in our lives, our schools, businesses and communities will continue for some time to come. More than ever before, modern libraries must keep current with these changes and their effects on our lives. Without sacrificing traditional roles, libraries must serve as information resource centers in many new and challenging ways in order to serve communities of the 21st century. Libraries must be capable of distributing information within the building, community, and within the larger context of the world. Specific issues relating to these areas include: Technology access within the library:

— Electronic card catalog access;

  i) up to date circulation information, including inventory information from other buildings and or libraries that are associated;

  ii) access to references including encyclopedias, dictionaries, etc.

  iii) areas for patrons to connect to the local building and community networks.

These access points may be used while working in the library, to access network resources throughout the library and/or community.

— Technology access within the community and to the world:

  i) The library technology systems can support access by the community from areas outside of the library, to information resources within the library, or resources that the library makes available to the community;

  ii) access to and from educational institutions, including colleges, K-12 schools, and educational institutions with a special partnering relationship.

— Access to and from other information resource consortiums.

Technology connection and resources can be subtly integrated into the structure of a library. Design objectives include:

— Providing appropriate, frequent, access to network and electrical connections.

— Appropriate areas for the main network equipment and related resources, including file servers, CD ROM towers, and related storage devices;

— Appropriate environmental controls including power conditioning, uninterruptible power supply, heating, ventilation and air conditioning to protect the technology equipment.

Furniture and seating that are appropriate and conducive to the use of technology. These include the ability to place keyboards at proper working height, to support monitors at appropriate angles, and other ergonomic factors. The functional areas for technology use within a Public library include:

— Areas for individual use:

  i) These are typically study desks and or work niches which are designed for individual use.

  ii) Work areas for research are often coordinated within the stacks and/or other reference area to allow work on both printed matter and electronic resources.

— Areas for small group use: These areas are required to support team or collaborative projects. These areas may include small rooms, group sized working alcoves, and other areas designed to support such work.

— Areas for large group use:

  i) Computer classrooms;

  ii) Large meeting rooms and presentation areas;

  iii) Lobbies or common areas, which might be used for large groups on special occasions.

Successful technology design for libraries must ensure appropriately sized easy access from the main technology area to the utility delivery area, typically outside of the library. This access will allow the connection to resources from the telephone company, cable TV company, and other network service providers. Care must be taken to ensure that future access is also provided to support implementation of future technologies that are not currently planned for in the design.

Video access, from the cable television provider should be carefully integrated, through the programming process, into appropriate areas within the libraries. Common and emerging applications for video will include:

— Teleconferencing may be used as a specific form of distance learning, a tool for communicating between peers whether students or faculty, or a tool for continued research;

— video connections for video origination and or display of video signals. The uses may include documentation and distribution of special guest lectures, town meetings, distribution of teacher presentations, and/or access to video resources in the main technology area of the library;

— access, as appropriate, to cable television resources. These resources may include institutional network access, Internet access, private programming, or public programming.

Sensitive technology systems design will preserve the aesthetic and functional objectives of the library, while providing predictable, frequent, and appropriate access to information technology resources. Appropriate design will also ensure that both current and future connections to internal and external resources may be implemented without structural or aesthetic changes to the library. This will allow modification of technology systems and resources without structural modifications or interruptions of use.

Incorporating information technology systems aesthetically into existing libraries, which were never designed to support such technologies, has far reaching impact on such issues as lighting, acoustics, power, environmental conditioning, cabling, space utilisation, furniture, and security to name a few. Transform the library into a model for the 21 st century through the deployment of infrastructure and technology systems to improve the accessibility of information.

Assist the library to better serve the community through close integration and collaboration with Trinity College and the Hartford Public Schools. Aid the library in awareness and exploration of technologies that will support community outreach through enhanced accessibility. Potential areas of benefit include branch libraries, the mobile library and other community centers. Provide the library with the capability to integrate print, data, multimedia and other emerging technologies through the thoughtful and comprehensive technological design of the library spaces. The infrastructure will take into account potential new uses of spaces within the Library, such as conference and group work areas wired to support videoconferencing for equipment to be purchased later. The network design will also take into account multimedia functions at "traditional" computer workstations and high-speed Internet access.

Cataloguing the Electronic Resource

As for all resources standard cataloguing principles and rules apply, such as supplying information where necessary, and use of standard notation where relevant information is not supplied. It is important to bear in mind that in most respects cataloguing e-resources is no different from cataloguing more traditional material. The chief source for the item is the entire resource itself, beginning with the home page. Accompanying material, not often associated with remote e-resources, is also a prescribed source of information. Load the page with images switched on if appropriate.

Problems of granularity may make identification of the home page difficult. Therefore clarify the actual resource being catalogued and how it relates to its immediate electronic environment, making relevant notes where necessary.

The URL or electronic location is that of the home page of the resource being catalogued—it can be copied and pasted from the location box into the 856 tag, subfield 'u'. When cataloguing pages within a website with frames it will be necessary to view the source file to identify the actual URL; right click mouse within frame. Where a discrete resource does not have direct access a related URL to the parent resource may be required, with appropriate indicators.

If information is lacking for the bibliographic record in the home page relevant information may be contained in the source page; click on View, source or right click on mouse. Otherwise the whole resource should be viewed. 'About' pages are also useful, especially for publisher information, dates of publication and coverage, and statements of responsibility. View copyright dates critically as these can be used flexibly in serial or continuing resources.

However the majority of library management systems assume a holding and problems and confusion may occur if holdings information is not attached to the bibliographic record. Also by assigning holdings sensibly to e-resources valuable management and statistical data can be generated from the system, as well as incorporating system functions that operate on the parameters of holdings data.

5

Metadata Resources

Metadata is a data about data, but basically it is a "structured data about data". It gives information about the data, which are stored on web. Each and every page of any website concerns with the metadata. Those metadata keeps information about the page on which the page talks. Different metadata standards are being used to represent the records in web such as MARC, Dublin Core, BIB-1, Text Encoding Initiative (TEI), and Electronic Archive Description (EAD) etc. Dublin Core is defined to be simple enough for people unschooled in the science of cataloguing to tag their documents for indexing by web harvesters while MARC has a richer description formats. Interoperability between digital libraries needs standardisation in metadata.

Metadata may be closely coupled with the object it describes as an intrinsic part of its composition; or it may have no intrinsic link with it at all. At the same time, the technical and service environments in which metadata services are being deployed are the subject of rapid change and development. Thus, the nature of the problem to be solved suggests a variety of solutions. It is helpful to consider a metadata spectrum, along which data becomes successively fuller, more structured, specialised, and expensive to create. This division into bands is presented for purposes of analysis only — as a way of presenting a view over an existing situation — and not as a set of fundamental distinctions. At one end is data used in services which currently support location and limited discovery. Terse metadata allows searching for known items, and for topics. This is the area inhabited by the webcrawlers which automatically extract data from resources. They currently provide web forms access onto proprietary databases.

There are moves to enhance the metadata on which they operate and to develop frameworks for interworking. At the other end of the spectrum is metadata which supports much richer functionality. It is often associated with research or scholarly activity, requires specialised knowledge to create and maintain, and caters for specialist domain-specific requirements.

Metadata formats being developed here can express a variety of formal and intellectual relationships, and are often part of a larger framework which provides for the encoding of the content they describe. Typically, they are looking at the creation of a variety of SGML document type definitions to cater for metadata and 'content'. Such initiatives include the Inter-university Consortium for Political and Social Research (ICPSR) SGML codebook initiative to describe social science data sets, the Encoding Archival Description (EAD), Content Standards for Digital Geospatial Metadata (FGDC) and the Consortium for Interchange of Museum Information (CIMI).

The Text Encoding Initiative can also be included here, and influenced some of these other developments. There has been some interest in the Z39.50 profile for access to digital collections for search and retrieval of such metadata. This has been taken furthest with CIMI where a companion profile is being developed for specific use with museum data.

The middle band contains services which contain full enough descriptions to allow a user to assess the potential utility or interest of a resource without actually having to retrieve it or connect to it, but not so full or complex as to require very specialist staff to create.

Typically, but not essentially, these descriptions are manually created, or are manual enhancements of automatically extracted descriptions, and they include a variety of descriptive and other attributes. They may be created to be loaded directly into a discovery service or may be harvested. Typically they are simple enough to be created by non-specialist users, or not to require significant discipline-specific knowledge. Descriptions tend to be of discrete objects and do not capture multiple relationships between objects.

Again, typically, they involve some selectivity in what they describe and may have more or less explicit criteria for selection. For these reasons, they may be expensive to create, again driving an interest in author- or publisher-generated description and automatic extraction techniques. Against this analytic background, one can note some likely future directions, especially across the boundaries of these bands.

Author- or site-produced metadata will become more important for crawlers and the middle band of services. This metadata may be harvested unselectively, or only from selected sites, depending on the service environment. An important motivation for such harvesting is to overcome some of the deficiencies of current crawlers without a provider incurring the cost of record creation.

At the same time, communities using the richer 'documentation' formats will wish to disclose information about their resources to a wider audience. How best to achieve this will have to be worked out: perhaps 'discovery' records will be exported into other systems. These directions suggest that the middle band will become more important as a general-purpose access route, maybe with links to richer domain-specific records in some cases. Incidentally, the current interest in the Dublin Core

Metadata Element Set can perhaps partly be explained by the fact that it has been positioned so that its target uses coincide with the trends outlined above: it provides the basis for a 'discovery' record; it can provide the basis for embedded content description which can be harvested by robot; and it aims to provide the basis for interoperability across richer description models.

Electronic Libraries Programme (eLib)

The Electronic Libraries Programme (eLib) is a three-year programme to modernise library services in the UK higher education community. The programme is spending approximately 15 million pounds over three years, and currently about 60 individual projects are in progress. Funding comes from the Joint Information Systems Committee of the Higher Education Funding Councils. UKOLN maintains the eLib information pages where further information about the programme and individual projects can be found.

eLib is organised around a number of project areas. One of these is Access to Network Resources. A major focus of this area is metadata and resource discovery services. Several subject-based information gateways have been funded, and are in various stages of start-up. They include:

- Social Science Information Gateway (SOSIG)
- Organising Medical Networked Information (OMNI)
- Edinburgh Engineering Virtual Library (EEVL)
- Art, Design, Architecture and Media Information Gateway (ADAM)
- Institute of Historical Research (IHR-info)

These are all organised in various ways but share certain characteristics. They are very much located in the middle band as outlined above: they aspire to provide discovery services to UK higher education. In some ways, they are rather like early abstracting and indexing services. They are developing databases of resource descriptions from which other services are derived. They are defining selection and quality criteria which determine which resources are included. They are aiming to have comprehensive coverage of resources within UK higher education, but take different approaches to resources elsewhere.

They are focusing on the server level — it is difficult to do otherwise and sustain this level of description — but aspire to move to the object level, however that might be achieved. Typically, their staff effort goes into management and administration, 'cataloguing', technical development, and promotion. Given the variety, volume, and volatility of relevant resources, it is likely that the subject services will consider how to lever their effort in a number of ways: by collaboration, by more proactive use of gathering, discovery and alerting technologies, and so on.

The services are considering various technical solutions to their services, and clearly have to make choices about metadata formats. The base service will have to provide web access to a searchable database of descriptions and some organised browsing facilities. Some of the services are using the ROADS software. There are also some other projects in the Access to Network Resources Area. CAIN and RUDI are looking at creating creating multimedia resources in the areas of conflict studies and urban design respectively. They are also looking at 'information gateways', but unlike the projects mentioned above, this is not their central purpose.

Resource Organisation and Discovery in Subject-based Services (ROADS)

ROADS is a development project, also in the Access to Network Resources area of eLib. A major objective of ROADS is to provide a set of software tools for the eLib subject-based services. These tools will allow the construction of distributed services and provide some data creation and other tools. An early motivation was that it should be possible to avoid the fragmentation of the current bibliographic environment and allow users have unified access to a distributed resource.

The development of ROADS has been guided by several strategic decisions. Wheels should not be reinvented: solutions should be based on Internet standards. Where those are being formed, ROADS experience will be put into their development. The system needs to support services in the middle band identified above, and certain decisions flow from that.

For this type of application, what is required is a description which is simple to create yet full enough for effective retrieval and relevance judgement. This implies a description which falls between the terseness of the crawlers and the fullness of a research library catalogue record. ROADS introduced the concept of 'trusted information provider', arguing that the collection of descriptions from approved authors and web-site administrators will be essential to a sustainable service. Again, a simple record structure will facilitate this and data creation and gathering tools are being prepared as part of the project.

A distributed framework is required: the user is best served by a solution which allows autonomously managed services to be accessible individually or as a navigable unit. Furthermore, we think this should be done in a network-friendly way and allow for multiple different configurations of service. The choice of IAFA and WHOIS++ was governed by pragmatic reasons: there is no ideological adherence to them as the 'one true path'. In the timescales of the project, it was important to have something which was immediately serviceable.

Importantly, the project acknowledges that there is no one solution. There will be several protocols and formats and much more on-the-wire conversions between them. It is in this context that ROADS includes a component which looks at interoperability with MARC and Z39.50. This will result in a report on semantic interoperability among USMARC, IAFA/WHOIS++ templates, and the Z39.50 BIB-1 attribute set and also a small demonstrator system.

At a wider level, ROADS aims to provide a collaborative framework through which the UK community can help contribute to the design and development of the future of such services. This is at the service and organisational level, and at the technical level where numerous issues are outstanding. Standards for the creation of descriptions and for the search and retrieve of such descriptions are still under development and open to influence. Omni and SOSIG are currently in production mode using ROADS version 0. This was developed so that services would have something to work with from an early stage. It provides a simple search engine, several tools for creation and processing of IAFA records, and a web interface.

At this stage, the services will continue to provide standalone servers accessed over the web. It includes a range of other functional enhancements. In early 1997, ROADS Version 2 will be released which will implement the Common Indexing Protocol. At this stage, we will test the ability of the system to provide unified guided access to a metadata resource distributed over several subject specific servers. Each server will generate a centroid, an inverted index style representation of its content, which will be collected in an index server.

The centroids provide 'forward knowledge' about the contents of servers in the distributed directory so that sensible decisions can be taken about navigation. A fuller description of the technical architecture of ROADS and its implementation of WHOIS++ can be found elsewhere. Further development may be possible at this stage, and will certainly take place within the Desire project. Although

ROADS aims to provide the eLib subject services with a systems framework, other users are not discouraged. As such it has a secondary aim in demonstrating the efficacy of a distributed solution in one compelling service environment. If successful it would hope to extend the scope to look at other directory applications. Users would benefit enormously from a simple to maintain, working directory service for distributing information about courses, research interests, 'white pages' data, and so on.

Digital Library Models

Much like a traditional library, a digital library can operate as a repository of objects that are identified using separate metadata records and subsequently disseminated as is. But more sophisticated digital libraries have evolved that are able to process objects both before and as they are delivered.

The processes or "services" customise the document to the user. Electronic texts are possibly the most frequently and most highly customised of objects disseminated by digital libraries. Digital models are characteristic of multimedia documents. That is to say, digital libraries typically treat models as immutable objects retrieved in toto on the basis of their cataloged metadata. If one assumes that a single model represents a logical whole, and that users will be interested in that whole, then in toto retrieval is a suitable method for model dissemination. These assumptions are not defensible, however, in the context of a cultural heritage digital library where the models' subjects themselves might not be complete and where user interest might be expected to lie solely in specific parts of a model.

The paradigm illustrates the need for enhanced integration between digital models and the services provided by the document management systems of digital libraries. One might argue that more detailed cataloging of metadata is all that is necessary. But, while resolving the problem of sub-object identification, more exacting practices will collide with cost-benefit barriers and still not provide a method for sub-object extraction.

A superior solution is to develop a way to parse the models and index their component geometry. The method proposed here is to masquerade digital models as XML (Extensible Markup Language) texts and to extend processing techniques that are already used by document management systems to these veiled models. There are additional benefits to this approach; the method provides a basis for the integration of models with automatic linking services and has the potential to improve integration with 3D shape-matching services. The proposed method is appropriate to models that have been stored in an ASCII format. For an object that is preserved in a cultural heritage digital library, the use of ASCII also makes archival sense.

Any structured ASCII format (e.g. IGES/STEP and DXF) for which an XML application might be composed is suitable. The research described here focuses on models encoded in X3D, an XML application of VRML (Virtual Reality Modeling Language, ISO/IEC 14772). The document management system of the Perseus Digital Library has multiple capabilities. The system is based on abstract structures to which elements of one or more DTDs are mapped, and on indices of these mappings.

The generation of the indices is automatic and can be configured to include descriptive content; this content is simultaneously extracted and stored in an RDF (Resource Description Framework) database to improve the discovery of resources. In the extension of the Perseus document management system to X3D models, an abstract structure is proposed for each culturally significant object The treatment of digital models as electronic texts illuminates the need for well-defined and well-named geometry. Object-oriented modeling, a common paradigm among the tools designed for mechanical engineers and artists, is suited to these requirements natively. Nested and related hierarchies of uniquely named components characterise models constructed with object-oriented tools.

Layer-oriented modeling, the most common paradigm for tools targeted to Architecture/Engineering/Construction professionals, is suited to these requirements only with forethought. Since a component is identified by the name of the layer on which it resides, several components grouped on the same layer effectively have identical names. And since layers are not nested, layer-oriented modeling flattens the hierarchies that establish name inheritances crucial to the identification and extraction of geometry. If a layer-oriented paradigm is used, a separate layer with an appropriately specific name should be created for every component of the model. However, this practice contradicts various standard layer naming conventions, which currently do not accommodate the necessary specificity.

Interoperability in Digital Libraries

Interoperability is a critical problem in the network environment especially, the Digital Libraries with increase in number of diverse computer systems, software applications, file formats, information resources and users.

But it becomes more critical problem in Indian digital libraries, with having those much differences it has another sharing problem of resources from one language to another as resources at Indian libraries are present in many Indian languages viz. English, Hindi, Sanskrit, Marathi, Gujarati, Oriya, Bengali, Punjabi etc. Thus it has problem of interoperability between multilingual digital library resources.

However there are so many true type fonts are being used to represent the Indian languages on web. But that's not sufficient tool to implement the multilingual. ISCII is also being used as a standard to represent the Indian languages on the web as well on the database part. But as we found that Unicode is the only solution, which represent the all languages being spoken in this world including the Indian languages.

It does not have any ambiguity and doesn't overlap, dealt with each and every characters of every language with unique values. To implement effectively interoperability function within the digital libraries following standards speak as tools:

— *UNICODE:* Unicode is an encoding scheme, provides a unique number for every character, no matter what the platform, no matter what the program, and no matter what the language is. It is not a hardware or software, it is a formal standard. It enables a single software product or a single website to be targeted across multiple platforms, languages and countries without re-engineering. As per the definition of the multilingual digital library "A multilingual digital library is a digital library that has all functions implemented simultaneously in as many languages as desired and whose search & retrieve functions are language dependent".

Thus the slogan given for the Unicode by the consortia becomes true, i.e. "When the world wants to talk, it speaks Unicode". It allows data to be transported through many different systems without corruption due to its platform independent capability. Technology for Multilingual digital libraries:

— *Unicode based Operating System:* Windows 2000/XP, NT, AIX, Sun Solaris, HP/UX

— *Unicode based Front-end Software:* HTML, XML, Java, JavaScript, .NET, PERL, XML, ASP, JSP, CORBA, etc

— *Unicode based Back-end Software (RDBMS):* MS SQL Server 2000, Sybase, Oracle 8i and DB2.

— OCR (Optical Character Recognition) Software.

— *Sorting Algorithm:* Sorting algorithm is defined as per the following three different techniques:

  — Primary Only means that only major differences are considered, such as different base letters.

  — Primary & Secondary means that a second level of differences is also considered, such as accents. However, these are only relevant if there are no primary differences anywhere else in the strings.

  — Primary - Tertiary means that a third level of differences is also considered, such as case. However, these are only relevant if there are no primary differences and no secondary differences anywhere else in the strings.

— *Harvesting protocol:* The Open Archive Initiative (OAI) for metadata harvesting is a new protocol dedicated to solving problems of digital library interoperability by defining simple protocols, most recently for the exchange of metadata. Although Z39.50 Information Retrieval Protocol is also one the harvesting protocol. Some digital library systems are using for retrieving and searching the records for example Maxwell System. It is crucial to explain, discuss, and disambiguate the concepts and terminology used among OAI implementers to harvesting approach to interoperability.

The harvesting protocol defined by the OAI is a request / response protocol with 6 request types, viz. Identity, ListMetadataFormats, ListSets, GetRecords ListRecord, and ListIdentifiers. It has defined in such a way to support a common set of principles and a technical framework to achieve interoperability. Functionality wise the multilingual digital library should have flexible with:

Comfortable to the user

Digital libraries are created in countries and, in general may be somehow specialised. It is expected that the users in the country where the library operates will want to use it in their native language. At the same time, users with other native languages than that of the country under consideration may need more international languages for English or Hindi.

Flexible in terms of the chosen languages

Digital libraries in different countries and aiming at different sets of users may operate with distinct sets of languages. As an example, in India a good set of languages is Hindi, Bengali, Gujarati, Marathi, Oriya, Sanskrit, Kannada, Telugu, Tamil and English etc. But in USA or in UK, it must be different.

Wide and accurate in terms of the information

In order to fulfill its functions, the digital library must be accurate in terms of information. This requires that the languages be kept track at any moment of operation by the user; he/she must know the languages of the catalogue entry and of the content, regardless the navigation language in use. For the search to be effective, no matter the navigation language, the user may submit search arguments in any language and all points of access must be possible to be searched in all languages, regardless of the navigation language of the session. In order to identify contents in original languages and corresponding translations into other languages, a strict translation control must exist.

Easy to operate

The digital librarian must control all cataloguing (original languages and translations) and all the contents (original languages and translations). For data integrity to be achieved, translation interfaces for the cataloguing and translation control applications must be available.

Language control Parameters

Language of the content: it is one of the metadata in metadata schemes The language of the content is the language in which the content is written and/or spoken

Language of the catalogue entry

The language of the catalogue is the language in which the attributes of the content and its instances are written

Language of navigation

The language of navigation is the language of all the interfaces and messages of the digital library system

Metadata is an emerging approach to organising structured digital collections, in order to support precise retrieval, long-term preservation, and interoperability on an extraordinary Internet scale. Although there are many metadata practices in digital libraries, few literatures have addressed the methodology of a best practice for developing metadata.

In the light of metadata provision, digital library projects often face a series of issues, including:

— how to get started,

— how to acquire metadata needs,

— how to choose a suitable metadata standard and adopt it,

— how to develop metadata specification,

— how to evaluate a metadata system, and so forth.

A set of effective methods to develop metadata is thus very important. Metadata Lifecycle Model (MLM) as a methodology of whole process of metadata provision for a digital library. Metadata provision for a digital library involves various processes. Hudgins, Agnew, and Brown recommend a workflow for a metadata project based on project management perspective. This approach demonstrates ten tasks to manage a metadata project, including: understanding the entire project, documentation, maximising existing infrastructure, choosing and evaluating the appropriate metadata standard, metadata record design, preliminary testing of workflow, initial staff design, workflow testing at midpoint, workflow testing at project conclusion, and reporting results.

Numerous attempts have been made by researchers to demonstrate how specific metadata formats are adopted and implemented at the digital library projects. The focus of metadata process includes:

— Methods of choice, evaluation, and adoption of existing metadata formats

— Methods of acquiring metadata needs in terms of lifecycle of digital objects

— Methods of preparation of metadata best practices

— Methods of development of metadata systems and tools

Metadata Lifecycle Model (MLM)

The MLM is a methodology involving a ten-step process by which digital library projects can design and implement metadata provision. It can be reviewed again once the project requirements have been changed. The purpose of the model is:

— To achieve a consistent method of developing metadata for digital library projects, so that they might achieve greater effectiveness and better.quality.

— To conduct a content-based analysis for digital collections, which takes into account knowledge mapping and metadata research needs while adopting any existing metadata formats.

The ten-step of the MLM can be classified into four main groups as follows.

Group I Requirement Assessment & Content Analysis

— *Step1:* Acquisition of Metadata Base Needs

— *Step2:* Review of Relevant Metadata Standards and Projects

— *Step3:* Investigation of Deep Metadata Needs

— *Step4:* Identification of Strategies for the Metadata Schemes

Group II System Requirement Specification

— *Step5:* Preparation of the Metadata Requirement Specification

— *Step6:* Evaluation of Metadata Systems

Group III Metadata System

— *Step7:* Preparation of Best Practice Guidance

— *Step8:* Development of the Metadata System

Group IV Service and Evaluation

— *Step9:* Maintenance of Metadata Service.4

— *Step10:* Evaluation of Metadata Performance

The first step of the metadata lifecycle is to interview the content experts or providers about their metadata requirements for each collection project, and analyse the attributes of collection projects through the four-layer for metadata selection.

— *Metdata scope*: Attributes of metadata are relating to thing, person, event, temporal, vocabulary control, and geographic name.

— *Legacy system*: basic information about the legacy system, including elements, structure, number of records, storage format, and input method and system. In addition, it is useful to understand the advantages and disadvantages of the system.

— *Metadata context*: Is only one metadata database constructed for this project? Are any other databases required to integrate with this metadata database, such as geographic information system (GIS)?

— *Metadata role and function*: What kind of metadata role is proposed for each project? What kind of function should be achieved by metadata, such as resources description, discovery, annotation, or administration?

After the four-layer for metadata selection is applied, the candidates of metadata schemes for a digital library are thus revealed. Current metadata trends and issues from around the world related to the profile of the digital library project can be collected and analysed as a reference for practical application and future development.

Through this stage the collection project members could well know what kind of differences exist with other similar or homogeneous collection projects, and also re-arrange the focus of expected project goals. Metadata scope and context are clarified, and related relationships are clearly drawn and attributed to a diversity of categories. It could ensure what kind of systems and databases are integrated by metadata mechanisms such as GIS.

The purpose of developing metadata services is to guarantee the quality assurance of metadata mechanisms. A service model is constructed to formulate the service items. The assessment of metadata record quality, including completeness, accuracy, record types, granularity levels, and records' serviceability. For example, an evaluation of the U.S. Government Information Locator Service (GILS) focused on assessing metadata quality from a set of criteria and procedures. The evaluation of the effectiveness of adopting a metadata scheme for retrieval, such as its capacity to facilitate access to title, creator, and subject. For many digital libraries, discovery, access, and description are the typical applications of metadata.

However, the case study shows that there are more functions needed, such as preservation, content rating, rights, data management, and e-Learning. In addition, domain-specific metadata sets are the core development of metadata practices in the case study. In other words, the generic metadata set, such as Dublin Core for resource discovery, is deployed in its top level of the union catalogue.

Intellectual Reality in Digital Library

A digital library might well be called something else—a digital information system, or a digital publishing system, to name two possible alternatives. But such alternatives have not been chosen. Instead, "library" has been the term of choice. And this choice has been made not by librarians but rather by computer and information scientists who have been in the forefront of the development of electronic information communications systems over the past three decades.

Library as a "Collection"

The traditional library has always been defined as a "collection"—an aggregation of informational objects. Usually, focusing on the idea of a collection is referenced to such things as its topical scope so as to determine what should be in it, or its proposed clientele so as to determine what access arrangements to it should be made. These are legitimate concerns, of course, but in quickly shifting to them we miss the most obvious thing that the idea of a collection conveys—its implied boundaries. A collection implies boundaries in the sense that, while collecting at its root simply means gathering, the act of gathering implies discrimination, some objects being included and others excluded. We might suppose that this simply means that informational objects are included and non-informational objects excluded. But this is not the case at all.

In a traditional library objects are normally included or excluded first of all on the basis of pragmatic considerations. It has always been that way. Expense both in acquiring and housing informational objects and the difficulty of obtaining certain ones of them have always demanded limits to collections. And the purpose for which a library is assembled has meant that not all possible objects have been wanted in the collection. After all, even where the informational objects might be few for some given realm, it may not serve the purpose of the collection to include all possible things—items in an unreadable foreign language, items which are plainly redundant or derivative, items representing incompetence, and the like.

A much more trenchant basis for boundaries is not pragmatic, however, but rather that boundaries appear to be necessary by the nature of things. When a collection is assembled it represents a segment of what Patrick Wilson has aptly called the "bibliographical universe" and which is defined elsewhere as, an abstraction of the accumulated items or objects of recorded knowledge of humankind in all of their various forms—for example, in the form of books, periodicals, graphics, sound recordings, motion pictures, electronic data compilations, business, governmental and personal records, and so on. The abstraction called the bibliographical universe has limitations, of course. For example, it includes only a single copy of each unique recorded knowledge object. And it necessarily excludes items which have become lost or which are intentionally kept from the public eye.

The result is that not every imaginable object of recorded knowledge is included in the abstraction. Even with such limitations, the bibliographical universe remains enormous. however. Think for a moment of the world's production of recorded informational objects even in a single year—perhaps a million new editions of books, countless periodical publications where even those recognised for scientific and scholarly merit number in excess of 150,000 titles, not to mention those which have ceased publication but are still useful.

These figures do not include serial publications of much more limited purview, government publications at any level, audio-visual items of all kinds, archival and other organisational records numbering in the trillions. To this we add a growing number of electronic sources, especially those representing visual images and multimedia. These may best be spoken of in terms of terrabytes of data and they are growing in numbers at exponential rates. All of the foregoing is mentioned because the reality of a collection, at least traditionally, is that it necessarily represents only a very small segment of a gigantic whole. Access to these materials has been traditionally provided by creating multiple libraries or collections, where the expense and labor in assembling, describing, storing, and making them available is shared among countless people and organisations.

Digital Library as a Collection of "Information Sources"

The traditional library ordinarily implies the idea of a collection of "information sources" which have the potential of informing in one way or another those who consult them. While the informative nature of an information source seems straightforward, there would appear to be more to the idea of such a source than its informativeness. One primary attribute among many that information sources have is that they have regularly been consulted and used in terms of their separate and unique identities as intellectual or artistic entities.

And as separate and unique entities they are by nature highly incommensurate in the ways they assemble information, the reasons for assembling information, the intended audiences for the act of assembling information, and the like. The idea that an information source has a separate and unique identity as an intellectual or artistic entity arises from the view that each such informational source has two different but interrelated kinds of attributes—those related to its content and those related to its container or medium of transmission.

Content attributes include such things as a source's intellectual form or genre, its topicality, its intended audience, and so on. But of special importance among content attributes are those which in library cataloging are clustered around the idea of the "work" or "works" an informational source contains.

A work is an entity constituting the intellectual or artistic effort of an intelligent being in representing his or her knowledge. It is called a work in the same sense that one designs and creates, say, a sidewalk or a flower arrangement. Each of the latter is the result of a direct effort that begins with the mind. In the case of information sources the result is a discrete intellectual or artistic entity or product which has an intentional structure, a storyline, arguments, and so on, with an identifiable beginning, middle, and end.

All information sources have the attribute of being a work in the sense spoken of here, although not all will have been expressed with equal amounts of intellectual or artistic skill and control. Indeed, there is enormous variety among them.

Some works may represent the expressions of single individuals, but others will represent layers of participation by several persons as in the creation of a work by one or more persons, its translation by one or more others, its augmentation with illustrations or commentary and its editing by still others. In contrast, other information sources represent the "utterances"of corporate agencies. Still others will represent the confluence of human and computer capabilities, as in a database software package. It will have been designed by a team of persons.

But, afterwards someone using the package will use the package to formulate a specific database structure , someone else will input data into the structure, still someone else may well devise a report program for the data, and a report will be produced by the computational power of the computer which runs the program. Likewise, there is immense variety in the way expression in information sources has been shaped, not simply in terms of intellectual structure, but also in the kind of expressive medium used—that is, whether the expression is textual and discursive, textual and elliptical, numeric, graphic, composed in a special language such as mathematical or chemical notation and the like. Indeed, some information sources may be distinctive by appearing to be combinations of many of these motifs or by appearing to be chaotic in their conception and execution, at least in terms of some standard of expression.

The intersection of all of these kinds of variation in information sources is so multifaceted, in fact, that it is fair to describe the whole universe of such sources as highly incommensurate in the way they present information. In fact, outside of differences that owe merely to variations in the container in which information sources are found, it seems fair to suppose that all information resources represent unique variants in intellectual structure, formatting, expression, etc. The reason for pointing out the "work" attributes of information sources as well as their incommensurateness is that much information seeking is shaped by and inextricably connected to these attributes.

Ever since information sources first came into existence they have regularly been consulted in terms of the intellectual or artistic entities they contain and in the light of the incommensurateness of their expressions of information.

Indeed, a large portion of humankind's intellectual activity has been devoted to the task of intellectually grappling with such objects in these terms, often assembling them as families of items based on how they refer to one another, or because they refer to common ancestor sources, or because they contain common text upon which comments are made, or because they have common sources or because of any number of other attributes which show their "family" relationships as whole intellectual or artistic entities.

This aspect of the phenomenon of information sources in the traditional library is pointed out because of undercurrents found in discussions of libraries in electronic environments that speculate that the new technology will and should promote something altogether different both in the nature of information sources within the environment and in the nature of their use.

The advent of digital libraries presents a plethora of challenges and opportunities for artificial intelligence technology. Extracting relevant information from large multimedia digital collections stresses technologies for information retrieval, text and image understanding, translation, and so on. Satisfying diverse user communities calls for advanced interfaces, user modeling, speech/gesture recognition, and other emerging mechanisms. Between users and collections is a gulf filled with a large, diverse, and evolving network of services that must be selectively marshaled to accomplish particular tasks.

A fundamental role for AI in digital libraries is to perform the underlying monitoring, management, and allocation of services and resources that bring together users and information. While user-interface or retrieval technologies are also important, it is obvious that such technologies will undergo ongoing and dramatic change, which in turn can lead to the restructuring of "how things are done" in the library.

6

Information Archival

The term, archive has come to be used to refer to a wide variety of storage and preservation functions and systems. Traditional archives are understood as facilities or organisations which preserve records, originally generated by or for a government organisation, institution, or corporation, for access by public or private communities. The archive accomplishes this task by taking ownership of the records, ensuring that they are understandable to the accessing community, and managing them so as to preserve their information content and authenticity. Historically, these records have been in such forms as books, papers, maps, photographs, and film, which can be read directly by humans, or read with the aid of simple optical magnification and scanning aids.

The major focus for preserving this information has been to ensure that they are on media with long-term stability and that access to this media is carefully controlled. The explosive growth of information in digital forms has posed a severe challenge not only for traditional archives and their information providers, but also for many other organisations in the government, commercial and non-profit sectors. These organisations are finding, or will find, that they need to take on the information preservation functions typically associated with traditional archives because digital information is easily lost or corrupted.

The pace of technology evolution is causing some hardware and software systems to become obsolete in a matter of a few years, and these changes can put severe pressure on the ability of the related data structures or formats to continue effective representation of the full information desired. Because much of the supporting information necessary to preserve this information is more easily available or only available at the time when the original information is produced, these organisations need to be active participants in the long-term preservation effort, and they need to follow the principles espoused in this Open Archival Information System (OAIS) reference model to ensure that the information can be preserved for the Long Term. Participation in these efforts will minimise the lifecycle costs and enable effective long-term preservation of the information. The explosion of computer processing power and digital media has resulted in many systems where the Producer role and the archive role are the responsibility of the same entity.

These systems, which are sometimes known as Active Archives, should subscribe to the goals of Long Term Preservation discussed in this document. The design process must realise that some of the Long Term Preservation activities may conflict with the goals of rapid production and dissemination of products to Consumers. The designers and architects of such systems should document the solutions that have been reached. A major purpose of this reference model is to facilitate a much wider understanding of what is required to preserve and access information for the Long Term. To avoid confusion with simple ,bit storage functions, the reference model defines an OAIS which performs a long-term information preservation and access function.

An OAIS archive is one that intends to preserve information for access and use by a Designated Community. It includes archives that have to keep up with steady input streams of information as well as those that experience primarily aperiodic inputs. It includes archives that provide a wide variety of sophisticated access services as well as those that support only the simplest types of requests. The OAIS model recognises the already highly distributed nature of digital information holdings and the need for local implementations of effective policies and procedures supporting information preservation.

This allows, in principle, a wide variety of organisational arrangements, including various roles for traditional archives, in achieving this preservation. It is expected that organisations attempting to preserve information will find that using OAIS terms and concepts will assist them in achieving their information preservation goals. Management is the role played by those who set overall OAIS policy as one component in a broader policy domain. In other words, Management control of the OAIS is only one of Management's responsibilities. Management is not involved in day-to-day archive operations.

OAIS archives are not shown explicitly. Such archives may establish particular agreements among themselves consistent with Management and OAIS needs. Some archives may interact with a particular archive for a variety of reasons and with varying degrees of formalism for any pre-arranged agreements. One OAIS may take the role of Producer to another OAIS; an example is when the responsibility for preserving a type of information is to be moved to this other archive.

One OAIS may take the role of Consumer to another OAIS; an example is when the first OAIS decides to rely on the other OAIS for a type of information it seldom needs and chooses not to preserve locally. Such reliance should have some formal basis that includes the requirement for communication between the archives of any policy changes that might affect this reliance. A person, or system, can be said to have a Knowledge Base, which allows them to understand received information. For example, a person who has a Knowledge Base that includes an understanding of English will be able to read, and understand, an English text. Information is defined as any type of knowledge that can be exchanged, and this information is always expressed by some type of data.

The information in a hardcopy book is typically expressed by the observable characters which, when they are combined with a knowledge of the language used, are converted to more meaningful information. If the recipient does not already include English in its Knowledge Base, then the English text (the data) needs to be accompanied by English dictionary and grammar information in a form that is understandable using the recipient's Knowledge Base.

Similarly, the information stored within a CD-ROM file is expressed by the bits (the data) it contains which, when they are combined with the Representation Information for those bits, are converted to more meaningful information as long as the Representation Information is understandable using the recipient's Knowledge Base. Assume the bits represent an ASCII table of numbers giving the coordinates of a location on the Earth measured in degrees latitude and East longitude. The Representation Information will typically include the definition of ASCII together with descriptions of the format of the numbers and their locations in the file, their definitions as latitude and longitude, and the definition of their units as degrees. It may also include additional meaning that is assigned to the table.

For digital information, this means the OAIS must clearly identify the bits and the Representation Information that applies to those bits. This required transparency to the bit level is a distinguishing feature of digital information preservation, and it runs counter to object-oriented concepts which try to hide these implementation issues. This presents a significant challenge to the preservation of digital information. As a further complication, the recursive nature of Representation Information, which typically is composed of its own data and other Representation Information, typically leads to a network of Representation Information objects.

Since a key purpose of an OAIS is to preserve information for a Designated Community, the OAIS must understand the Knowledge Base of its Designated Community to understand the minimum Representation Information that must be maintained. The OAIS should then make a decision between maintaining the minimum Representation Information needed for its Designated Community, or maintaining a larger amount of Representation Information that may allow understanding by a larger Consumer community with a less specialised Knowledge Base. Over time, evolution of the Designated Community's Knowledge Base may require updates to the Representation Information to ensure continued understanding.

As a practical matter, software is used to access the Information Object, and it will incorporate some understanding of the network of Representation Information objects involved. However, this software should not be used as rationale for avoiding identifying and gathering readily understandable Representation Information that defines the Information Object, because it is harder to preserve working software than to preserve information in digital or hardcopy forms.The OAIS reference model emphasizes the preservation of information content. As digital technology evolves, multimedia technology and the dependency on complex interplay between the data and presentation technologies will lead some organisations to require that the look and feel of the original presentation of the information be preserved.

This type of preservation requirement may necessitate that the software programs and interfaces used to access the data be preserved. This problem may be further complicated by the proprietary nature of some of the software. Various techniques for preserving the look and feel of information access are currently the subject of research and prototyping. These techniques, which include hardware level emulation, emulation of various common service APIs, and the development of a virtual machine, investigate the preservation of the original bit steam and software across technology.

Though the OAIS reference model does not focus on these emerging techniques, it should provide architectural basis for the prototyping and comparison of these techniques. An Information Package is a conceptual container of two types of information called Content Information and Preservation Description Information (PDI). The Content Information and PDI are viewed as being encapsulated and identifiable by the Packaging Information. The resulting package is viewed as being discoverable by virtue of the Descriptive Information.

The Content Information is that information which is the original target of preservation. It consists of the Content Data Object (Physical Object or Digital Object, i.e., bits) and its associated Representation Information needed to make the Content Data Object understandable to the Designated Community. The CDO may be an image that is provided as the bit content of one CD-ROM file together with other files, on the same CD-ROM, that contain Representation Information. Only after the Content Information has been clearly defined can an assessment of the Preservation Description Information be made.

The Preservation Description Information applies to the Content Information and is needed to preserve the Content Information, to ensure it is clearly identified, and to understand the environment in which the Content Information was created. The Preservation Description Information is divided into four types of preserving information called Provenance, Context, Reference, and Fixity. Briefly, they are the following:

— Provenance describes the source of the Content Information, who has had custody of it since its origination, and its history.

— Context describes how the Content Information relates to other information outside the Information Package. For example, it would describe why the Content Information was produced, and it may include a description of how it relates to another Content Information object that is available.

— Reference provides one or more identifiers, or systems of identifiers, by which the Content Information may be uniquely identified. Examples include an ISBN number for a book, or a set of attributes that distinguish one instance of Content Information from another.

— Fixity provides a wrapper, or protective shield, that protects the Content Information from undocumented alteration. For example, it may involve a check sum over the Content Information of a digital Information Package.

The Packaging Information is that information which, either actually or logically, binds, identifies and relates the Content Information and PDI. For example, if the Content Information and PDI are identified as being the content of specific files on a CD-ROM, then the Packaging Information would include the ISO 9660 volume/file structure on the CD-ROM, as well as the names and directory information of the files on CD-ROM disk. The Descriptive Information is that information which is used to discover which package has the Content Information of interest. Depending on the setting, this may be no more than a descriptive title of the Information Package that appears in some message, or it may be a full set of attributes that are searchable in a catalog service.

OAIS and the Information Package

It is necessary to distinguish between an Information Package that is preserved by an OAIS and the Information Packages that are submitted to, and disseminated from, an OAIS. These variant packages are needed to reflect the reality that some submissions to an OAIS will have insufficient Representation Information or PDI to meet final OAIS preservation requirements. In addition, these may be organised very differently from the way the OAIS organises the information it is preserving. Finally, the OAIS may provide information to Consumers that does not include all the Representation Information or all the PDI with the associated Content Information being disseminated. These variants are referred to as the Submission Information Package (SIP), the Archival Information Package (AIP), and the Dissemination Information Package (DIP).

The Submission Information Package (SIP) is that package that is sent to an OAIS by a Producer. Its form and detailed content are typically negotiated between the Producer and the OAIS. Most SIPs will have some Content Information and some PDI, but it may require several SIPs to provide a complete set of Content Information and associated PDI to form an AIP. A single SIP may contain information that is to be included in several AIPs. The Packaging Information will always be present in some form.

Within the OAIS one or more SIPs are transformed into one or more Archival Information Packages (AIP) for preservation. The AIP has a complete set of PDI for the associated Content Information. The Packaging Information of the AIP will conform to OAIS internal standards, and it may vary as it is managed by the OAIS. In response to a request, the OAIS provides all or a part of an AIP to a Consumer in the form of a Dissemination Information Package (DIP). The DIP may also include collections of AIPs, and it may or may not have complete PDI.

The Packaging Information will necessarily be present in some form so that the Consumer can clearly distinguish the information that was requested. Depending on the dissemination media and Consumer requirements, the Packaging Information may take various forms.

Management provides the OAIS with its charter and scope. The charter may be developed by the archive, but it is important that Management formally endorse archive activities. The scope determines the breadth of both the Producer and Consumer groups served by the archive.

The first contact between the OAIS and the Producer is a request that the OAIS preserve the data products created by the Producer. This contact may be initiated by the OAIS, the Producer or Management. The Producer establishes a Submission Agreement with the OAIS, which identifies the SIPs to be submitted and may span any length of time for this submission. Some Submission Agreements will reflect a mandatory requirement to provide information to the OAIS, while others will reflect a voluntary offering of information. Even in the case where no formal Submission Agreement exists, such as a World Wide Web (WWW) site, a virtual Submission Agreement may exist specifying the file formats and the general subject matter the site will accept.

Within the Submission Agreement, one or more Data Submission Sessions are specified. There may be significant time gaps between the Data Submission Sessions. A Data Submission Session will contain one or more SIPs and may be a delivered set of media or a single telecommunications session. The Data Submission Session content is based on a data model negotiated between the OAIS and the Producer in the Submission Agreement. This data model identifies the logical components of the SIP (e.g., the Content Information, PDI, Packaging Information, and Descriptive Information) that are to be provided and how (and whether) they are represented in each Data Submission Session.

All data deliveries within a Submission Agreement are recognised as belonging to that Submission Agreement and will generally have a consistent data model, which is specified in the Submission Agreement. A Data Submission Session may consist of a set of Content Information corresponding to a set of observations, which are carried by a set of files on a CD-ROM. The Preservation Description Information is split between two other files.

All of these files need Representation Information which must be provided in some way. The CD-ROM and its directory/file structure are the Packaging Information, which provides encapsulation and identification of the Content Information and PDI in the Data Submission Session. The Submission Agreement indicates how the Representation Information for each file is to be provided, how the CD-ROM is to be recognised, how the Packaging Information will be used to identify and encapsulate the SIP Content Information and PDI, and how frequently Data Submission Sessions will occur. It also gives other needed information such as access restrictions to the data.

Each SIP in a Data Submission Session is expected to meet minimum OAIS requirements for completeness. However, in some cases multiple SIPs may need to be received before an acceptable AIP can be formed and fully ingested within the OAIS. In other cases, a single SIP may contain data to be included in many AIPs. A Submission Agreement also includes, or references, the procedures and protocols by which an OAIS will either verify the arrival and completeness of a Data Submission Session with the Producer or question the Producer on the contents of the Data Submission Session.

Responsibilities of OAIS

The minimal responsibilities that shall be discharged by an OAIS.

Mandatory Responsibilities

Mandatory responsibilities that an organisation must discharge in order to operate an OAIS archive. The OAIS must:

— Negotiate for and accept appropriate information from information Producers.

— Obtain sufficient control of the information provided to the level needed to ensure Long-Term Preservation.

— Determine, either by itself or in conjunction with other parties, which communities should become the Designated Community and, therefore, should be able to understand the information provided.

— Ensure that the information to be preserved is Independently Understandable to the Designated Community. In other words, the community should be able to understand the information without needing the assistance of the experts who produced the information.

An organisation operating an OAIS will have established some criteria that aids in determining the types of information that it is willing to, or it is required to, accept. These criteria may include, among others, subject matter, information source, degree of uniqueness or originality, and the nature of the techniques used to represent the information (e.g., physical media, digital media, format).

The information may, in general, be submitted using a wide variety of common and not-so-common forms, such as books, documents, maps, data sets, and moon rocks using a variety of communication paths including networks, mail, and special delivery. The OAIS negotiates with the Producer to ensure it acquires appropriate Content Information and associated PDI for its mission and the Designated Community. Considerable iteration may be required to agree on the right information to be submitted, and to get it into forms acceptable to the OAIS. For example, this may include digitising audio or video material, or scanning text.

The OAIS should extract, or otherwise obtain, sufficient Descriptive Information to assist the Designated Community in finding the Content Information of interest. It also should ensure that the information meets all OAIS internal standards.

Content Information and Ownership of Intellectual Property Rights

It is important for the OAIS to recognise the separation that can exist between physical ownership or possession of Content Information and ownership of intellectual property rights in this information. If it has created the information and is the legal owner of the Content Information, the OAIS already has the independence to do what is required to preserve the information and make it available. When acquiring the Content Information from any other producer or entity, the OAIS must ensure that there is a legally valid transfer agreement that either transfers intellectual property rights to the OAIS, or clearly specifies the rights granted to the OAIS and any limitations imposed by the rightsholder(s).

The OAIS must ensure that its subsequent actions to preserve the information and make it available conform with these rights and limitations. When the OAIS does not acquire the intellectual property rights, the agreement should specify what involvement the rightsholder(s) will have in preservation, management or release of the information. In most cases, it will be preferable for the OAIS to negotiate an agreement that specifies the rightsholder(s) requirements and authorises the OAIS to act in accordance with those requirements without active involvement of the rightsholder(s) in individual cases.

The OAIS must assume sufficient control over the Content Information and Preservation Description Information so that it is able to preserve it for the Long

Term. There is no issue with the AIP's Packaging Information because, by definition, this is under internal OAIS control. The problems of assuming sufficient control of the Content Information and Preservation Description Information, when they are largely digital, are addressed in three related categories, as follows:

— copyright implications; intellectual property and other legal restrictions on use;

— authority to modify Representation Information;

— agreements with external organisations.

Legal Restrictions

An archive will honour all applicable legal restrictions. These issues occur when the OAIS acts as a custodian. An OAIS should understand the copyright concepts and applicable laws prior to accepting copyright materials into the OAIS. It can establish guidelines for ingestion of information and rules for dissemination and duplication of the information when necessary. It is beyond the scope of this document to provide details of national and international copyright laws. Authority to modify Representation Information: Although the Fixity information within the Preservation Description Information of an AIP ensures that the Content Information-related bits have not been altered, there will come a time when Content Information bits are not in a form that is convenient for the Consumers from the Designated Community.

The Content Information bits may be fully documented in available hardcopy forms, so technically the information has not been lost, but practically the information has become inaccessible. The OAIS needs the authority to migrate the Content Information to new representation forms. If it is acting as a custodian, it may need to seek additional permission to make such changes. If the information is copyrighted, the OAIS should already have negotiated permission to make the changes needed to meet preservation objectives.

It may employ subject matter experts, from outside the OAIS, to help ensure that information is not lost. Ideally, when this situation arises, both the original AIPs and new AIPs will be retained. An OAIS may establish a variety of agreements with other organisations to assist in its preservation objectives. It may establish an agreement with another OAIS so that it does not have to preserve all the common Representation Information objects related to its Content Information objects. Agreements with other organisations should be monitored to be sure they are being followed and remain useful. The submission, or planned submission, of Content Information and associated PDI requires a determination as to who the expected Consumers, or Designated Community, of this information will be.

This is necessary in order to determine if the information, as represented, will be understandable to that community. For example, an archive may decide that certain Content Information should be understandable to the general public and, therefore, this becomes the Designated Community. For some scientific information, the Designated Community of Consumers might be described as those with a first year graduate level education in a related scientific discipline. This is a more difficult case as it is less clear what degree of specialised scientific terminology might actually be acceptable.

The Producers of such specialised information are often familiar with a narrowly recognised set of terminology, so it is especially critical to clearly define the Designated Community for their information and to make the effort to ensure that this community can understand the information. The possible evolution of the definition of the Designated Community also needs consideration.

Information originally intended for a narrowly defined community may need to be made more widely understandable at some future date. For example, information originally intended to be understandable to a particular scientific community may need to be made understandable to the general public. This is likely to mean adding explanations in support of the Representation Information and the Preservation Description Information, and it can become increasingly difficult to obtain this information over time. Selecting a broader definition of the Designated Community when the information is first proposed for Long-Term Preservation can reduce this concern and also improve the likelihood that the information will be understandable to all in the original community. The degree to which Content Information and its associated PDI conveys information to a Designated Community is, in general, quite subjective.

Nevertheless, it is essential that an archive make this determination in order to maximise information preservation. Digital Content Information and PDI need adequate Representation Information to be Independently Understandable to the Designated Community. Consider Content Information from a digital set of observations of rainfall, temperature, pressure, wind velocities, and other parameters measured all over the world for a year. This type of information is very extensive, and is not usually in a form intended for direct human browsing or reading, but it is in a form appropriate to searching and manipulation by application software.

Such content may only be understandable to the original Producers, unless there is adequate documentation of the meaning of the various fields and their interrelationships, and how the values relate back to the original instrumentation that made the observations. In such specialised fields extra effort is needed to ensure that the Content Information and the Preservation Description

Information are understandable to a Designated Community.

If the archive does not have this level of expertise in-house, it may have outside community representatives review the information for long-term understandability. Otherwise some of the information may be understandable to only a few specialists and be lost when they are no longer available.

Even when a set of information has been determined to be understandable to a particular Designated Community, over time the Knowledge Base of this community may evolve to the point that important aspects of the information may no longer be readily understandable. At this point it may be necessary for the OAIS to enhance the associated Representation Information so that it is again readily understandable to the Designated Community.

Software is needed for efficient access to Digital Content Information. However, maintaining Content Information-specific software over the Long Term has not yet been proven cost effective due to the narrow application of such software. The danger of information loss is great when such software is relied upon for information preservation and understanding because it may cease to function under only small changes to the hardware and software environment. This may not be recognised unless there is a vigorous, ongoing, testing and validation program.

Preservation Policies

It is essential for an OAIS to have documented policies and procedures for preserving its AIPs, and it should follow those procedures. The appropriate policies and procedures will depend, at minimum, on the nature of the AIPs and any ,backup relationships the archive may have with other archives. The Producer and Consumer communities should be provided with submission and dissemination standards, policies, and procedures to support the preservation objectives of the OAIS.

The Designated Community should be monitored to be sure the Content Information is still understandable to them. The Designated Community may lose its familiarity with some terminology, and the definition of the community may be broadened to include other members with different backgrounds. A long-term technology usage plan, updated as technology evolves, is essential to avoid being caught with very costly system maintenance, emergency system replacements, and costly data representation transformations.

By definition, an OAIS makes its AIPs visible and available to its Designated Communities. Multiple views of its holdings, supported by various search aids that may cut across collections of AIPs, may be provided.

Some AIPs may only exist as the output of algorithms operating on other AIPs. They appear as DIPs that, upon dissemination, should include documentation on how they were derived from other AIPs. The expectations of OAIS Consumers regarding access services will vary widely among archives and over time as technology evolves. Pressures for more effective access must be balanced with the requirements for preservation under the available resource constraints.

Some AIPs may have restricted access and therefore may only be disseminated to Consumers who meet access restrictions. The OAIS should have published policies on access and restrictions so that the rights of all parties are protected.In general, DIPs may be distributed by all varieties of communication paths, including networks and physical media.

Preservation Planning also designs IP templates and provides design assistance and review to specialise these templates into SIPs and AIPs for specific submissions. Preservation Planning also develops detailed Migration plans, software prototypes and test plans to enable implementation of Administration migration goals. Access: This entity provides the services and functions that support Consumers in determining the existence, description, location and availability of information stored in the OAIS, and allowing Consumers to request and receive information products. Access functions include communicating with Consumers to receive requests, applying controls to limit access to specially protected information, coordinating the execution of requests to successful completion, generating responses and delivering the responses to Consumers.

In addition to the entities described above, there are various Common Services assumed to be available. Modern, distributed computing applications assume a number of supporting services such as inter-process communication, name services, temporary storage allocation, exception handling, security, backup and directory services. Much excellent work has already been done in the area of open system environment reference models. Operating system services provide the core services needed to operate and administer the application platform, and provide an interface between application software and the platform. These services include the following:

— Kernel operations provide low-level services necessary to create and manage processes, execute programs, define and communicate signals, define and process system clock operations, manage files and directories, and control input-output processing to and from the external environment.

— Commands and utilities include mechanisms for operations at the operator level, such as comparing, printing, and displaying file contents; editing files;

pattern searching; evaluating expressions; logging messages; moving files between directories; sorting data; executing command scripts; and accessing environment information.

- Real-time extension includes the application and operating system interfaces needed to support those application domains requiring deterministic execution, processing, and responsiveness. The extension defines the applications interface to basic system services for input/output, file system access, and process management.
- System management includes capabilities to define and manage user resource allocation and access, configuration and performance management of devices, file systems, administrative processes, queues, machine/platform profiles, authorisation of resource usage, and system backup.
- Operating system security services specify the control of access to system data, functions, hardware, and software resources by users and user processes. Network services provide the capabilities and mechanisms to support distributed applications requiring data access and applications interoperability in heterogeneous, networked environments. These services include the following:
  - Data communication includes API and protocol specifications for reliable, transparent, end-to-end data transmission across communications networks.
  - Transparent file access to available files located anywhere in a heterogeneous network.
  - Personal/micro computer support for interoperability with systems based on other operating systems, particularly microcomputer operating systems, which may not be formally specified in a national or international standard.

— Remote Procedure Call services include specifications for extending the local procedure call to a distributed environment.

— Network security services include access, authentication, confidentiality, integrity, and non-repudiation controls and management of communications between senders and receivers of information in a network.

Security services capabilities and mechanisms to protect sensitive information and treatments in the information system. The appropriate level of protection is determined based upon the value of the information to the application end-users and the perception of threats to it. These services include the following:

— Identification/authentication service confirms the identities of requesters for use of information system resources. In addition, authentication can apply to providers of data. Access control service prevents the unauthorised use of information system resources. This service also prevents the use of a resource in an unauthorised way. This service may be applied to various aspects of access to a resource or to all accesses to a resource.

— Data integrity service ensures that data is not altered or destroyed in an unauthorised manner. This service applies to data in permanent data stores and to data in communications messages.

— Data confidentiality service ensures that data is not made available or disclosed to unauthorised individuals or computer processes. This service will be applied to devices that permit human interaction with the information system. In addition, this service will ensure that observation of usage patterns of communications resources will not be possible.

— Non-repudiation service ensures that entities engaging in an information exchange cannot deny being involved in it. This service may take one or both of two forms. First, the recipient of data is provided with proof of the origin of the data. This protects against any attempt by the sender to falsely deny sending the data or its contents. Second, the sender of data is provided with proof of delivery of data. This protects against any subsequent attempt by the recipient to falsely deny receiving the data or its contents.

Digital SIPs may be delivered via electronic transfer (e.g., FTP), loaded from media submitted to the archive, or simply mounted (e.g., CD-ROM) on the archive file system for access. Non-digital SIPs would likely be delivered by conventional shipping procedures. The Receive Submission function may represent a legal transfer of custody for the Content Information in the SIP, and may require that special access controls be placed on the contents. This function provides a confirmation of receipt of a SIP to the Producer, which may include a request to resubmit a SIP in the case of errors resulting from the SIP submission.

The Quality Assurance function validates (QA results) the successful transfer of the SIP to the staging area. For digital submissions, these mechanisms might include Cyclic Redundancy Checks (CRCs) or checksums associated with each data file, or the use of system log files to record and identify any file transfer or media read/write errors.

The Generate AIP function transforms one or more SIPs into one or more AIPs that conform to the archive's data formatting and documentation standards. This may involve file format conversions, data representation conversions or reorganisation of the content information in the SIPs. The Generate AIP function may issue report requests to Data Management to obtain reports of information needed by the Generate AIP function to produce the Descriptive Information that completes the AIP.

The Generate Descriptive Information function extracts Descriptive Information from the AIPs and collects Descriptive Information from other sources to provide to Coordinate Updates, and ultimately Data Management. This includes metadata to support searching and retrieving AIPs (e.g., who, what, when, where, why), and could also include special browse products to be used by Finding Aids.

The Coordinate Updates function is responsible for transferring the AIPs to Archival Storage and the Descriptive Information to Data Management. Transfer of the AIP includes a storage request and may represent an electronic, physical, or a virtual transfer. After the transfer is completed and verified, Archival Storage returns a storage confirmation indicating the storage identification information for the AIP.

The Coordinate Updates function also incorporates the storage identification information into the Descriptive Information for the AIP and transfers it to the Data Management entity along with a database update request. In return, Data Management provides a database update response indicating the status of the update. Data Management updates may take place without a corresponding Archival Storage transfer when the SIP contains Descriptive Information for an AIP already in Archival Storage.

Archival Storage

The Receive Data function receives a storage request and an AIP from Ingest and moves the AIP to permanent storage within the archive. The transfer request may need to indicate the anticipated frequency of utilisation of the data objects comprising the AIP in order to allow the appropriate storage devices or media to be selected for storing the AIP. This function will select the media type, prepare the devices or volumes, and perform the physical transfer to the Archival Storage volumes. Upon completion of the transfer, this function sends a storage confirmation message to Ingest, including the storage identification of the AIPs.

The Manage Storage Hierarchy function positions, via commands, the contents of the AIPs on the appropriate media based on storage management policies, operational statistics, or directions from Ingest via the storage request. It will also conform to any special levels of service required for the AIP, or any special security measures that are required, and ensures the appropriate level of protection for the AIP. These include on-line, off-line or near-line storage, required throughput rate, maximum allowed bit error rate, or special handling or backup procedures. It monitors error logs to ensure AIPs are not corrupted during transfers.

This function also provides operational statistics to Administration summarising the inventory of media on-hand, available storage capacity in the various tiers of the storage hierarchy, and usage statistics. The Replace Media function provides the capability to reproduce the AIPs over time. Within the Replace Media function the Content Information and Preservation Description Information (PDI) must not be altered. However, the data constituting the Packaging Information may be changed as long as it continues to perform the same function and there is a straight forward implementation that does not cause information loss.

The migration strategy must select a storage medium, taking into consideration the expected and actual rates of errors encountered in various media types, their performance, and their costs of ownership. If media-dependent attributes have been included as part of the Content Information, a way must be found to preserve this information when migrating to higher capacity media with different storage architectures. The Error Checking function provides statistically acceptable assurance that no components of the AIP are corrupted during any internal Archival Storage data transfer. This function requires that all hardware and software within the archive provide notification of potential errors and that these errors are routed to standard error logs that are checked by the Archival Storage staff.

The PDI Fixity Information provides some assurance that the Content Information has not been altered as the AIP is moved and accessed. Similar information is needed to protect the PDI itself. A standard mechanism for tracking and verifying the validity of all data objects within the archive may also be used. For example, CRCs could be maintained for every individual data file. A higher level of service, such as Reed-Solomon coding to support combined error detection and correction, could also be provided.

The storage facility procedures should provide for random verification of the integrity of data objects using CRCs or some other error checking mechanism.The Disaster Recovery function provides a mechanism for duplicating the digital contents of the archive collection and storing the duplicate in a physically separate facility. This function is normally accomplished by copying the archive contents to some form of removable storage media, but may also be performed via hardware transport or network data transfers. The Provide Data function provides copies of stored AIPs to Access. This function receives an AIP request that identifies the requested AIP(s) and provides them on the requested media type or transfers them to a staging area. This function also sends a notice of data transfer to Access upon completion of an order.

Logical Model for Archival Information

A basic concept of the OAIS Reference Model is the concept of information being a combination of data and Representation Information. The Information Object is composed of a Data Object that is either physical or digital, and the Representation Information that allows for the full interpretation of the data into meaningful information.

The Data Object may be expressed as either a physical object together with some Representation Information, or it may be expressed as a digital object (i.e., a sequence of bits) together with the Representation Information giving meaning to those bits. The Representation Information accompanying a physical object like a moon rock may give additional meaning, as a result of some analysis, to the physically observable attributes of the rock. This information may have been developed over time and the results, if provided, would be part of the Information Object. The Representation Information accompanying a digital object, or sequence of bits, is used to provide additional meaning. It typically maps the bits into commonly recognised data types such as character, integer, and real and into groups of these data types. It associates these with higher-level meanings that can have complex inter-relationships that are also described.

The purpose of the Representation Information object is to convert the bit sequences into more meaningful information. It does this by describing the format, or data structure concepts, which are to be applied to the bit sequences and that in turn result in more meaningful values such as characters, numbers, pixels, arrays, tables, etc. These common computer data types, aggregations of these data types, and mapping rules which map from the underlying data types to the higher level concepts needed to understand the Digital Object are referred to as the Structure Information of the Representation Information object. These structures are commonly identified by name or by relative position within the associated bit sequences.

The Representation Information provided by the Structure Information is seldom sufficient. Even in the case where the Digital Object is interpreted as a sequence of text characters, and described as such in the Structure Information, the additional information as to which language was being expressed should be provided. This type of additional required information is referred to as the

Semantic Information. When dealing with scientific data, for example, the information in the Semantic Information can be quite varied and complex. It will include special meanings associated with all the elements of the Structural Information, operations that may be performed on each data type, and their inter-relationships.

International Standard Organisation (ISO) 9660 describes text as conforming to the ASCII standard, but it does not actually describe how ASCII is to be implemented. It simply references the ASCII standard which is additional Representation Information that is needed for a full understanding. Therefore the ASCII standard is a part of the Representation Net associated with ISO 9660 and needs to be obtained by the OAIS in some form, or the OAIS needs to track the availability of this standard so that it may take appropriate steps in the future to ensure its ISO 9660 Representation Information is fully understandable.

Representation Networks

Representation Information, which is itself an Information Object, may be expressed in physical forms (e.g., a paper document) or in digital forms. When the Representation Information is in digital form, additional Representation Information is needed to understand the bits of the Representation Information. In principle, this recursion continues until physical forms are encountered. For example, Representation Information expressed in ASCII needs the additional Representation Information for ASCII, which might be a physical document giving the ASCII standard.Each item of Representation Information can have multiple components, including multiple referenced Representation Information components; each with is own Representation Information

To preserve the meaning of an Information Object, its Representation Information must also be preserved. This is most easily accomplished when the Representation

Information objects are expressed in forms that are easily understandable, such as text descriptions that use widely supported standards such as ASCII characters for electronic versions. One problem with the use of only text descriptions is that such descriptions can be ambiguous.

This is addressed by the use of standardised, formal description languages containing well-defined constructs with which to describe data structures. These languages may need to be augmented with text descriptions to fully convey the semantics of the Representation Information Two special types of Representation Information are Representation Rendering Software and Access Software. Representation Rendering Software is able to display the Representation Information in understandable forms.

The file and directory structure of many CD-ROMs conforms to ISO 9660. This standard is Representation Information describing how most CD-ROM file structures are to be implemented, and it may be obtained as a paper document. However it may also be obtained as a digital object that needs to be understood as a PDF object. Rather than actually obtaining the documentation of PDF and writing software to understand the ISO 9660 object, an OAIS may use available PDF display software to render the ISO 9660 documentation humanly visible and readable. In this role the PDF display software is referred to as Representation Rendering Software because it is used to render the Representation Information.

If the OAIS does not also obtain the associated description of PDF, it needs to record and track this fact because when PDF objects are no longer cost-effective for access and display, the ISO 9660 documentation expressed as a PDF object will need to be migrated to a new form. Access Software presents some or all of the information content of an Information Object in forms understandable to humans or systems. It may also provide some types of access service, such as displaying, manipulating, processing, or sub-setting, to an Information Object. For some types of Digital Objects, such software may be widely available. It is not necessary for the OAIS to maintain or provide such software. The OAIS may want to maintain and provide this software for more specialised types of Digital Objects.

Since Access software will incorporate some understanding of the Representation Information, some archives may attempt to use Access Software as a substitute for full Representation Information. Access Software source code, which embodies at least a partial understanding of the associated Representation Information, may be used as documentation expressing such Representation Information.

A problem with this approach is that the desired Representation Information may not be clearly identifiable as it may be mixed with various processing and display algorithms, and may be incomplete since the code assumes an underlying operating environment. It may be difficult to tell, from the software code, what Representation Information is missing. The use of Access Software executables, without the source code, such as may occur with proprietary formats, presents a much greater risk for loss of information because it is more difficult to maintain an operating environment for software than to migrate documentation over time. The practical use of emulation techniques, to preserve working software, has not yet been shown to be cost-effective. This is a significant issue for those desiring to preserve a look and feel to information access.

Types of Information

There are many types of information involved in the long-term preservation of information in an OAIS. Each of these types can be viewed as a complete Information Object in that it contains a data object and adequate Representation Information to understand the data.

The Content Information is the set of information that is the original target of preservation by the OAIS. Deciding what is the Content Information may not be obvious and may need to be negotiated with the Producer. The Representation Information for a digital Content Data Object (both semantic and syntactic) is needed to fully transform the bits into the Content Information. In principal, this even extends to the inclusion of definitions (e.g., dictionary and grammar) of any natural language (e.g., English) used in expressing the Content Information.

Over long time periods the meaning of natural language expressions can evolve significantly in both general and in specific discipline usage. As a practical matter, the OAIS needs to have enough Representation Information associated with the bits of the Content Data Object in the Content Information that it feels confident that the members of the Designated Community can enter the Representation Network with enough knowledge to begin accurately interpreting the Representation Information. This is a significant risk area for an OAIS, particularly for those with an expert Designated Community, because jargon and apparently widely understood terms may be short-lived. In such cases extra care needs to be exercised to ensure that the natural evolution of the Designated Community Knowledge Base does not effectively cause information loss from the Content Information.

As described above for an Information Object in general, the Representation Information can also be viewed as being augmented by Access Software that supports the presentation of the Content Information to the Consumer. Examples of this type of software include word processors supporting complex document format representations of Content Information and scientific visualisation systems supporting representations of Content Information as a time series or a multidimensional array. The software uses its knowledge of the underlying Representation Information to provide these services. Often required information will be embedded in the software packages used by the Designated Community to present and analyse the Content Information. A reason for preserving working Access Software arises from a convenience factor. Even with a complete set of Representation Information, practical access to all or part of a digital Content Data Object requires the use of Access Software. Thus a software module that provides useful access to a digital Content Data Object may be preserved in a working state as a matter of convenience. This is not difficult to do as long as the environment, which supports the software module, is readily available.

This environment consists of some underlying hardware and an operating system, various utilities that effectively augment the operating system and storage and display devices and their drivers. A change to any of these may cause the software module to no longer function, to function incorrectly, or to be unable to present results to the application or human user. The complexity of these interactions is what traditionally makes the preservation of working software such an arduous task. In short, the use of Access Software to replace Representation Networks is attractive from the point of view of minimising the resources needed to ingest data and provide current users with access to data.

However the reliance on working software can provide major problems for Long-Term Preservation when that software ceases to function. Indefinite long-term information preservation requires a full and understandable description of the Representation Information. An important function of the OAIS is deciding what parts of the Content Information are the Content Data Object and what parts are the Representation Information. This aspect is critical to a clear understanding of what is being preserved.

Preservation of Archival Description

In addition to Content Information, the Archival

Information must include information that will allow the understanding of the Content Information over an indefinite period of time. The specific set of Information Objects, which are required for this function, is collectively called Preservation Description Information (PDI). The PDI must include information that is necessary to adequately preserve the particular Content Information with which it is associated. It is specifically focused on describing the past and present states of the Content Information, ensuring it is uniquely identifiable, and ensuring it has not been unknowingly altered.

This information is typical for all types of archives and has been classified in the context of traditional archives. However, the class definitions must be extended for digital archives. The following definitions are preserving Digital Information:

— *Reference Information*: This information identifies, and if necessary describes, one or more mechanisms used to provide assigned identifiers for the Content Information. It also provides those identifiers that allow outside systems to refer, unambiguously, to this particular Content Information. Examples of these systems include taxonomic systems, reference systems and registration systems. In the OAIS Reference Model most if not all of this information is replicated in Package Descriptions, which enable Consumers to access Content Information of interest.

— *Context Information*: This information documents the relationships of the Content Information to its environment. This includes why the Content Information was created and how it relates to other Content Information objects existing elsewhere.

— *Provenance Information*: This information documents the history of the Content Information. This tells the origin or source of the Content Information, any changes that may have taken place since it was originated, and who has had custody of it since it was originated. This gives future users some assurance as to the likely reliability of the Content Information. Provenance can be viewed as a special type of context information.

— *Fixity Information*: This information provides the Data Integrity checks or Validation/Verification keys used to ensure that the particular Content Information object has not been altered in an undocumented manner. Fixity Information includes special encoding and error detection schemes that are specific to instances of Content Objects. Fixity Information does not include the integrity preserving mechanisms provided by the OAIS underlying services, error protection supplied by the media and device drivers used by Archival Storage.

The Fixity Information may specify minimum quality of service requirements for these mechanisms. The OAIS needs to explicitly decide what the exact definition of Content Information is in order to be able to ensure that it also has the PDI needed to preserve the Content Information. Once the Content Information has been determined, it is possible to assess the Preservation Description Information.

— *Packaging Information*: The Packaging Information is that information which, either actually or logically, binds or relates the components of the package into an identifiable entity on specific media. For example, if the Content Information and PDI are identified as being the content of specific files on a CD-ROM, then the Packaging Information may include the ISO 9660 volume/file structure on the CD-ROM.

These choices are the subject of local archive definitions or conventions. The Packaging Information does not necessarily need to be preserved by an OAIS since it does not contribute to the Content Information or the PDI. However, there are cases where the OAIS may be required to reproduce the original submission exactly. In this case the Content Information is defined to include all the bits submitted.

The OAIS should also avoid holding PDI or Content Information only in the naming conventions of directory or file name structures. These structures are most likely to be used as Packaging Information. Packaging Information is not preserved by Migration. Any information saved in file names or directory structures may be lost when the Packaging Information is altered.

— *Descriptive Information:* To preserving information, the OAIS must provide adequate features to allow Consumers to locate information of potential interest, analyse that information, and order desired information. This is accomplished through a specialisation of the Information Object called Descriptive Information, which contain the data that serves as the input to documents or applications called Access Aids.

  The Descriptive Information is generally derived from the Content Information and PDI. The Descriptive Information can be viewed as an index to enable efficient access to the associated Information Package via associated Access Aids. Access Aids are documents or applications that can be used to locate, analyse, retrieve, or order information from the OAIS.

Information Life Cycle Management

The project managers from the "cutting edge" projects emphasised the importance of considering best practices for archiving at all stages of the information management life cycle. Acknowledging this important philosophy, the best practices identified by the study are presented in the framework of the information life cycle — creation, acquisition, cataloging/identification, storage, preservation and access.

— *Creation* : Creation is the act of producing the information product. The producer may be a human author or originator, or a piece of equipment such as a sensing device, satellite or laboratory instrument. Creation is viewed here in the broadest sense, as increasingly science is based on a variety of data types, products and originators.

All project managers acknowledged that creation is where long-term archiving and preservation must start. Even in rigorously controlled situations, the digital information may be lost without the initial awareness on the part of the originator of the importance of archiving. Practices used when a digital object is created ultimately impact the ease with which the object can be digitally archived and preserved.

In addition, there are several key practices involving the creator that are evolving within the archiving projects. First, the creator may be involved in assessing the long-term value of the information. In lieu of other assessment factors, the creator's estimate of the long-term value of the information may be a good indication of the value that will be placed on it by people within the same discipline or area of research in the future. The U.S. Department of Agriculture's Digital Publications Preservation Steering Committee has suggested that the creator provide a preservation indicator in the document. This would not take the place of formal retention schedules, but it would provide an indication of the long-term value that the creator, as a practicing researcher, attaches to the document's contents.

Secondly, the preservation and archiving process is made more efficient when attention is paid to issues of consistency, format, standardisation and metadata description in the very beginning of the information life cycle. The Oak Ridge National Laboratory recently announced guidelines for the creation of digital documents. Limits are placed on both the software that can be used and on the format and layout of the documents in order to make short and long-term information management easier. Many project managers acknowledged that the best practice would be to create the metadata at the object creation stage, or to create the metadata in stages, with the metadata provided at creation augmented by additional elements during the cataloging/identification stage.

However, only in the case of data objects is the metadata routinely collected at the point of creation. Many of the datasets are created by measurement or monitoring instruments, and the metadata is supplied along with the data stream. This may include location, instrument type, and other quality indicators concerning the context of the measurement. In some cases, this instrument-generated metadata is supplemented by information provided by the original researcher. For smaller datasets and other objects such as documents and images, much of the metadata continues to be created "by hand" and after-the-fact. Metadata creation is not sufficiently incorporated into the tools for the creation of these objects to rely solely on the creation process.

As standards groups and vendors move to incorporate XML (eXtensible Mark-up Language) and RDF (Resource Description Framework) architectures in their word processing and database products, the creation of metadata as part of the origination of the object will be easier.

— *Acquisition and Collection Development* : Acquisition and collection development is the stage in which the created object is "incorporated" physically or virtually into the archive. The object must be known to the archive administration. There are two main aspects to the acquisition of digital objects — collection policies and gathering procedures.

— *Collection policies:* In most countries, the major difference in collection policies between formal print and electronic publications is the question of whether digital materials are included under current deposit legislation. Guidelines help to establish the boundaries in such an unregulated situation. It is also the case that there is just too much material that could be archived from the Internet, so guidelines are needed to tailor the general collection practices of the organisation. The collection policies answer questions related to selecting what to archive, determining extent, archiving links, and refreshing site contents.

— *Selection:* Both the National Library of Canada (NLC) and the National Library of Australia (NLA) acknowledge the importance of selection guidelines. The NLC's Guidelines state, "The main difficulty in extending legal deposit to network publishing is that legal deposit is a relatively indiscriminate acquisition mechanism that aims at comprehensiveness.

In the network environment, any individual with access to the Internet can be a publisher, and the network publishing process does not always provide the initial screening and selection at the manuscript stage on which libraries have traditionally relied in the print environment.

While the scope of NLA's PANDORA (Preserving and Accessing Networked Documentary Resources of Australia) Project is only to preserve Australian Internet publishing, the NLA also acknowledges that it is still impossible to archive everything. Therefore, the NLA has formulated guidelines for the Selection of Online Australian Publications Intended for Preservation by the National Library of Australia.

These guidelines are key to the successful networking of the state libraries into the National Collection of Australian Electronic Publications, since they provide consistency across multiple acquisition activities. Scholarly publications of national significance and those of current and long term research value are archived comprehensively. Other items are archived on a selective basis "to provide a broad cultural snapshot of how Australians are using the Internet to disseminate information, express opinions, lobby, and publish their creative work." Directly connected to the question of selection is the issue of extent. What is the extent or the boundary of a particular digital work? This is particularly an issue when selecting complex Web sites.

Archiving Links : The extensive use of hypertext links to other digital objects in electronic publications raises the question of whether these links and their content should be archived along with the source item. This issue has been addressed by the selected projects in a variety of ways.

Most organisations archive the links (the URLs or other identifiers) but not the content of the linked objects. The American Institute of Physics archives the links embedded in the text and references of its electronic journal articles but not the text or content of any of these links, unless the linked item happens to be in its publication archive or in the supplemental material which it also archives.

Similarly, the Office of Scientific and Technical Information of the U.S. Department of Energy (DOE OSTI) does not intentionally archive any links beyond the extent of the digital object itself. However, the document may be linked to another document if that document is another DOE document in the OSTI archive. NLA's decision about archiving the content of linked objects is based on its selection guidelines. If a linked item meets the selection guidelines, it's contents will be archived, otherwise it will not be. In a slightly different approach, the NLC has chosen to archive the text of the linked object only if it is on the same server as the object that is being archived.

The NLC cites difficulties in tracking down hypertext links and acquiring the linked objects as the reason for its decision not to include the content of other links. The previous issue of the same periodical, accessed through a hypertext link, would be considered a part of the original publication. Another publication accessed through a hypertext link would not be considered part of the original publication. Only two of the reviewed projects archive the content of all links. Internet guru Brewster Kahle's Internet Archive retains all links, because the aim of the project is to archive a snapshot of the entire Internet.

Within a specific domain, the American Astronomical Society also maintains all links to both documents and supporting materials in other formats, based on extensive collaboration among the various international astronomical societies, researchers, universities, and government agencies. Each organisation archives its own publications, but links are maintained not only from references in the full text and cited references of the articles, but between and among the major international astronomical databases. Within this specific domain, the contents of all linked objects are available.

Refreshing the Archived Contents : In cases where the archiving is taking place while changes or updates may still be occurring to the digital object, as in the case of on-going Web sites, there is a need to consider refreshing the archived contents. A balance must be struck between the completeness and currency of the archive and the burden on the system resources. Obviously, the burden of refreshing the content increases as the number of sources stored in the archive increases.

Gathering Approaches: There are two general approaches to the gathering of relevant Internet-based information -- hand-selected and automatic. In the case of the NLA, the sites are reviewed and hand-selected. They are monitored for their persistence before being included in the archive. Alternatively, the Royal Library, the National Library of Sweden, acquires material by periodically running a robot to capture sites for its Kulturarw project without making value judgments.

Intellectual Property Concerns: Intellectual property remains a key issue in the acquisition process. The approaches to intellectual property vary based on the type of organisation doing the archiving. In the case of data centers or corporate archives where there is a close tie between the center and the owner or funding source, there is little question about the intellectual property rights related to acquisition. However, in the case of national libraries, the approaches to intellectual property rights differ from country to country. The differences are based on variant national information policies or legal deposit laws.

In many countries, the law has not yet caught up with the digital environment, and the libraries must make their own decisions. In the absence of digital deposit legislation, the PANDORA Project seeks permission from the copyright owner before copying the resource for the archive. In contrast, the Swedish and Finnish national library projects have an automated system and do not contact the owners.

— *Identification and Cataloging:* Once the archive has acquired the digital object, it is necessary to identify and catalog it. Both identification and cataloging allow the archiving organisation to manage the digital objects over time. Identification provides a unique key for finding the object and linking that object to other related objects. Cataloging in the form of metadata supports organisation, access and curation. Cataloging and identification practices are often related to what is being archived and the resources available for managing the archive.

Metadata: All archives use some form of metadata for description, reuse, administration, and preservation of the archived object. There are issues related to how the metadata is created, the metadata standards and content rules that are used, the level at which metadata is applied and where the metadata is stored. The majority of the projects created metadata in whole or part at the cataloging stage. However, there is increasing interest in automatic generation of metadata, since the manual creation of metadata is considered to be a major impediment to digital archiving.

A project is underway at the U.S. Environmental Protection Agency to derive metadata at the data element level from legacy databases. The Defense Information Technology Testbed (DITT) Project within the U.S. Department of Defense is also investigating automated metadata generation. A variety of metadata formats are used by the selected projects, depending on the data type, discipline, resources available, and cataloging approaches used. Most national libraries use traditional library cataloging standards with some fields unable to be filled and others taking on new meaning.

All titles in the NLA's PANDORA Archive receive full MARC cataloging by the Electronic Unit Staff. However, several newer abbreviated formats developed specifically for Web-based resources are also in use. EVA uses a Dublin Core-like format. It is anticipated that an abbreviated format such as the Dublin Core may facilitate receipt of metadata directly from the publisher, eliminating the need for extensive library cataloging. There is even a greater variety of content standards used by the projects when entering data into the metadata fields.

The national libraries tend to use traditional library cataloging rules such as AACR2. Some communities, such as the geospatial community, have information standards, such as latitude and longitude, which are easily incorporated as metadata content standards. However, work remains to identify the specific metadata elements needed for long-term preservation as opposed to discovery, particularly for non-textual data types like images, video and multimedia. The level at which metadata is applied depends on the type of data and the anticipated access needs. Datasets are generally cataloged at the file or collection level.

Electronic journal articles may be cataloged individually, sometimes with no concern about metadata for the issue or journal title levels. Homepages provide a particularly difficult problem for determining the level at which metadata should be applied. Generally, the metadata is applied to whatever level is considered to be the full extent of the intellectual resource. In the projects reviewed, the metadata files generally are stored separately from the archives themselves. Libraries may store the metadata in their online public access catalogs. Publishers may store the metadata in a bibliographic or citation database.

However, in some instances, such as electronic journals with tagged headers for title, authors, author affiliation, etc., the information may be stored with the object itself and extracted for the catalog. In the case of distributed archives, the metadata may be stored centrally, with the objects distributed throughout the network, or the metadata may be stored as embedded tags in the digital resource. Discussions surrounding the interoperability of archives, both within and across disciplines, focus on the need to be able to crosswalk or translate between the various metadata formats. This is key to the development of networked, heterogeneous archives.

The Open Archival Information System (OAIS) Reference Model developed by the ISO Consultative Committee for Space Data Systems addresses this issue by encapsulating specific metadata as needed for each object type in a consistent data model. The Long Term Environmental Research (LTER) Network has developed mechanisms for "fitting" its network-specific metadata information into the broader scheme of the Federal Geographic Data Committee content standard for geographic data and other standards related to ecology.

For those archives that do not copy the digital material immediately into the archive, the movement of material from server to server or from directory to directory on the network, resulting in a change in the URL, is problematic. The use of the server as the location identifier can result in a lack of persistence over time both for the source object and any linked objects.

Despite possible problems, most archives continue to use the URL when referencing the location for the digital object. However, there are some projects that are changing this practice. The OCLC archive uses PURLs, persistent identifiers to which the changeable URL is mapped. The American Chemical Society uses the Digital Object Identifier for its journal articles and also maintains the original Manuscript Number assigned to the item at the beginning of the publication process.

A multifaceted identification system is used by the American Astronomical Society (AAS). Name resolution is used instead of URLs. In addition, the AAS uses astronomy's standard identifier, called a "Bibcode", which has been in use for fifteen years. In the spring of 1999, AAS added PubRef numbers; other identifiers can be added as needed to maintain links.

— *Storage* : Storage is often treated as a passive stage in the life cycle, but storage media and formats have changed with legacy information perhaps lost forever. Block sizes, tape sizes, tape drive mechanisms and operating systems have changed over time. Most organisations that responded to the question about the periodicity of media migration anticipate a 3-5 year cycle.

The most common solution to this problem of changing storage media is migration to new storage systems. This is expensive, and there is always concern about the loss of data or problems with the quality when a transfer is made. Check algorithms are extremely important when this approach is used.

The most rigorous media migration practices are in place at the data centers. The Atmospheric Radiation Monitoring (ARM) Center at the Oak Ridge National Laboratory plans to migrate to new technologies every 4-5 years. During each migration, the data is copied to the new technology. Each migration will require 6-12 months.

— *Preservation* : Preservation is the aspect of archival management that preserves the content as well as the

> look and feel of the digital object. While the study showed that there is no common agreement on the definition of long-term preservation, the time frame can be thought of as long enough to be concerned about changes in technology and changes in the user community. Depending on the particular technologies and subject disciplines involved, the project managers interviewed estimated the cycle for hardware/software migration at 2-10 years.

New releases of databases, spreadsheets, and word processors can be expected at least every two to three years, with patches and minor updates released more often. While software vendors generally provide migration strategies or upward compatibility for some generations of their products, this may not be true beyond one or two generations. Migration is not guaranteed to work for all data types, and it becomes particularly unreliable if the information product has used sophisticated software features. There is generally no backward compatibility, and if it is possible, there is certainly loss of integrity in the result.

Plans are less rigorous for migrating to new hardware and applications software than for storage media. In order to guard against major hardware/software migration issues, the organisations try to procure mainstream commercial technologies. For example, both the American Chemical Society and the U.S. Environmental Protection Agency purchased Oracle not only for its data management capabilities but for the company's longevity and ability to impact standards development.

Unfortunately, this level of standardisation and ease of migration is not as readily available among technologies used in specialised fields where niche systems are required because of the interfaces to instrumentation and the volume of data to be stored and manipulated. Emulation, which encapsulates the behavior of the hardware/software with the object, is being considered as an alternative to migration. A MS Word 2000 document would be labeled as such and then metadata information provided that indicates how to reconstruct such a document is at the engineering — bits and bytes — level. An alternative to encapsulating the software with every instance of the data type is to create an emulation registry that uniquely identifies the hardware and software environments and provides information on how to recreate the environment in order to preserve the use of the digital object.

At this time, there is no system in place to provide the extensive documentation and emulation information required for this approach to be operable, particularly to allow an archive to deal with the variety of older technologies. Most importantly, there is no policy that requires the manufacturers to deposit the emulation information. The best practice for the foreseeable future will be migration to new hardware and software platforms; emulation will begin to be used if and when the hardware and software industries begin to endorse it.

At the specific format level, there are several approaches used to save the "look and feel" of material. For journal articles, the majority of the projects reviewed use image files (TIFF), PDF, or HTML. TIFF is the most prevalent for those organisations that are involved in any way with the conversion of paper backfiles.

JSTOR, a non-profit organisation that supports both storage of current journal issues in electronic format and conversion of back issues, processes everything from paper into TIFF and then scans the TIFF image. The OCR, because it cannot achieve 100% accuracy, is used only for searching; the TIFF image is the actual delivery format that the user sees. However, this does not allow the embedded references to be active hyperlinks. HTML/SGML (Standard Generalised Mark-up Language) is used by many large publishers after years of converting publication systems from proprietary formats to SGML.

The American Astronomical Society (AAS) has a richly encoded SGML format that is used as the archival format from which numerous other formats and products are made. The SGML version that is actually stored by the publisher is converted to HTML. PDF versions can also be provided by conversion routines. For purely electronic documents, PDF is the most prevalent format. This provides a replica of the Postscript format of the document, but relies upon proprietary encoding technologies. PDF is used both for formal publications and grey literature.

The National Library of Sweden transforms dissertations that are received in formats other than PDF to PDF and HTML. While PDF is increasingly accepted, concerns remain for long-term preservation and it may not be accepted as a legal depository format, because of its proprietary nature.

Preserving the "look and feel" is difficult in the text environment, but it is even more difficult in the multimedia environment, where there is a tightly coupled interplay between software, hardware and content. The U.S. Department of Defense DITT Project is developing models and software for the management of multimedia objects. Similarly, the University of California at San Diego has developed a model for object-based archiving that allows various levels and types of metadata with distributed storage of various data types.

The UCSD work is funded by the U.S. National Archives and Records Administration and the U.S. Patent and Trademark Office.A key preservation issue is the format in which the archival version should be stored. Transformation is the process of converting the native format to a standard format.

On the whole, the projects reviewed favored storage in native formats. However, there are several examples of data transformation. AAS and ACS transform the incoming files into SGML-tagged ASCII format.

The AAS believes that "The electronic master copy, if done well, is able to serve as the robust electronic archival copy. Such a well-tagged copy can be updated periodically, at very little cost, to take advantage of advances in both technology and standards.

The content remains unchanged, but the public electronic version can be updated to remain compatible with the advances in browsers and other access technology." The data community also provides some examples of data transformation. For example, the NASA Data Active Archive Centers (DAACs) transform incoming satellite and ground-monitoring information into standard Common Data Format.

The U.K.'s National Digital Archive of Datasets (NDAD) transforms the native format into one of its own devising, since NDAD could not find an existing standard that dealt with all their metadata needs. These transformed formats are considered to be the archival versions, but the bit-wise copies are retained, so that someone can replicate what the center has done. In some countries, there are intellectual property questions related to native versus transformed formats.

According to Canadian Copyright Law, an author's rights are infringed if the original work is "distorted, mutilated or otherwise modified." After much discussion, the NLC decided that converting an electronic publication to a standard format to preserve the quality of the original and to ensure long-term access does not infringe on the author's right of integrity. However, this assumption has not been tested in court.

One of the paradoxes of the networked environment is that in an environment that is so dynamic and open to change, there is a greater and greater emphasis on standards. Those projects that have been archiving for a long period of time indicated that while they started out with a large number of incoming formats — primarily textual — the number of formats have decreased. DOE OSTI began its project with a limited number of acceptable input formats, because there were so many different native formats. In the political environment of that time, it was difficult to gain support for the standardisation of word processing packages. However, documents are currently received in only a few formats. Text is received in SGML (and its relatives HTML and XML), PDF (Normal and Image), WordPerfect and Word. Images are received in TIFF Group 4 and PDF Image.

The market forces have reduced the number of major word processing vendors. To a lesser extent, consolidation has occurred in the number of spreadsheet and database formats. However, there is less consistency in the modeling, simulation and specific purpose software areas; much of this software continues to be specific to the project. Therefore, the emphasis in these areas is on the development of standards for interoperability and data exchange, realising that perhaps the market forces will not play as large a role here as with more general purpose software applications.

— *Access :* The previous life cycle functions that have been discussed are performed for the purpose of ensuring continuous access to the material in the archive. Successful practices must consider changes to access mechanisms, as well as rights management and security requirements over the long term.

Most project managers interviewed consider the access and display mechanisms to be another source of change in the digital environment. Today it is the Web, but there is no way of knowing what it might be tomorrow. It may be possible in the future to enhance the quality of presentation of items from the digital archive based on advances in digitisation and browser technologies. The electronic archive is used to create new access versions as the access mechanisms change. However, the originals are always retained.

7

Role of Internet in Digital Preservation

Today, we need again to take a fresh and holistic look at what we are trying to do, to examine the nature of all types of resources that we acquire, describe, organise, arrange, preserve, access, select, and use. We need to understand characteristics of users, their abilities, inquiries, and information tasks, retrieval models, and operational standards. Finally, we need to educate current and future professionals about the evolving nature of virtual public service components. We all read papers on important issues of digital libraries, on declining uses of cumbersome traditional reference services, on sharply increased uses of convenient search engines, on early experiences of collaborative digital reference services, and on uses of various chat technologies.

Consumers will be increasingly remote rather than in-house, diverse in their capabilities and needs, and will have high expectations from 24/7 real-time virtual reference (similar to the ones in banking, automated gas stations, food services, and other self-help industries). This area has been mainly studied by the cataloging community and at a generic level only. In addition, we need better linkages between different types of resources. At one level, there is the 856 field, electronic location and access, between a MARC catalogue record and networked documents. It links a bibliographic record that is displayed on WebOpacs with full text documents. Other issues will be related to attaching tags for quality assurance, especially to fluid digital-born documents. Examples include authenticity, provenance, permanency, methodological integrity-reliability and validity. Another area that will be equally important to consider is the capability to use seamless languages both by the reference provider and the consumer in various question negotiations and answering settings.

The word seamless here means that clients need a series of gentle transformation of search languages on the Web, ranging from a pictorial representation of a "thing" for the elementary school child, to conceptual maps and DDC for the high school student. More than ever before, we need a search language that would ensure consistency, accuracy, precision, and negotiation power between the remote parties.

Controlled languages typically include subject headings, classifications, names, and unified titles. This area has been traditionally studied by catalogers and classification researchers; it has recently been studied by others and renamed into knowledge organisation tools, ontologies, and meta languages. Research is needed to investigate level of compatibility between and among languages for different user groups.

Here, we have not touched upon communication languages that are needed for disadvantaged users if we are to provide equitable CDRS for all potential clients. Search engines are likely to index more popular and US sites. With billions of digital documents out there, even with embedded tiny networked sensors and actuators, it will be mandatory to delineate reference tasks to be performed by trained and experienced people and others to be computer mediated at different levels of intervention.

According to the new library act the virtual library is THE new item especially for the public libraries, where the use of information technology until recently was not so well established.

So the government has initiated several projects in order to promote the public libraries as local information centres, and to experience the library staffs in using the internet to communicate with the end users. In October 2000 a new national service to the public was opened: bibliotek.dk - financed by the government. It is an online catalogue where you can search amongst all the Danish libraries' - public libraries as well as research libraries - books, CDs, articles, CD-ROMs, videos, reviews, talking books and research reports. You can order what you want and collect it at the library of your preference.

All you need is an internet access and a borrower's number to the library where you want to collect. You can order what you wish from your home PC or from any internet access. If your own library has not got what you need, your library can get it from another library in the interlending network. This database is based on the national professional online catalogue DanBib, which still serves as the national bibliographic interlending tool.

The principal goal is to simplify the complexity of a professional database for the benefit of the non-professional user. For example a title should only be shown once though the libraries may have different principles of registration. The public libraries use the national classifications system where the research libraries use Dewy. Search facilities will be extended, and the interface to the end user will go on being developed.

A future intention is that it will be possible to be told immediately if there is any waiting time. Via e-mail you can get information about the latest links. Also the children's library is a net guide for children and young adults. The guide gives access to links on the internet which have been chosen according to the same guidelines as those the librarians normally apply when selecting material for children and young adults. Global information for ethnic minorities is offered at: finfo.dk It is a global guide with links to the countries particularly relevant to ethnic minorities in Denmark. You can also get general information about the rights, obligations and possibilities of ethnic minorities in the Danish society.

In addition most public Danish information according to the national information policy is to be found on the official web sites and there is a tendency to publish online versions in stead of printed. Regarding reference material the DEF-project has initiated projects for research libraries and for public libraries to get licenses to databases and reference material with relevance for the local users. This of course is a challenge to the reference librarians and time has come to consider whether we can quit the past and the good old reference sources.

However there is no doubt that time has come to improve the librarians' competencies in being "virtual librarians". Skills in handling desk top facilities, downloading and file handling is still not "common knowledge" among the middle aged librarians. Also it is obvious, that the public libraries have competitors in delivering information via the internet, and that people often help themselves searching and finding via the most popular search engines. For the users it must make a difference to ask a librarian: you must get correct and sufficient information on time. The Danish libraries have skilled workers and competence to deliver information even to specific groups of users - but this is often a secret to the public.

An explanation in many libraries will be that we have not got the time, the experience and other resources for marketing our services. The public library is well established in peoples' minds and our statistics show that we are busy and that the number of users is increasing - especially when it comes to the education area. So it is easy to forget, that there actually is a much bigger market for information in the local area among professionals as well as amateurs: businesspeople, lawyers, doctors, people looking for jobs, genealogists and people dealing with local history. Through the years the libraries have built up competencies and resources to serve the local areas with proper information; in a near future these investments will be changed into virtual services delivered from as well small as big public libraries - the only tool you need is access to the internet.

In many aspects the reference work in the Danish libraries must go back to basics if the library service shall make the difference for the user. And marketing must be priority. It is necessary that the service offered is accessible: there must be someone there to answer the phone and chat. For many years we have kept on taking up new tasks - now is the time to look back and find out if services are no longer needed.

It is obvious that we cannot go on compiling new activities and services - we simply have not got the resources for that. We have noticed, that the users' needs are changing. Many users still come to the library for leisure, but the number of students and people searching for lifelong learning is growing and their demands are becoming more sophisticated. The quick reference service will change into information management and document delivering and that the librarian will have to deal with more complicated subjects on an expert basis. Users want access to the library virtually as well as physically 24 hours round the clock. Having the reference sources online makes them invisible - especially to the users frequenting the physical library.

Treaties, artifacts of social institutions, are negotiated in order to respond collectively to issues that states have been unable to resolve without institutional support. However, the multilateral treaty-making process is not always productive. Take the Moon Treaty for example, the fifth in a series of U.N. outer space treaties which after nine years of negotiations finally culminated in consensus at the U.N. Committee on the Peaceful Uses of Outer Space (COPUOS) before being sent to the General Assembly. It entered into force in 1984 but has since only attained five signatures and nine ratifications.

There are many treaties similar to the Moon Treaty that are currently gathering dust on bureaucratic bookshelves. Simply put, the present system has not always been effective. Despite such problems as fraud, terrorism, and security breaches, the World Wide Web is not powerless in such a setting as the U.N. Office of Outer Space Affairs (OOSA) web site demonstrates.Inaugurated in March 1994 as the first official U.N. presence on the WWW, the OOSA web site disseminates on-line documents and maintains archives to help promote space technology and space law as an integral part of sustainable development efforts in developing countries where the Internet is becoming more readily available.

One of the most compelling roles of the Internet in multilateral treaty-making is its capacity-building function which links diplomats, institutions, and practices to enable states to achieve their objectives. Priority areas for capacity-building on the Internet are:

— *Information dissemination and access*: The Internet fosters creation of political and administrative forums which allow negotiating parties to understand, formulate, and share their own interests and concerns. It also stimulates a multiplier effect by harnessing domestic opinion and facilitating the linkage of policies with issues. Moreover, uncertainty regarding other parties' positions on issues will no longer restrain otherwise willing countries from helping to bring multilateral treaties to fruition.

— *Alliances, domestic and international networks, and bilateral and multilateral partnerships through negotiation*: Even micro-states or coalitions of weaker states can share a flexible forum to more vigorously participate in agenda-setting and bargaining rather than be overwhelmed by current consensus "bullying."

— *Dynamics*: Once treaties are in force, the role of the Internet is dynamic- allowing multilateral treaties to be monitored as well as sustaining and documenting the levels of international cooperation on a continuing basis. The U.N. Office of Outer Space Affairs for creating a web site which enhances multilateral treaty-making.

Although the Moon Treaty was negotiated before the advent of the Internet, and will examine some of the reasons why the youngest of the outer space treaties has suffered such low levels of state ratification and how the Internet could have been instrumental in helping the treaty acquire universal acceptance. The following reasons for the failure of many developing countries to ratify the Moon Treaty:

— lack of knowledge of the benefits of space technology

— lack of sharing and transfer of space technology with space faring nations

— lack of general involvement in space activities, and

— lack of domestic regulatory mechanisms to ensure compliance with treaties.

In addition, current research indicates that the ambiguity of terminology concerning property rights, the common heritage of mankind, and a future legal regime to govern exploitation of the moon "as such exploitation is about to become feasible " have hindered states' ratification process.

One of the key requirements in this regard is capacity-building and the recognition that OOSA's web site is more than the sum of its individual components. Its horizontal networks across agencies and its vertical networks from individuals to communities disseminate valuable information which facilitates cooperation for the mutual benefit of all countries. The OOSA web site builds capacity by striving to improve the use of space science and technology for the economic and social development of all nations.

The Opening Page also lists agendas of committee meetings, current regional space workshops, indexes of on-line reports of the Legal Subcommittee, the Scientific and Technical Subcommittee, and international space symposiums. The web site is also user-friendly. It should be noted that the site's PDF and HTML files are available in all the official languages of the United Nations: Arabic, Chinese, English, French, Russian, and Spanish. However, it is not uncommon to find documents in other languages such as German, Norwegian, or Portuguese.

The availability of important documents in different languages is applaudable considering the astronomical costs of translating the colossal amount of written text.In addition to these documents, direct links are also available for accessing the original outer space treaties on the United Nations web site.

The What's New page announces new upcoming events including committee meetings, summits, and workshops. Because the web site has a global focus and is built on the premise of improving communications and information access, it requires a broad and holistic view of capacity development ranging from space applications for disaster management to youth programs and space education.

The Programme on Space Applications (PSA) page helps address two of the reasons why the Moon Treaty has failed to achieve universal acceptance:

(1) lack of knowledge of the benefits of space technology, and

(2) lack of sharing and transfer of space technology with spacefaring nations.

Since its creation the PSA has made substantial progress in furthering the knowledge and experience of space applications around the world. The OOSA web site helps to promote education, research and development support, and technical advisory service.

In sum, the mission of the PSA web pages is to enhance the understanding and subsequent use of space technology for peaceful purposes in general, and for national development, in particular, in response to expressed needs of different geographic regions of the world. The site also builds capacity by promoting greater cooperation and exchange of actual experiences in space science and technology; for example:

— Development of a fellowship program for in-depth training of scientists, technologists and applications specialists

— Organisation of seminars on advanced space applications and new system

— Stimulation of the growth of indigenous nuclei and an autonomous technological base in space technology in developing countries

— Dissemination of information and advanced technologies and applications.

One of the reasons offered for the low level of signature and ratification of the Moon Treaty was the lack of states' general involvement in space activities. The OOSA web site helps attract states' attention by linking space technology with domestic issues in a number of ways. For example, in 1999 the Third Conference on the Exploration and Peaceful Uses of Outer Space (UNISPACE III) was organised with two main goals:

— To promote the use of space technology in solving problems of a regional and global nature; and

— To further strengthen the capability of Member States, particularly developing countries, in the use of space-related technologies for economic, social and cultural development.

— To meet these goals, the OOSA web site announces symposiums and workshops to attract domestic interest.

Moreover, the UNISPACE III pages allow access to valuable background papers, General Assembly resolutions, international treaties, and other documents; for example:

— Disaster Prediction, Warming and Mitigation

— Management of Earth Resources

— Space Communications and Applications

During World Space Week in 2001 Secretary-General Kofi Annan addressed the United Nations: Space technology has produced tools that are transforming weather forecasting, environmental protection, humanitarian assistance, education, medicine, agriculture and a wide range of other activities.

And of course, a fascination with space leads many young people to pursue careers in science and technology, helping developing countries in particular to build up their human resources, improve their technological base and enhance their prospects for development. By promoting World Space Week, the OOSA web site helps the organisation to:

— educate people around the world about the benefits they receive from space,

— encourage greater use of space for sustainable economic development,

— demonstrate public support for space programs,

— excite children about learning and their future,

— promote institutions around the world that are involved in space, and

— foster international cooperation in space outreach and education.

Other events promoted by the OOSA web site are essay contests, summer camps, and student internships. For example, the OOSA web site provides links to UNESCO pages which sponsor an annual student essay contest.

The contest is open to all high school students between 15 and 18 years old and girls are encouraged to participate. The OOSA site also provides links to the International Institute of Spatial Informationa Technology (IISIT) of the People's Republic of China, the Institute of Remote Sensing and GIS of Peking University and UNESCO (Beijing Office) which hold summer camps in Peking. The objective is to enhance the knowledge, understanding and interest of high school students in aviation and aerospace.

Internet Dynamics

The OOSA web site is a prime example of Internet dynamics. Transparency and accountability on the part any international organisation are powerful influences in reducing conflict and in improving cooperation. Such willingness to open processes and decisions to public scrutiny curbs distrust and thus enhances adherence to treaties. Many of OOSA's on-line reports are devoted to documenting the space activities of its member states. In fact, every year COPUOS invites its member states to submit updates on their space activities including information on national and international programs.

One of the reasons why the Moon Treaty may have failed to achieve universal achievement is due to the lack of domestic regulatory mechanisms to ensure compliance with treaties. The United Nations Office for Outer Space Affairs is the Secretariat for the Legal Subcommittee of the United Nations Committee on the Peaceful Uses of Outer Space (COPUOS), which is the primary international forum for the development of laws and principles governing outer space.

The Space Law pages are thus a valuable resource for states, non-governmental organisations and the general public in order to promote understanding, acceptance and implementation of the international space law agreements concluded under United Nations auspices. The On-line Index of Objects Launched into Outer Space provides a quick and easy reference to data submitted to the United Nations in conformity with the Registration Convention and General Assembly Resolution 1721 B (XVI). It provides links between space objects and their relevant documents of registration.

In addition, the Index also contains information on space objects not registered with the United Nations in order to provide a complete data set to users. Currently the Index contains information on satellites launched from 1957 to the present. Space debris and other non-functional objects are not included.

New information technologies currently provide excellent opportunities for improving the efficiency and effectiveness of decision-making and negotiation as witnessed by new business and commercial auction applications.

8

Digital Libraries and World Wide Web

The Web is not a library but library material can be selected from the Web. This matter seeks then to further understanding of the dynamics of Web page and Web site lifecycles. These patterns challenge the integrity and the usefulness of libraries with Web content. The focuses on individual Web page and site attrition rather than the Web as a whole. Web pages and Web sites can be collected and categorised. They can be aggregated and included as parts of library collections. These libraries can take one of two forms.

Web libraries can consist of native documents linked to the library, which provides access to the document but do not exercise control or ownership over the document. Web libraries can also "collect" Web documents through caching or archiving, thus creating a local electronic record on an historical Web document. Digital libraries, including Web-based collections, are redefining both the role of electronic information storage and retrieval as well as the role of traditional libraries. Digital libraries include collections of books, journal articles, graphics, newspapers, and other material in digital format; in sum, collections of digitised content. To be a library, that collection should be organised according to some standard. There are many examples of digital libraries. The Digital Library Federation offers one definition of digital libraries: "Digital libraries are organisations that provide the resources, including the specialised staff, to select, structure, offer intellectual access to, interpret, distribute, preserve the integrity of, and ensure the persistence over time of collections of digital works so that they are readily and economically available for use by a defined community or set of communities."

Because sometimes try to treat information on the Web similarly to the way organise information in a library, does that necessarily mean that the Web is a library? On one level, the Web can be seen as an extension of and as a tool for libraries. If the Web is a tool, it is a complex tool serving to modify the information management and retrieval functions of both librarians and libraries. The Web can be employed as a transfer and distribution mechanism for the digital and digitised collections of libraries.

Web users can organise Web documents into document clusters that can be managed, searched, and accessed. These clusters or libraries have taken many forms. The vast majority of these attempt an in situ organisation and categorisation of Web content. Perhaps the most common are the jumppages, or Web page collections of hypertext links that point to other Web pages or Web sites with a defined content.

There are also a growing number of limited area search engines (LASE) that are restricted to development of indexes for Web documents with specific content. These include Argos, the Limited Area Search of the Ancient and Medieval Internet LASE, the Ananzi LASE providing access to material from or about South Africa, or the directory of LASEs provided by Internet Sleuth.

The Web differs from the more traditional information media in several substantial ways. The Web as a whole may not be organised to the degree that Chen might want it to meet the standard of a library, but neither is the entire corpus of print or electronic media so organised either. Part of the problem lies in part in definition of the Web: sometimes process and sometimes content.

Some argues there are four-point argument against the Web as library:

— despite appearances to the contrary, the Web does not offer access to all information;

— the Web lacks authority and quality control;

— the Web is inadequately catalogueed;

— Web search interfaces and other tools are ineffective and simplistic.

The Web lacks authority and quality control, but so do many print publications. Much of the Web is reminiscent of the political and religious pamphleteering so prevalent in Europe and North America over the past 200 years. The Web can resemble that archetypal forgery in print The Protocols of the Elders of Zion raised to some major order of magnitude. It can be an intentional or unintentional vehicle for poor or wrong information. It is a conduit for pornography. It can also provide effective and timely access to useful and accurate information.

One difficulty with the Web is that it is today far more difficult for third parties to assess quality and authority using methods developed for more traditional publications. There are six approaches to bring quality control to the Web. These are the programming, procedural, structuring, bibliographical, evaluative or indexed, and organisational approaches. Variations and additions to these approaches have been offered as well. Bibliometric or Webometric approaches may provide additional quality control.

These include citation analysis, link following and word counts. Others have adopted bibliometric approaches by following hypertext link trails to authoritative or substantive sites. Recent work suggests that following link trails to clusters of clusters can identify authoritative Web sites. There is no doubt that the indexes of the major search engines and directories are inadequate. The fact is do not even know how big the Web is much less how to define big. The Web contains many documents, pages, sites, and objects. Sizing the Web has proven to be a complex and uncertain enterprise. In an eloquent defense of Web catalogueing, and dispel what are for them the three most persuasive arguments against the practice. These are:

1) Web content is trash,
2) Web content is too ephemeral, and
3) Catalogueing technologies were designed for print and are not applicable to the Web.

Some Web resources are trash as is some print. But even trash needs at times to be classified or catalogueed. Their other two observations are more telling. Others recognise that Web document changes are important to their bibliographic control and still others have found it necessary to modify practice in response to those changes. Much attention has been paid to Web size and growth, as defined by server and host counts, packet traffic (MIDS) and other indicators. While we recognise both functions, we tend to concentrate more attention on the informatics of the transfer function rather than on the growth and change of the information content of the medium. That said, reasonably certain of at least two things: the Web is a big place and that it is ever-changing and ever-growing. There have been a number of approaches and proposals to categorise, index, and catalogue the Web. Let us concede that the Web is not and is not meant to be a library any more than the authoring, publication, production, distribution, and marketing of traditional media constitute libraries.

Libraries are collections of these information products, organised in some useful fashion, and made available to the appropriate client or patron pool. Perhaps not or perhaps it does not matter, for libraries can be libraries if their collections either are not universally comprehensive or if their collections do not address all points of view concerning a specific issue. In fact, no library can ever fully meet the "access to all information" test. It can also be argued that in time the Web may more likely provide access to all points of view than print because of the very ease of publication to the Web. Like other information streams, the Web can be organised, collected, and managed. Libraries, necessarily digital libraries, can be and are constructed from Web resources. The Internet is a moving target in two ways. First, there is a constant stream of technical change and computing upgrades and improvements. New capabilities, concepts and terminology challenge the practitioner, but these are manageable.

The other change is, from the perspective of managing Web content, far more profound. Web pages and Web sites undergo constant modification. These changes take two general forms. The first is existence. Both Web pages and Web sites exhibit varied longevity patterns. The second is content modification. Efforts to organise, categorise, index, or catalogue the Web all contain one inherent and fatal flaw. Before one can successfully organise Web content, one must recognise and compensate for the dynamic nature of the Web.

Once a Web site is removed from its server, unless it is cached or archived it is gone. It is true that the media that traditional materials are produced on deteriorate over time. It is also possible for societies to seek to eliminate whole bodies of literature either from neglect or active eradication. Conceivably, Web documents are not subject to physical deterioration but they are subject to the technological. There is an even more important difference between Web documents and traditional ones.

Once an author or publisher ceases to support a traditional publication, so long as copies are maintained in libraries, the document continues to exist and more often than not continues to be available for use. This is not so with the Web. Moreover, when a Web document is edited or updated, the edited version replaces and erases the earlier edition. New traditional editions may update older ones but they do not erase them. Creating Web document archives and caches can solve some of these issues.

A Web cache may be considered a very short term Web archive. In caching, Web documents are stored then accessed at some location closer to or faster for the end user than the original host is. Caching creates ethical, legal, as well as timeliness concerns. Archiving raises additional problems including what to archive and how often should the archive be updated. Storage and retrieval can quickly become a major problem. The library of native documents rather than with the library of cached documents. The literature suggests for example that change and attrition effect information retrieval. Changing pages are the more frequently visited pages.

The organisation of Web sites may help predict document longevity. Web pages located at the server-level domain are zero level pages, those one file removed are at the first level, and so on. This is not particularly surprising in that many zero and first level pages are navigational and will necessarily change as the Web site as a whole changes, while those pages located deeper on the file structure are more likely to be content in nature.Web sites and Web pages undergo content change and attrition. While content and structural changes can and have been measured the limits its focus to Web site and Web page persistence. Persistence is the most fundamental form of change. Either a document exists or it does not. Both Web pages and sites manifest one of three forms of persistence behavior. They may persist of a given period of time - which is to say each time the URL is queried, the specific page addressed is accessed, it responds. The Web page may fail to respond. Any Web page that fails to respond, but subsequently responds after one of two additional queries in a forty-eight hour period is considered present. Web page data are collected on a weekly basis.

A Web page is defined here as comatose if on the sixth and subsequent weekly queries including the most recent when data were taken, that Web page failed to resolve. The term comatose is chosen purposefully, for as the data which follow demonstrate, once a Web page goes comatose, this in itself is no guarantee that a Web page will not return at some time to the same URL. If a Web page were to return after the sixth collection period or five weeks, it would no longer be counted in subsequent assessments as comatose. Web pages that fail but return are labeled intermittent.

Two forces effect library collection development from the Web. In order to provide patrons with both broad and exhaustive resources libraries will necessarily have to turn to digital and Web resources to expand and augment their collections. In the end, digital and hybrid libraries, will have to incorporate native Web documents into their collections to a degree far greater than is now the practice. The Web and for that matter traditional publishing are in constant flux.

New Web documents are constantly being added to the available resource pool, just as new print and digital materials are. This offers no original challenge to libraries. The original challenge to libraries brought by the Web lies in its ephemeral nature. Both Web pages and Web sites undergo metamorphosis, attrition, and return.

Any library that seeks to incorporate Web materials into its collection must take into account this dynamic or the quality of the bibliographic representation as well as of the collection itself will rapidly erode. If indeed the half lives of Web sites and Web pages are about two years, information managers must pay attention to the process. Document death is never trivial, for in the absence of an archive, the information contained in that document is lost.

Comatoseness is not necessarily as tragic as document death in that some documents are intermittent and do return. This may not be unique to the Web, librarians have had extensive experience managing changing technology, changing media, and controlling for document demise.

The document lifecycle is far more prevalent on the Web than for print; it is in fact an accepted norm. If this lifecycle is both ubiquitous and normal, those who seek to manage Web content must develop new systems and adapt old standards that specifically address it. To manage the lifecycle, the digital library community has begun to address the dynamic and the impact that change has on the quality of collections; indexing, search, and retrieval algorithms, end user and intermediary behavior; document storage, caching, and archiving; and other related issues.

There are two main approaches to providing Web services: the Simple Object Access Protocol (SOAP) and Representational State Transfer (REST). REST is the simpler of the two. It is a codification of the style of interaction that has formed the basis of the Web over the last decade. REST, whenever possible uses existing mechanisms to communicate, such as HTTP put and get. The main advantages of this approach to us are the simplicity of REST services and the ease in which they can in turn be used within other services.

Since REST services can often be invoked directly from a Web browser, this offers additional possibilities for interaction with services. SOAP takes a more procedural view of Web services. Functions, their parameters and return values are defined, often using an XML language called Web Services Definition Language (WSDL). This enables a very formal and easily portable description of the Web service that makes it fairly easy for a programmer to create a client that will make use of it, or a server to implement the service. The main disadvantage of SOAP is more complication and overhead in the messages compared to REST.

This can be a factor in efficiency and ease of integration for those not conversant with SOAP. REST advocates also feel that SOAP hides too much within opaque function calls that would be better exposed using standard HTTP functions whose semantics are well understood. As a Web service provider we take the rather pragmatic view that we will provide services in the form our users want them, whether REST, SOAP, or some other approach.

REST takes a very simple approach: requests are sent in as HTTP requests, often as simply a URL. The response is sent back in XML. In some of our services we now include stylesheets to format the XML so that someone coming to the service through a Web browser will see a nicely formatted page rather than the raw XML. To a great extent, this is how the whole Web works, except that HTML (or now XHTML, the XML variant of HTML) is used in replies. SOAP is complex enough that including even one simple SOAP example in its full XML within a paper is difficult. SRW (Search and Retrieve on the Web) is a good example of a digital library SOAP service, offering the same functionality as SRU, but using SOAP wrappers to move the data.

This brings with it a WSDL definition of the service that can ease the implementation of a SRW server within an HTTP server such as Apache. The WSDL definitions and software such as Apache Axis 9 hide much of the complexity of SOAP from the implementer.

Classification of Web Services

There are a number of classifying digital library Web services. Users and systems need to register different types of objects, search for them, resolve references, navigate hierarchies and other types of links, decompose objects into simpler objects, enhance objects, and transform objects from one format to another.

— *Registration:* Registration services provide persistent identifiers to concepts or objects. They often serve up metadata about metadata. Examples of this include Dublin Core extensions, and the OpenURL formats of digital objects. Physical or digital items can also be registered, and cataloguing services such as OCLC's offer that sort of registration and control. A similar service is associating identifiers with names agents, such as people and institutions, such as name authority services.

— *Searching:* Search services are all familiar to us. Some sort of search string is typically mapped to a list of records. Searching Web services put this basic functionality in XML wrappers to make it available to higher-level programs the user interacts with. The leading example of this in digital libraries is the Z39.50 work on SRU/SRW.

Rather than having to understand BER and ASN.1, programs interact in XML over HTTP. In this case, the main reason not to change over from classic Z39.50 is probably the investment in the current systems. Newly designed systems would find SRU/SRW much easier to implement and use. Slightly outside the library world, systems such as Google are making their services available using SOAP, and finding many different institutions integrating Google in their applications.

— *Resolution:* Resolution services come in many different flavours. Typically, they map from identifiers to data. An example might be a service that accepts an ISBN and returns bibliographic data about the items that ISBN is associated with. Other examples include mapping controlled names to metadata about the people identified, and mapping a subject class number to a textual description of that class.

— *Navigation:* It is possible to create Web services that facilitate the navigation through a set of links. Of course, the Web itself is an example of general network movement using links, but more specialised services may also be of use.

— *Decomposition:* There are a number of decomposition services appearing. Decomposition services offer the possibility of applying concentrated knowledge and expertise to these problems and making them widely available. These services might be as simple as identifying individual names from a list of names or breaking a class number into its constituent parts, to the more complex problems of exposing the structure of a document or identifying letters/words/sentences within an image.

— *Enhancement:* Digital library systems could use any number of enhancement services. An important enhancement are normalisation services, such as adding controlled forms of names to metadata containing uncontrolled forms, or adding classification numbers selected on the basis of the text of a document. If links can be identified within metadata records it would also be possible to expand incomplete data.

OCLC does that now internally in some of our online services where tables of contents and cover art are added to book catalogue records for display. Web services are a way this type of information could be integrated into distributed and disparate services at less cost than maintaining and integrating all the data locally.

— *Transformation:* Many of the above services offer some sort of 'transformation,' so there is overlap between types of services. Transformation services operate at a higher level than many of the other services, e.g. translating the syntax of metadata records from MARC21 to MARC-XML.

Somewhat harder to accomplish is the translation of a Dublin Core record (in whatever format) into MARC-21 or between classification systems. At the high-end of these services might be natural-language translations.

Catalog as Portal to the Internet

Libraries are awash in contradictions. Gate counts are up; circulation is down. While one set of constituents eschews traditional library services, another group pushes statistics for catalog searching steadily upward. Inside the profession, librarians engage in spirited debates about their role. In the face of doubters, librarians argue that only ignorant or naïve individuals would believe that the Web could satisfy all their information needs, particularly in the scholarly community.

At the same time, they energetically acquire or license digital resources. With the addition of digital materials to the library's portfolio a debate about the role of the catalog has also developed. Proponents of the catalog and of libraries believe strongly that the catalog has enduring value and that it can evolve to be a useful tool for Web access, whereas critics do not foresee any role for the library catalog as a research tool for networked information. It is always humbling to learn that something you regard as a great and very contemporary problem echoes an experience from the past.

In America, large libraries are getting very large. They are being run for wide constituencies on broad lines. More and more the practical American spirit is seeking for coordination and cooperation. It is by no means certain that the card form of catalog will continue indefinitely as the chief tool of library workers. It is highly probable that selected catalogs will take the place of huge general repertories. Dimly one can see the possibilities of mechanical changes and alterations, of the use of photography, instead of printer's ink, possibilities of compression or even total change of form.

Certainly present card catalogs will require intelligent direction of the highest order to make them respond to the demands of readers, to the needs of the community. Changes such as these will require an intelligent and sympathetic oversight to insure their success. The librarians who will carry them out, who will guide and mold the development of cataloging, must perforce have been experienced and trained catalogers. Union catalogs expanded the function of the catalog to serve as an index to the holdings of multiple institutions, increasing their importance in the process.

Concomitant with the emergence of the union catalog was an increase in the standardisation of cataloging practice. Early in this century, The Library of Congress revolutionised catalogs through the provision of printed cards. A key catalyst for the development of more uniform cataloging was the MARC format, created in the 1960s through major leadership and innovation at the Library of Congress.

MARC enabled electronic dissemination of bibliographic records and engendered networks of libraries in such entities as OCLC and the Research Libraries Group. While initially MARC's power was felt in the economies realised through copy cataloging, first of records emanating from the Library of Congress, and subsequently, from original cataloging contributed through thousands of libraries, large and small, in the last two decades, MARC's potency has increasingly derived from unleashing the potential of the large-scale union catalog for resource sharing. Standardised bibliographic records conveyed using the MARC format also led to the rise of local systems for the management of local library holdings.

The OPAC (Online Public Access Catalog) assumed rising importance, and some librarians noted with dismay that the ease and convenience of the OPAC sometimes (often) lured searchers and lulled them into a complacency with results that were incomplete. Many institutions accelerated retrospective conversion of the card catalog to ensure that historical collections and fundamental publications acquired and cataloged prior to going online did not suffer from benign neglect.

Some unconventional thinkers loaded records for titles not held by their library, such as the catalog of the Center for Research Libraries, or UMI's Dissertation Abstracts, so that their clients might encounter resources, while not directly owned by their host organisation, were readily accessible to them. RLG's Eureka databases and WorldCat were also considered logical extensions of the bibliographic universe available to students and researchers using a campus library.

A constant lament throughout the decades has been the insufficiency of resources to catalog all the titles acquired by libraries. Administrators exhorted catalogers to be more productive, and in an effort to address the inexorable growth in workload as the volume of publications and acquisitions increased, catalogers, often led by the Library of Congress, introduced a number of collaborative programs to share cataloging and achieve economies. Their success in achieving enhanced productivity, though a combination of cooperative cataloging and enhanced tools, such as the cataloger's workstation, can be measured by noting that the number of catalogers employed in ARL university libraries has declined by 25% from 1990 through 1998 while the number of titles cataloged continues to rise. Although some catalogers feared loss of job security if they successfully eliminated arrearages, new categories of materials to include in the catalog emerged to absorb any slack.

Manuscript finding aids, guides to images, records for electronic resources, tables of contents, and other "non-book" materials competed for the attention of technical services specialists. In 2001, the information landscape appears to be considerably more complex than the one our predecessors populated. There is more information, the pace of change is more rapid, and the means and formats for communication are more diverse. The catalog, at the level of the local institution, provides the information-seeker with bibliographic description and access to content imbued with several critical features. There is an implicit assumption that the works cited in the catalog are readily available for consultation.

Furthermore because libraries have generally had a commitment to preserve and maintain those items they acquired, readers anticipate that a source identified today will be available in the future as well. Because they have been assembled according to standard practices and rules, by human intelligence, there is a high consistency in description, which in turn creates a high degree of predictability in results. This dependability generates an aura of trust. The user familiar with a catalog will have a high degree of confidence in the credibility of the sources contained in it. Another function of the catalog has been to link disparate materials. Until recently, the subject linkage has been chiefly among books, but in the past few years, catalogs have begun to incorporate a variety of formats, including manuscripts, visual images, audio recordings, and now, in great numbers, digital objects. Finally, although catalog searching is a seemingly free good, with host institutions assuming the cost of maintaining local catalogs and paying for the subscription costs. Even the titles and proprietary information referenced by the catalog are more often than not purchased or licensed by a library and made freely available to its users.

Recent enhancements in online catalogs have improved the quality of access. Some of the features found in state-of-the art catalogs are Web access, relevance ranking, more refined keyword searching, ability to limit by date or other information, and reference linking. Thus, the functionality of the online catalog is increasing, and its proponents are convinced that it can continue to remain an essential tool for the identification and location of documents and materials of importance for researchers.

Today's OPAC holds records for books and journals, films, finding aids, audio recordings, computer files, maps, and graphic images, although the preponderance of surrogates are still for monographs and printed materials. As libraries subscribe to more and more online journals, full text documents, and other digital materials, catalog records refer to publications accessible to a community through a variety of authorisations. No longer are all the citations in a catalog to holdings owned by a library; pointing to materials served remotely has become commonplace.

The purity of the principle that the local catalog provides access to materials held by the host institution has become diluted slightly to accommodate items selected for community use and readily accessible, although not physically controlled by the library. On the other hand, some librarians have balked at the introduction of certain types of electronic resources into the catalog, particularly those likely to have transient URLs or which require heavy maintenance.

The catalog represents stability, dependability, reliability, and quality. Its holdings have not typically been ephemeral in nature. It goes against the grain for librarians to invest in the creation of an expensive and detailed bibliographic record if the resource for which it is a surrogate, is not likely to endure for the foreseeable future, if not permanently. Recognising that some patrons may prefer to connect directly with online resources without being routed through the catalog, some libraries have developed separate gateways to networked resources. These gateways facilitate access to electronic materials selected by the library by providing a single point of entry, by organising them into categories, and using metadata, often derived from their catalog records, to assist users in locating networked resources.

The gateway concept appeals strongly to those for whom speedy access to online resources is a priority, and it offers many of the desirable features of the catalog, since the bibliographic control over its contents is carefully managed by librarians. Although patrons have enthusiastically adopted the gateway at many organisations, there are some flaws in its design. Of concern for the library is the expense of maintaining synchronicity between the catalog and the gateway. Although clever programs enable the cloning of bibliographic records, entries in the catalog and the Gateway are not always identical. Another issue that has burdened catalogers has been the matter of database aggregations. The phenomenon of bundling journals or databases or other electronic materials into a single resource, has led to a heavy workload in those institutions which have chosen to analyse each individual title in an aggregation.

The dynamic nature of these aggregations, in which titles are added and dropped by the host provider on a continual basis, sometimes without notification, has significantly increased the labor entailed in adding, dropping, or modifying bibliographic records. Confoundingly, only a few suppliers of aggregations have to date seen the desirability of providing bibliographic records as a service, forcing each subscriber to repeat the effort of incorporating references to the titles they provide separately in their catalogs and/or gateways. The Program for Cooperative Cataloging has worked with some vendors, such as EBSCO, ProQuest, CIS, and Gale, to stimulate the provision of wholesale bibliographic records to accompany subscriptions to its database aggregation.

These records can be loaded into a library's local system, increasing the standardisation of access and saving local catalogers from the task of creating them from scratch or searching, downloading, and modifying for local use records existing in a national database. This approach has had some success, but many publishers and vendors have lacked the staff expertise to create records of the quality expected by libraries.

In some cases librarians have been unable to convince them that this is a service that would be worth the expense and effort of improvement. In July 2000 OCLC put into production a service called CORC, the Cooperative Online Resource Catalog. Over 400 libraries are participating in the development of a Web-based product that uses a combination of automated tools and library collaborators to create a database of records to Web resources.

URL maintenance is improved over its present, labor-intensive mode in local catalogs through the application of automated functions in concert with shared effort through the partners to distribute the workload. A library may export CORC records to a local catalog or gateway in either MARC or Dublin Core formats. OCLC will include CORC records in its WorldCat database.

Still another variation on the desire to manage access to Internet resources through the catalog, thereby maintaining the elements of predictability, authority, and stability of the traditional catalog, is the creation of a digital library architecture that embraces different formats and permits crossfile searching of materials cataloged, indexed, or otherwise controlled through a number of metadata schemes. Endeavor's ENCompass, currently under development, expands the view of the OPAC to enable users to direct a single query to multiple databases constructed using different encoding languages.

The product is an open framework that uses metadata standards such as Dublin Core, EAD (Encoded Archival Description), and TEI (Text Encoding Initiative) to provide access to full-text resources, finding aids, and other digital objects that the ENCompass host has identified as relevant to its user community. ExLibris is developing a similar product called MetaLib. VTLS has developed a three-part approach, "Library Automation in 3V," which includes a system to handle internal library processes, a second component to support digitisation, indexing, linking, and access of multimedia materials, and a third part to facilitate integration with external sources and technologies.

These initiatives offer promise for the immediate future for effective access to a broader range of materials. As noted, libraries have struggled for years to stay ahead of the rising tide of printed publications as they labored to provide bibliographic control. The Library of Congress, for example, heroically reduced its backlog of monographs over the past decade. Yet, despite some measure of success through a combination of cooperative initiatives, new technological advances, and occasional staff increases, the essential problem of cataloging or otherwise describing and analysing the world of knowledge has remained an enormous challenge.

As print indexes morphed into online databases, some voices admonished that libraries ought never to have allowed the indexing business to migrate from their domain into the commercial sector in the 1930's. The penetration of visual culture into scholarly activity necessitates improved access and more widespread dissemination of records about visual images. Other formats and materials, such as manuscripts and audio transcriptions, have ascended in importance. The interest in these materials, which have often been sequestered in special collections, has risen in part as digital technology has facilitated their visibility and accessibility. Although the backlogs in these formats (manuscripts, music, photographs, moving images, sound recordings, and maps) were even more egregious than those of books and serials, LC has sought to increase formal control over them in the past few years, and other institutions have raised the priority of their special collections as well.

The numbers remain daunting, however. At one large research library, the task of converting all existing finding aids using EAD and gaining descriptive control over its entire collection of manuscripts was estimated to exceed $3 million, and since its technical services operations, using its present methodology to organise its collections, is chronically understaffed, it expected to increase this figure by a quarter of million dollars per year, taking into account the rate of new acquisitions. During the same period that libraries have been asserting control over their backlogs of printed publications and have been shining their light on the hidden resources found in archives and special collections, the World Wide Web sprang to life.

Few people had the clairvoyance to anticipate its astonishing growth and vitality. Today it registers 1.5 million new pages per day, and with a present size estimated to be in excess of 2 billion pages, it represents a major challenge to the traditional library practices. As there is mounting evidence that students, faculty, researchers, and the general public are making the Internet their information resource of the first and last resort, library values of careful selection, standardised description, and enduring access to publications are questioned as both costly and futile.

A common assertion by those conversant with the Web is that library tools such as AACR and MARC won't scale in the Web environment. One digital library specialist has advanced the theory that an Internet search engine, such as Google, could replace the expensive, labor-intensive aspects of librarianship, obviating the need for catalogers, reference librarians, or selectors, or at least significantly reducing the university's dependence on them. As Bill Arms ventures in an article entitled *Automated Digital Libraries*:

Quality of service in automated digital libraries will not come from replicating the procedures of classical librarianship. More likely, automated libraries will provide users with equivalent services that are fundamentally different in the way they are delivered. For example, within the foreseeable future, computer programs are unlikely to be much good at applying the Anglo-American Cataloguing Rules to monographs. But cataloguing rules are a means to an end, not the end itself. They exist to provide services to users, notably information discovery.

Automatic methods for information discovery may not need traditional cataloging. The criterion for evaluating the new methods is whether the users find what the information they require. With the Web estimated to be increasing by 10 million pages weekly, the task of indexing Internet resources is clearly gargantuan, and not something that can be accomplished by even the most industrious honeybee hive of catalogers. Instead of relying on the catalog to identify and retrieve relevant web pages, users have turned instead to Web portals. Internet portals originated as the librarians of the Web.

The word "portal," meaning "door," has been used to characterise Web sites commonly known for offering search and navigation tools. Now portals are more than just a launching pad to content at other sites. They offer a broad array of online resources and services. Although there is no single model for what constitutes a portal, all portals offer at least five core features: Web searching, news, reference tools, access to online shopping venues and some communication capabilities.

According to Looney and Lyman, "portals gather a variety of useful information resources into a single, 'one-stop' Web page, helping the user to avoid being overwhelmed by 'infoglut' or feeling lost on the Web." Portals differ significantly from library catalogs in several key ways. Like the catalog, they are built around the concept of a community, although a considerably larger body of users than the typical library catalog user. Unlike the catalog, they integrate all manner of information in their scope, rather than concentrating exclusively on "published" information. Frequently they contain a strong commercial element, with advertising prominent on their pages, and often affecting the display of search results.

The search engines they employ use programs to harvest URLs and generate responses. Search queries yield large response sets, often in the thousands, and the items retrieved include duplicates, false drops, results skewed by deliberate manipulation of terms by their authors, materials of dubious heritage: in short a vast flea market of junk, collectibles, and genuine antiques. Large numbers of the URLs retrieved lead to dead ends, where the site has moved or dropped off the face of the earth or where the information has ceased to be updated.

Users spend an inordinate amount of time sifting through the vast finds, often failing to locate the best resource. The Internet portals are rife with deficiencies. They lack the very characteristics which are the virtues of the catalog. Their value, on the other hand, is lacking in the catalog. The information they access is prolific, and is often very current. With the hyperlinked aspect of the Web, it is easy to move from document to document, and the generous amount of full-text resources allows the user to mine very specific terms. There is vastly more audio and visual data available for consultation.

The user can conduct her research without the inconvenience or disruption of leaving her computer, and she can readily cut and paste the results of her searches into her own documents. Result sets are ranked by relevance, and can be tailored to personal specifications. These characteristics, along with many other positive features of the Internet, excite an enthusiasm for the Internet that outweighs the deficiencies for large numbers of the population of information seekers.

The scholars portal would foster standards and provide cross database searching. Even a collaborative endeavor such as CORC could not fulfill this role, as the quantity and diversity of Web resources defy such comprehension. Even if one were to limit the candidates for control to the high quality resources contemplated as links in the "scholars portal", one should assume that the catalog would serve as only one point of access to web resources by users, who would likely have several other portals they would consult, based on their affinity groups.

Instead of striving for comprehensiveness, the goal of the catalog as portal must be to increase the ability of a community of users to meet their information needs by doing as much "one-stop shopping" as possible. By including access to web resources in the catalog, libraries would be extending to some Internet materials the same level of control that they have traditionally provided for analog formats. They would convey, through their integration in the online catalog, the credibility conferred through an affirmative selection by an intelligent being.

The presence of a citation in a catalog has come to signify for the user that the source discovered is readily obtainable, that it has been chosen for its relevance to past and present foci of the community of which the searcher is a member; that the material possesses authenticity, in that the rigor of the selection process vouches in some way for its scholarly value; and that the document consulted today will be persistently available for future examination. The wrapper of the catalog conveys respectability on its contents. Readers recognise that the texts and documents referenced in the catalog represent a diversity of viewpoints, but that the universe of publications on a particular topic has been screened to separate out those objects which have traditionally had the greatest value for a particular constituency.

In the past, those publications have had a heavy concentration of highly edited, peer-reviewed, frequently cited publications, and the virtue of the catalog for discovering materials meeting these and other unwritten standard of quality still continues.

On the Web, most information does not have an institutional warranty behind it, which really means you have to exercise much more judgment. There is a strong argument for libraries providing access to Internet resources for their clients. By creating a mechanism that offers a particular subset of information seekers the ability to search citations to a pool of information that includes all formats, libraries can offer a service that increases the productivity of the searchers.

A number of Internet search tools are commonly used by the library community. Many libraries, maintain their own Web pages of selected Internet resources. This approach presents filtered and arranged information geared to a specific user community, but usually offers poor user interface and limited search options, may require surfing hyperlinks page after page, and segregates Internet resources from the library's catalog. Furthermore, since the creation and maintenance of these web pages depend entirely on scarce and expensive human resources, the databases produced by this approach are seldom comprehensive. Another prominent tool is the robot-based search engine, such as Lycos or Harvest. These engines automatically navigate through Web spaces, searching for hyperlinks, retrieving relevant documents, indexing them, and creating a database out of them.

An advantage of this type of search is quantitative recall. One of the drawbacks is lack of precision. With the size of the Internet expanding exponentially, it will become more and more difficult to sift through these massive indiscriminate search results. At the same time, the databases created by these search engines could potentially become bigger than the Internet resources themselves. Furthermore, none of these search engines adequately address the issue of indexing non-textual files such as executable, image, compressed, sound, or moving image files. Such problems lead us to conclude that using metadata—data about data—is an important long-term approach for finding information on the Internet.

Network-based Library Information System

User-friendliness of library information systems is important, because they are used not only by professional librarians but also by novice users. Advanced hardware and software technologies have brought us new concepts to build user-friendly library information systems such as GUIs, multimedia user interfaces, collaboration support tools, etc.

The digital library will provide us with an intellectual environment where users can interactively retrieve and read documents, books, audio-visual materials, etc. However, from a practical point of view, we cannot build such environments in one day, because not all libraries can afford high-performance computing and network facilities. Since library information systems are data-centered, it is not easy to modify data-dependent functions or to add new information to an existing database in order to create new functions and user interfaces. These points imply that we need to build toward the digital library gradually, starting from existing library information systems.

OPAC

OPAC has been the most common tool for library users and librarians, and it will be also commonly used in digital libraries. It is obvious that well-designed GUI improves user-friendliness especially for novice users. OPAC with a bookshelf-like browser of bibliographical data would be useful from a practical point of view, even if the bookshelf on a display does not look like a physical bookshelf. The advantages of the bookshelf-like interface are:

1) users can find not only a book retrieved via retrieval commands but also from a glance at other books placed on the same bookshelf,

2) the structure of bookshelves is semantically organisable, and

3) the display order of books is modifiable as needed.

HOPAC[hopac] has a bookshelf-like interface organisation based on the Dewey Classification System. Its hierarchical structure helps a user move his/her viewpoint in the space of books and documents. The Book Shelf window of HOPAC does not look like a physical bookshelf. In addition to the text-based presentation, the authors consider that images of books and bookshelves would help users find books. The number of book images displayable on a display at a same time is obviously smaller than the number of book title texts. This fact looks disadvantageous, but too much information on a display is not friendly to users. The image-oriented bookshelf has the advantage that users can immediately see the size of a book without reading detailed bibliographic information. In addition, we can embed icons into a book image which represent such information as the book being checked-out, having duplications, one of series books, and so on.

Collaboration by Library Users and Librarian

The librarian is an important information resource in a library, and we cannot fully take advantage of a library without his/her help. A digital library will not necessarily be a fully automated librarian-less library, but will have to provide intelligent collaborative services of librarians.

Yamamoto mentioned the roles of librarians in the era of digital libraries as follows:

— Gateway between users and digital library networks,

— Reference via networks,

— Read-aloud via networks, and

— Intermediary as an information creator, editor, and publisher.

He also mentioned the types of reference services via network as follows:

— *Network Navigation:* support to find and approach information sources,

— *Cooperative Search:* support to search information,

— *Cooperative Translation:* multi-linguistic support to access foreign information, and

— *Instruction of Information Tools*: support to learn what tools users should use and how they should use the tools.

In addition to the collaborative services of librarians, the digital library will have to provide environments for group work. For example, researchers sometimes use a conference room in a library for research meetings using journals and other materials in the library. They store their new knowledge and information which are got from their discussion into the library. This means that the digital library should provide a virtual conference room where users can hold discussions through the same displays where library materials such as electronic journals and digitised images are shown.

Thus, collaboration support is one of the important features that should be explored in order to build the digital library. Reference services could be carried out using conventional media such as telephone, facsimile and email. However, these media do not offer the face-to-face communication that is quite important both for librarians and users; librarians must be able to correctly understand questions and needs of users, and users would be able to appropriately express their questions in their conversation with librarians.

SOPAC

SOPAC has been implemented based on the client-server model on a unix workstation which has the Motif GUI environment. The database of SOPAC is identical to the database used by XOPAC, which has 110,000 titles.

Users communicate with SOPAC via multiple windows. A SOPAC GUI includes the following windows:

— *Retrieval Command Window*: accepts retrieval commands as well as set operations AND, OR, and DIFF for intersection, union, and difference operations on retrieved data.

— *Result Window*: displays retrieved data. Users can get detailed bibliographic data of a member of the list on the Detailed Information Sub-window.

— *Memopad Window*: for user annotation.

— *Bookshelf Window*: browse a portion of bookshelf by designating a book on a result window. A bookshelf image of the designated book and its neighboring books is displayed. The order of the book images is primarily determined by the identification numbers of the books.

— *Detailed Information Sub-window*: all of the bibliographic information of a book which is selected on a result window or a bookshelf window.

Bookshelf Window

SOPAC displays a bookshelf with the book highlighted on the Retrieval Window and placed in the center. The order of books is the same as that on a physical bookshelf. The order is determined by the unique identification number given to each book, and users can scroll the bookshelf horizontally.

Each book image is a push-button to request detailed bibliographic information, which is displayed on a Detailed Information Sub-window attached below the bookshelf window. The shape of a book image is determined by the bibliographic description of the book, i.e., height and number of pages. The book title is presented from top to bottom and can be vertically scrolled.

It is not easy to re-create an OPAC database or to modify the scheme of its records. SOPAC has been developed on the XOPAC database. It would be better for bookshelf-like browsers to be able to show physical images of books, i.e., covers and title pages. However, it was not practical to scan in the physical image of every holding and to add it to an existing OPAC database, so the SOPAC book image is created only from existing data.

Books are displayed vertically in order to enhance realism. This means that title texts on the images are drawn vertically. This is convenient for titles in Japanese.

Several issues remain unsolved in the current SOPAC system:

— Bookshelf reorganisation: functions to re-organise bookshelves in accordance with semantical requests from users,

— Browsing Support Tools based on Semantical Structure of Bookshelves: tools to show classification hierarchy and thesauri, and

— Active Information Tools: icons to show active information such as "checked out", "in bindery", etc.

Modeling Reference Work as Librarian's Desk

The principal components of reference work in conventional libraries are as follows:

— a librarian,

— a library user,

— library materials, which include primary information sources in a library such as books, journals, etc., and secondary information sources such as OPACs, thesauri, dictionaries, and encyclopedias,

— user's materials such as books and memos, and

— a librarian's desk.

The library user and librarian are modeled as the participants in a conversation carried out via the system. Library materials and user materials, which may or may not be in digital form, are modeled as objects to be displayed on the terminals in front of the participants. The librarian's desk is modeled as a display screen in front of each participant where the participants can see their partners and view the same materials.

It is natural to design a library collaboration support system based on the librarian's desk metaphor. We can find memo pads, a computer terminal, a telephone, a copy machine, and so on in addition to the library materials on/ around a librarian's desk. These things should be modeled as system components visible to the participants.

System Structure

The CSS has been developed on two workstations of the ULIS campus LAN. The graphical environment of the workstation is OSF/Motif on X-window.

The following paragraphs are brief descriptions of the components.

— *Control Tool*: The control tool manages initiation and termination of a session between a user and a librarian.

— *TV-phone*: The TV-phone displays real time video pictures taken by a video camera placed at and digitised by the workstation. The captured image is digitised and transferred through the LAN. Sound communication is half-duplex, requiring a talk control panel to switch talking direction.

— *Shared Virtual Display (SVD)*: SVD is a window which realises a virtual display where multiple windows are displayed and input/output operations are performed on them. The participants share the virtual display where the user can see every operation by the librarian, and vice versa. This feature is crucial in order to enhance the quality of communication between the participants; that is, a participant needs to view all operations performed on the terminal of the other participant, for example mouse movement, mouse clicking, etc.

— *White Board*: The participants can input character text and draw images on the board which is equally accessible to both participants. The participants can use the white board to explain things which are difficult to express on the TV-phone.

— *Image Tool:* The participants can input images using a color image scanner. The input images are shown on both workstations.

Web Archiving

The Web is the largest document ever written, with more than 4 billion public pages and an additional 550 billion connect-ed documents on call in the "deep" Web. The Web is written in 220 languages (although 78 percent of it is in English) by authors from every nation.

Ninety-five percent of Web pages are publicly accessible, a collection 50 times larger than the texts collected in the Library of Congress (LC), making the Web the information source of first resort for millions of readers. Nonetheless, the Web is still less than 10 years old, and the economic, social, and intellectual innovation it is causing is just beginning. The Web is growing quickly, adding more than 7 million pages daily. At the same time, it is continuously disappearing. The average life span of a Web page is only 44 days, and 44 percent of the Web sites found in 1998 could not be found in 1999.

Web pages disappear every day as their authors revise them or servers are taken out of service, but users become aware of this only when they enter a Universal Resource Locator (URL) and receive a "404-Site Not Found" message. As ubiquitous as the Web seems to be, it is also ephemeral, and much of today's Web will have disappeared by tomorrow. The implication is clear: if we do not act to preserve today's Web, it will disappear. In the past, important parts of our cultural heritage have been lost because they were not archived-in part because past generations did not, or could not, recognise their historic value. This is a cultural problem. In addition, past generations did not address the technical problem of preserving storage media-nitrate film, videotape, vinyl recordings-or the equipment to play them. They did not solve the economic problem of finding a business model to support new media archives, for in times of innovation the focus is on building new markets and better technologies.

Finally, they did not solve the legal problem of creating laws and agreements to protect copyrighted material yet at the same time allow for its archival preservation. The very pace of technical change makes it difficult to preserve digital media. How many people can retrieve documents from old word processing diskettes or even find yesterday's e-mail?

All documents follow a life cycle from valuable to outdated, but then, perhaps, some become historically important. Archivists often rescue boxes of documents as they are being transported from the attic on their way to the dump. But the Web is not stored in attics; it just disappears. For this reason, conscious efforts at preservation are urgent. The hard questions are how much to save, what to save, and how to save it. Every new technology takes a few generations to become stable, so we do not think to preserve the hardware and software necessary to read old documents.

Digital documents are particularly vulnerable, since the very pace of technical progress continuously makes the hardware and software that contain them outmoded. A Web archive must solve the technical problems facing all digital documents as well as its own unique problems. First, information must be continuously collected, since it is so ephemeral. Second, information on the Web is not discrete; it is linked. Consequently, the boundaries of the object to be preserved are ambiguous. Who has the responsibility for collecting and preserving the Web and the resources to do so? The economic problem is acute for all archives. Since their mission is to preserve primary documents for centuries, the return on investment is very slow to emerge, and it may be intangible hence hard to measure.

Archives serve the public interest in the very long run, with immediate benefits for only a few scholars. For this reason, they tend to be small and specialised. However, a Web archive will require a large initial investment for technology, research and development, and training-and must be built to a fairly large scale if it is continuously to save the entire Web.

New intellectual property laws concerning digital documents have been optimised to develop a digital economy, thus the rights of intellectual property holders are emphasized. Copyright holders have reason for caution, because the technology is so new and the long-term implications of new laws are unknown.

Although the Web is popularly regarded as a public domain resource, it is copyrighted; thus, archivists have no legal right to copy the Web. And yet it is not preservation that poses an economic threat, it is access to archives that might damage new markets.

Finding a balance between preservation and access is the most urgent problem to be solved, because if today's Web is not saved it will not exist in the future. Access is a political as well as a legal problem. The answer to the access problem, like the answers to all political problems, lies in establishing a process of negotiation among interested parties. Who are the stakeholders, and what are the stakes, in building a Web archive?

— For librarians and archivists, the key issue is to ensure that historically important parts of the documentary record are preserved for future generations.

— For owners of intellectual property rights, the problem is how to develop new digital information products and to create sustainable markets without losing control of their investments in an Internet that has been optimised for access.

— The constitutional interest is twofold: the innovation policy derived from Article I, Section 8 of the U.S. Constitution ("progress in the useful arts and sciences"), and the First Amendment.

— The citizen's interest is in access to high-quality, authentic documents, through markets, libraries, and archives.

— Schools and libraries have an interest in educating the next generation of creators of information and knowledge by providing them with access to the documentary record; this means access based on the need to learn rather than on the ability to pay.

In sum, the policy problem is to find a process for balancing these interests in the long run, including finding a means through which each of the parties can conduct and evaluate significant experiments and reach solutions that strike a balance among legitimate contending interests.

Howard Besser has identified five key technical problems necessary for digital preservation:

1. The viewing problem is the maintenance of an infrastructure and the technical expertise necessary to make digital documents readable.
2. The scrambling problem is decoding any compression or technical protection service software protecting the Web page.
3. The interrelation problem is preserving the contexts that give information meaning, such as links to other Web pages.
4. The custodial problem is defining the standards, best practices, and collection policies that define the boundary of the work and its provenance and authenticity.

5. The translation problem concerns the way in which the experience and meaning of the Web page are changed by migrating it into new delivery devices.

When one is building a Web archive these problems translate into three questions: What should be collected? How do we preserve its authenticity? How do we preserve or build the technology needed to access and preserve it?

Ultimately, the scope and scale of a Web archive will be determined by the definition of the digital object to be collected-the "Web page." This is not a simple matter. From a user's point of view, a Web page is the image called forth by placing a URL address into a Web reader.

This operational definition is necessary but not sufficient, for an archive also must be sure that the document is translated in an authentic manner. In this case, authenticity means that the document must both include the context and evoke the experience of the original. The average Web page contains 15 links to other pages or objects and five sourced objects, such as sounds or images. For this reason, the boundaries of the digital object are ambiguous. If a Web page is the answer to a user's query, a set of linked Web pages sufficient to provide an answer must be preserved.

From this perspective, the Web is like a reference library; that is, it is the totality of the reference materials in which a user might search for an answer. If so, the object to be preserved might include everything on the Web on a given subject at a given point in time, for example, the 2000 election or the World Trade Center terrorist attack. None of these possibilities would be easy to realise, for the Web is not a fixed collection of artifacts. Today, the "surface" Web contains all of the static hypertext markup language (HTML) pages that can be accessed by URLs. Some of the surface Web, especially in the commercial sector, requires passwords or encryption keys; this area might be called the "private" Web. To archive these Web pages would require permission of the owners. The private Web is often encased in security protection services that make copying and preservation doubly difficult. Beyond these problems, surface Web pages are often generated on the fly, customised on demand from databases in the "deep" or "dark" Web.

The deep Web is estimated to be 500 times larger than the surface Web. It includes huge data sources and software code that provides information services for surface Web pages on the fly. The deep Web is the information architecture that produces what we read on the surface; the surface itself exists only as long as a reader is using it.

This deep Web cannot easily be archived, since the data are guarded by technical protection services. It is also potentially protected by privacy concerns, since if Amazon.com owns a profile of one's use of information, it is not necessarily available for archiving without his/her consent. Here there are not only tensions between markets and archives but also conflicts between privacy concerns and the interest of history. The ambiguous boundaries of Web objects are also problematic because they are compounds of design elements, including texts, pictures, graphics, digital sound, movies, and code-the list expands as innovation continues.

Each of these elements has intellectual property rights attached to it, although they are rarely marked and sometimes impossible to trace. Yet, at least in principle, a digital archive would have to have permission from each of these rights holders. In the words of the US National Research Council's report, The Digital Dilemma: Intellectual Property in the Information Age, "for the digital world, one must sort out and clear rights, even of ephemera". Even if the Web page could be copied technically and we knew what we wanted to preserve, Web pages are protected by copyright law. Even now there are sophisticated debates about how a Web archive should collect data: Should the default be that copyrighted information is collected and the owner has to opt out; or should it not be collected or disclosed unless the owner actively gives permission ("opts in")? This is a question that may be resolved by legislation or the courts.

It is important to remember that the Web is a global document; consequently, there are likely to be many jurisdictions making laws and rules, and enforcement across national borders will be difficult without treaty agreements. Defining the boundaries of the object to be collected also requires decisions about authenticity and provenance. These decisions must be recorded as part of the archive; the preservation community calls this kind of information "metadata," or information about information, and often builds records of what is in the collection using these metadata.

A standard way of recording the metadata must be created to record the historical and technical context in which the document(s) were found.

Technologies to reproduce the Web object-however defined-must be preserved, including the hardware and software necessary to access the information in an authentic context or to recreate it. This is difficult in the best of cases. Have we authentically preserved a computer game if we preserve only the graphics, or must we preserve the look and feel of the game in use? Every solution changes the context of information in ways that affect its authenticity.

One strategy tries to preserve the original equipment; another uses contemporary technology to emulate the original "look and feel" of the information in use; still another migrates the digital signal to new storage media. Migration is not just a technical problem. Storage media for digital documents are not yet stable for long-term preservation. Magnetic storage media such as tape and discs eventually deteriorate. Moreover, hardware and software eventually become obsolete, hence very expensive to preserve and operate.

A Web archive must migrate from one technical environment to another as generations of technology succeed one another. Nevertheless, under today's law such migration could be a violation of copyright law because it involves copying the signal from one medium to another. These problems are typical of those that occur in the early stages of every innovation, when getting to market quickly is more important than is perfecting the product. Digital information products are not designed for longevity, and even if they were, it is likely they would become obsolete quickly. As a consequence, the technologies of digital preservation are complex and expensive. The problems are understood far better than are the solutions at this point, but it is already clear that a Web archive will require substantial investment in technological infrastructure and technical research and development, and that commercial entities are unlikely to lead this effort unless there is short term economic value in doing so. Both archives and libraries collect, organise, preserve, and provide access to the documentary record.

The distinguishing function of archives is to preserve the integrity of documents for the long run. Preservation for centuries invariably requires new technologies; hence, the Council on Library and Information Resources and other organisations are investigating long-term storage and migration of data.While the technical problem of preservation is difficult, it is well understood.

The problem of access, by contrast, involves legal and economic issues that have not yet been adequately explored. While print archives provide a useful model, the economic and legal environments surrounding print are quite different from those surrounding digital documents. Economic and legal issues cannot be separated. In 1998, the Digital Millennium Copyright Act (DMCA) gave copyright owners rights to protect their works in digital formats. The DMCA implements the 1996 WIPO Copyright Treaty and WIPO Performances and Phonograms Treaty. Among the purposes of these treaties was harmonising copyright policy around the world to encourage global commerce in digital information.

As a public policy, the DMCA was focused upon making the Internet safe for intellectual property. If digital information is easily moved from place to place on a network, such movement is considered to be copying and is protected by copyright. If Internet information is easily accessed, making it difficult for a rights holder to control distribution, the DMCA encourages the development of technical protection services (such as encryption) by making it illegal to develop technologies to break them.

For printed information, copyright policy has balanced information markets with public goods, such as education, the First Amendment, and libraries to provide access to information.

— The first-sale doctrine allows libraries to circulate copyrighted works to library patrons. In the digital realm, however, information may be licensed by contract rather than sold under copyright. With licenses, the provisions of the contract determine the uses that are allowed, which are unlikely to include library circulation or fair use. While printed works may also be sold with "shrink-wrap" licenses, the print market has not accepted them as readily as have markets for digital information.

— The fair-use doctrine allows for copying for personal educational purposes, within limits that are designed to protect information markets from damage. Here again, if licenses govern commerce in digital information, these copyright provisions do not govern the contractual agreement reached between buyer and seller.

The Digital Dilemma makes a constructive case for extending the fair-use doctrine to digital information in the future. The rationale for the market approach, embodied in the DMCA, was twofold.

— First, new information markets are expensive to develop, and from the industry perspective, public interest doctrines such as first sale and fair use are taxes on this investment.

— Second, the global scale of the Internet means that millions of copies can be made and distributed in seconds, causing economic damage that cannot be repaired. Thus, while copyright laws governing print place emphasis upon ex post facto remedies such as litigation, the DMCA emphasizes prevention.

Every digital copy, perhaps even copies made temporarily for system management purposes, thus requires the permission of the copyright holder. The DMCA explicitly allows archives to make digital copies of print works for the purpose of preservation. To prevent illegal copying, the DMCA encourages the use of technical protection services such as encryption by making it illegal to use software to break them, and also making it illegal to develop and distribute such software. Software developers feel that this provision raises free-speech issues and perhaps property issues if it makes it illegal for the owner of a legal copy to make a backup.

Congress recognised the complexity of some of these issues, empowering the LC to advise Congress whether this provision in Section 104 prevents noninfringing uses of certain classes of copyrighted works. Print archives are permitted to collect copyrighted materials and copy them for preservation purposes. For example, it is legal to copy print materials from one medium to another as part of a migration strategy over time, but it may not be legal to do so with digital collections, or to reformat them (e.g., from CD-ROM to a hard disk). Differences between the production and distribution of printed and digital works raise additional legal issues for Web archives. When something is published in the print world, it is registered for copyright; thereafter, the laws governing it are largely unambiguous. On the Internet, it is not always clear when something has been "published." At this point, it is not clear to most users whether placing information on the Web places it in the public domain or under copyright protection.

The Digital Dilemma concludes that the Web is copyrighted in principle, but notes public confusion on the issue and explores ambiguities that make it unclear whether archives have the right to make preservation copies and preserve them using migration strategies. In the print world, it has been possible to develop a copyright regime that balances the needs of markets and those of archives.

The Internet makes it difficult simply to transfer copyright doctrine from the print to the digital environment. Yet many of the problems for the Web archive outlined earlier seem to be unanticipated consequences of laws intended to support the digital marketplace and might, in principle, be resolved by negotiation. This process might begin by discussing the possible damage to the marketplace caused by long-term archives and seeking solutions.

Inevitably, a Web archive will be a new kind of organisation, one that responds to the problems and interests surrounding the Web. It may not be a place at all-it may be a function distributed among institutions over many locations on a global network. The starting point for building a Web archive is to envision organisational strategies to manage this process.

Two organisational strategies are emerging-one from the archival and library professions and the other from computer scientists. These strategies are not opposites and are not mutually exclusive, but contrasting them helps frame the strategic choices. In US, one library and archival strategy for organising digital archives is presented in Preserving Digital Information, a report of the Task Force on Archiving of Digital Information, published by the Commission on Preservation and Access and the Research Libraries Group.

One technical strategy is offered by the library community, which has developed sophisticated cataloging strategies. The MARC record is used to build print library catalogs that may be searched by users to identify the best information resources. MARC records include fields to describe every aspect of printed documents; the Dublin Core metadata project is defining a standard for cataloging digital documents.

Computer scientists funded by the National Science Foundation (NSF) Digital Library program are developing a second model. While the Dublin Core is designed to enable searches of library catalogs of digital collections, the NSF digital library projects are developing search engines that directly parse the digital documents themselves. Records identify the best information source described in a catalog, while search engines and data-mining technologies go to the source itself. Each has its advantages.

The point is that these technologies are optimised for two different kinds of archive. The computer science paradigm allows for archiving the entire Web as it changes over time, then uses search engines to retrieve the necessary information. An archival catalog supports high-quality collections built around select themes, saving only the Web sites judged to have potential historical significance or special value, and describing these special qualities in collection records and catalogs that could be searched. This is a fundamental debate about the nature of the Web as a technical object as well. The librarian tends to look at the content of the Web page as the object to be described and preserved.

The computer scientist tends to look at the Web as a technology for linking information-a system of relationships (hence the name "Web"). This implies not only a difference in scale: it is a difference in philosophy. Should Web archives include everything or only carefully selected samples? Should the end user make decisions about the quality of the Web page, or should they be made by a selector who chooses which Web pages to save?

Social and Political Framwork for Web Archive

If the social and political framework for the Web archive is still evolving, so, too, are other key elements. These include the following:

Evolving technology

The Web has grown to global scale very rapidly; it may represent the fastest diffusion of a new technology in human history. At the same time, the technology of the Web has not stopped evolving. Even now, significant evolution is occurring as, for example, new architectures replace static Web pages with customised Web pages generated on the fly. Because innovation is not linear, the development of the Web is unpredictable. For stakeholders, the best option is to participate in the new organisations that, if they do not govern the future of the Web, at least attempt to analyse and influence its direction. To participate in discussions about the technical future of the Web, it is worthwhile to follow the discussion of the World Wide Web Consortium.

Evolving law

Copyright law protects the entire Web. However, the Web is global, and a practice that is legal in one jurisdiction may violate the law in another. For this reason, Web law needs to become harmonised, which suggests that international treaty making (e.g., the WIPO treaty) may be as important as is national legislation.

Evolving economic issues

The Web began as software for the exchange of documents among scientists and researchers, using an Internet that was subsidised for education and research purposes. Today the Internet is increasingly commercial, and the Web has been the subject of vigorous investment as a technology for the digital economy.

The search for sustainable business models for Web business has undergone a rapid evolution, ranging from Web advertising models to banner ads, sponsorship ads, subscription models, and business to consumer (B2C) enterprises. Investment in these enterprises and technologies has slowed for the moment because there is little sense that viable economic models have been identified.

9

Networked Information

Many universities are now implementing institutional authentication and access management systems to support specific application and security requirements; typically this work is being overseen by the institution's information technologists and it is often motivated by policy imperatives and priorities that are very different from those of the library. Because authentication and access management represents a common infrastructure that will ultimately need to serve many purposes, it is essential that libraries and information technology groups establish a dialog now to ensure that the systems which are ultimately deployed honour the complete set of campus community requirements. Organisational readiness within the content provider community is also a barrier to the use of advanced technology-based approaches; content site operators are no more able than libraries to obtain commercial turnkey solutions.

But as libraries offer a growing portfolio of network-based information resources, they face immediate and pragmatic needs for access management. In developing strategies, it is important to recognise that technical choices about access management have policy implications. A library negotiates a license agreement on behalf of its patron community-for example, the faculty, staff, and students of a university.

This license agreement gives members of the community the right to use some network-based resource-perhaps a commercially offered electronic encyclopedia or scholarly journal at a publisher website, or a specialised research database at another university that is part of a resource-sharing agreement. Users connect to the site using web browsers running on their personal workstations or on public workstations.

As the site hosting the licensed resource processes these requests for web pages, it must determine whether the requesting user is in fact a member of the appropriate user community. If so, he or she is given access; if not, access is refused. Obviously, this basic scenario can be elaborated upon-for example, there is a need for finer-grained systems that can be used to allow only registrants in a specific multi-institutional course access to electronic reserve materials provided by the library at one of the institutions.

These more elaborate situations raise additional problems both in terms of scale and system design and are useful to have in mind to understand the extent of the requirements; however, we will concentrate on the basic scenario here. Access management needs to be routine and easy to implement; once a contract is signed, lengthy technical negotiations between institution and content supplier should not be necessary before users can have access.

In a world of networked information resources, access management needs to be a basic part of the infrastructure, and must not become a barrier to institutional decisions to change or add resource providers. While it may be a complex administrative question to determine the membership of the patron community in a world of extension students, affiliated medical professionals, visiting scholars, and others who may blur the boundaries, libraries have a great deal of experience in devising these policies.

In the physical world of circulating materials, the "technical" problem is dealt with through the presentation of a library card indicating that the holder is indeed an authorised borrower; this library card is issued upon the presentation of policy-specified documents that identify the user and prove that he or she meets the policy criteria for authorised community membership. Historically, many computer systems employed user IDs and passwords. When a user ID was first defined, it would have certain rights and privileges associated with it. The user would then supply a password upon demand to demonstrate his or her rights to use a given ID.

Leaving aside technical problems associated with the use of passwords on an insecure network and the possible technical remedies, there is a more basic architectural issue. We are in a world where users may routinely want access to many different network resources controlled by many different organisations, such as publishers; but with the ability to follow links on the Web it may not even be clear to the user which publisher owns what resource.

Users will not be able to remember and manage a large number of different user IDs and passwords issued by different publishers; further, each publisher will need some cumbersome procedure to validate the user as a community member prior to issuing a user ID and initial password. This does not scale up in a practical way to a world filled with electronic information resources. The library might issue the user a single ID and password for all licensed external network resources, and then transmit lists of these IDs and passwords to each content supplier so that the supplier can use the list to validate users.

However, there are architectural problems here, as well: a very large number of publishers would need to be notified every time the list of user IDs and passwords changes, with inevitable timeliness and synchronisation problems. Also, each publisher takes on an enormous responsibility for protecting the security of the ID/ password list; a security breach at any publisher will mean a security breach at every publisher doing business with the library for networked resource access, an unacceptable liability. Here the networked information scale-up means that too many independent parties must rely on each other to maintain security, and that the cost of accurately maintaining a synchronised common-access management database will be very high. As a stopgap measure, many institutions are currently using electronic "place"-the user's source IP network address-as a substitute for other methods of demonstrating proof of community membership. If the user's connection request came from a network that belonged to the university, it is assumed to be from a community member.

Network ownership does not change too frequently, so maintaining a list of valid network numbers and making this available to publishers is a tractable administrative burden. Further, since the list of network numbers, unlike IDs and passwords, doesn't need to be kept secret, there is little interdependence. This approach works well and, indeed, has the virtues of simplicity and transparency to the user, as long as all users come to the resource providers through the campus or library network.

However, in an era when many institutions are discontinuing dial-up modem pools in favour of commercial Internet service providers, and when new access technologies to the home, such as cable television modems for Internet access, are beginning to deploy, a great deal of legitimate user access now takes place from sources other than the campus or library network. With growing needs to support distance learners, part-time students who may do academic work from their place of business, and people who want to exploit the "anytime, anywhere" promise of networked information resources from their homes, limiting access by source IP network address disenfranchises more users every day.

For most universities, for example, it is clearly no longer acceptable to tell community members they can only access networked information resources from on-campus workstations. Two general approaches are emerging to address the access management problem. The first is the use of proxies.

Here, an institution develops an internal authentication system and uses it to validate user access to a special machine on the institutional network, called a proxy. Once a user is validated, he or she can ask the proxy to contact an external resource; in some variations, the proxy mediates the user's entire interaction with the external resource, while in other variations the proxy drops out of the interaction after making the introduction.

From the resource operator's point of view, it is only necessary to know that the institution's proxy server can be trusted to pre-validate all users before contacting the external resource host. Proxies have a number of advantages: authentication is an internal matter to the institution and external service providers need not be concerned with the details of how this is accomplished; at least in theory, the institution has complete flexibility in deciding what resources a user can have access to through the proxy and when; and the proxy can act as a central control point for the institution in access management.

On the negative side, the proxy is a high-impact central point of vulnerability for outages or capacity problems (though, of course, it's possible to have multiple proxy machines), and configuration management in the proxy can become extremely complex and labour-intensive, particularly if not every valid proxy user has access to all resources. Further, proxies do not eliminate the need for an authentication system; they only isolate its scope to the proxy and the members of the institutional community. The other approach is based on credentials.

The basic idea here is that the institution issues each user the electronic analog of a community ID card. The user, or the user's browser, presents these credentials upon demand to any resource provider that requests them; the resource provider can then, through a fast electronic transaction, validate the credentials with the issuing institution.

The validation process shares with proxies the vulnerability to outages or capacity problems on the part of institutional systems that verify credentials, though these vulnerabilities are more circumscribed. A compromise of the credential-verification system may be more serious than compromise of a proxy: proxy compromise usually means that unauthorised users get access to resources for the period during which the proxy is compromised, while a compromise in the credentialing system may well mean that new credentials need to be issued to the entire authorised user community. The major practical difficulties with the credentials-based approaches, however, involve technical problems, standards, cost, and software integration. The simplest credentials-based approach would be to have the institution just issue the user a user ID and password for external resources, and to have external resource providers validate the ID/password pair with the institution.

This reduces, but doesn't eliminate, the interdependence among external resource providers in the maintenance of security; further, standards don't exist for such a validation process and no off-the-shelf software supports it. The industry is moving towards a technology based on public key cryptographic certificates (X.509) in off-the-shelf software, and, at least in theory, this should work well for personal machines.

X.509 removes the interdependent security issue because credentials are computed for each use from information that is held only by the user and never directly transferred to the content provider. The problems with this approach include integration with browsers, the mechanics of issuing and distributing these electronic cryptographic certificates to users, the cost and complexity of acquiring and operating the infrastructure for managing and validating public key certificates, and government regulation of the export and use of cryptography in various countries, which causes problems in an increasingly international world of scholarly resources. All of these problems with cryptographic certificates are slowly but steadily getting better (except, perhaps, for the government regulation issues), but, at least today, implementation of such an approach is an enormous challenge. Finally, it is important to note that X.509 was really designed to support applications such as electronic commerce.

The development of any access management strategy raises policy issues in areas such as privacy, accountability, and the collection of management data. It is important to recognise that libraries must decide whether to address these issues through legal means, through technical means, or by a combination of the two. Library experience in other contexts offers some insights. Libraries have aggressively championed and defended the privacy of their patrons. They have done this through both legal means-by developing privacy policies and by requiring a legal subpoena as a condition for divulging records-and also by technical means by not keeping historical circulation data on an individual basis, which then limits the amount of information that they can be compelled to disclose under any circumstances. Patron privacy has been such an important value to libraries that they have, by and large, used a dual technical/legal strategy to provide their patrons with the strongest possible protection.

In the electronic environment, it is easy for a publisher to track the use of content in great detail-what material is being viewed, for how long, and how often. Depending on how the access management system is structured, particularly when credential-based approaches are employed, the publisher may be able to correlate this usage information to a specific individual by name, to a long-term "pseudonymous" identity that the publisher can link to an institution but not to an actual individual within that institution's community, or simply to a transient and anonymous member of the institution's user community.

Clearly, the license contract between institution and publisher can speak to the collection, retention, use, and disclosure of such usage data on a policy basis, but libraries and patrons may find it desirable to limit the ability of the publisher to collect information by the design of the access management system on a technical basis, as well. One important point needs to be made about user privacy that underscores the need for contractual constraints even in conjunction with an access management system that provides some level of anonymity: often users will make their actual identities known to content providers for other reasons, independent of the access management system, such as to take advantage of email-based current awareness services or personalisation options in a user interface.

The access management system is not the only way in which privacy can be compromised, or bargained away for increased function or convenience. A license agreement represents a commitment on the part of the licensee institution to honour the terms of the license, and to educate members of its community about their obligations under the license.

The publisher and library share a need for some level of accountability by community members: if a single user accesses publisher content hundreds of times a day from three continents, it's likely that something is wrong; perhaps that user doesn't understand his or her obligations, or perhaps credentials have been compromised. There is a need for the publisher and the library, acting together, to be able to investigate such situations effectively, and, if need be, to block access by specific individuals who seem to be violating the terms of a license agreement.

But, in order to do this effectively, a publisher needs to be able to at least provide an institution with enough information to permit the individual in question to be identified; note that this does not necessarily mean that the publisher can directly identify the individual in question, but only that the publisher can provide the institution with enough information to identify the user. The need for accountability contradicts, to some extent, the mandate to design anonymity into an access management system, and argues for a pseudonymous approach. This can be achieved with credential-based approaches, but is more difficult with proxy-based architectures. Finally, there is the issue of management data.

Electronic information resources promise libraries much more accurate and detailed data about what content is actually being used and how often-though even at this level libraries may want to make contractual stipulations to protect patron privacy; for instance, it is not clear how many universities would be comfortable having a list of all the articles read by members of their community posted on the Web every week. But greater problems arise when libraries want to have these usage statistics, at whatever level of aggregation, demographically faceted-for example, to drive internal cost allocation processes within the library's institution.

The simplest solutions are often to pass demographic attributes to the publisher along with identities or pseudonyms and to get the publisher to do the work of generating management data for the library-but this path can rapidly compromise the privacy of pseudonymous users by making them more identifiable and, if actual identities are used, it makes the privacy problem even more acute by raising the stakes on the amount of information disclosed. Demographically faceted usage data offers a good illustration of the scaling issues that we face in the move to network-based electronic information. If a library were dealing with just a single publisher, it would be reasonable to have the publisher return detailed (transactional) usage data with pseudonyms to the library. The library could then look up the pseudonyms to obtain demographic data and summarise the transaction data into management information. Here privacy is protected by library policies and does not depend on the publisher, who knows only pseudonyms. But this is intractable with hundreds of publishers, each supplying transaction data at different time intervals and in different formats.

Licence Agreements and Inter Library Loans

Some licences restrict fair dealing, for example where a licence agreement for an electronic publication states that copies of any part of the publication may only be made by, or for, members of the institution to which the publication is licensed. This would appear to strike at the heart of the Inter-Library Loan (ILL) system that is part of the library privilege.

Transient, or disk cache, copies of parts of, or all of, an electronic publication, where such copies occur automatically as a result of a permissible electronic transaction, should not be considered a breach of copyright. This is subject to the proviso that deletion of such transient copies should take place as soon as possible after they are no longer required for the purposes of that permissible electronic transaction. The use of such transient copies to make further copies after the permitted electronic transaction is not fair dealing.

Where an image is incidental to the textual material being copied, then any digital copying of such images is fair dealing. This applies to drawings, photographs and all other types of image. For fair dealing to apply, the image must be integral to, and integrated in the text - in other words it must support the text, not the other way around. Copying and transmitting an image, or a set of images, with little or no text associated with them is probably not fair dealing if carried out by an individual, and is certainly not part of library privilege.

Databases

Early in 1998, the UK implemented a revision to copyright law to implement a European Union Directive on databases. The revisions provide for protection for databases. If the selection of materials, or organisation of the database involves original creative effort, the database itself enjoys copyright protection, and the usual ground rules for fair dealing apply. In addition, all databases, whether enjoying copyright or not, also receive a new database right that protects the maker of the database against unauthorised extraction or reutilisation.

An exception to the database right allows copying "for the purposes of illustration for teaching or research, other than teaching or research for a commercial purpose, but only by a lawful user and subject to acknowledgement of source." These revisions to the law raise a number of important questions, such as: do the materials typically handled by those in academic institutions qualify as databases?

In some cases, they clearly do, such as dictionaries, almanacs, encyclopaedias, abstracting and indexing services, and so on. It is not clear whether books or journals will do so. Secondly, it is not clear how the term "illustration for teaching or research" will be interpreted. It could be interpreted very tightly, permitting copying solely for illustration purposes, or it could be interpreted as broadly as fair dealing has traditionally been treated.

10

Information Handling

It is commonly difficult to accept is that a large amount of library material is reaching the end of its natural life, and the few years that it has left can only be prolonged by careful handling and storage. The type of library and how it is used reflect the preservation needs of its collections. The preservation requirements of a local public lending library are obviously different from those of a national library. However, both are obliged to maintain and keep accessible their collections, whether for a few years or indefinitely. Economically, libraries cannot afford to let their holdings wear out prematurely. Replacing library material, even when possible, is expensive. Preservation makes good economic sense. It cannot be easily predicted what will be of interest to researchers in the future. Preserving current collections is the best way to serve future users. Responsible and professional library staff should be committed to caring for and preserving the material with which they work. Everyone is responsible.

While preservation and conservation specialists can advise and carry out specific activities, it is the duty of all library staff, from the head of the library downwards, to safeguard the welfare of their holdings. Preservation measures have to be endorsed, supported, and encouraged from the most senior level to the most junior in the library. Those who are responsible for managing the library and maintaining the external and internal fabric of the buildings must liaise closely with those who are responsible for the welfare of the collections. If money has been set aside to rewire and replace the lighting of a building, then the opportunity should be used for ensuring not only that energy-saving lighting is used but also that it meets particular preservation lighting requirements.

When plumbing is being installed or replaced, all concerned should be working towards ensuring that risks to the collections are reduced, and not increased by having pipes running through areas where library material is present. In such instances clear communication is the key. The preservation needs of a library have to be considered in line with the social and political climate in which the organisation operates. The organisation's purpose, collecting policies, and available resources also have to be taken into account. Consequently, preservation policies must be made in consultation with various departments for the following reasons: The acquisitions and collecting sections of a library should be prepared to purchase additional copies of heavily used material, like reference works, when the cost of repairing such items is greater than replacing them. It is also necessary to calculate whether surrogate copies (i.e., microform or electronic versions, and the machines to read them) are a more economical and effective way of providing access to heavily used material than 'hard' copy.

A policy should be agreed with the cataloguing and record-creating activities of the library together with readers' services to direct users to surrogates rather than originals and to the most appropriate copy. Departments should plan for sufficient, good-quality accommodation for acquisitions.Reading room staff should be kept informed of any restrictions concerning the use of original material and briefed on limitations to photocopying. Resources should be provided for training staff on security for themselves and for library material, on how to handle library material correctly, and on how best to pass this knowledge on to users.

An exhibition policy should be drawn up which ensures that items will not come to harm while on exhibition, whether within the library or on loan to other institutions. Librarians and conservation staff should agree on whether items are fit for display. Adequate support and security, and suitable environmental conditions for material to be exhibited, should be enforced.

Preservation staff and those responsible for the collections, whatever their level of experience, should not only have some technical and scientific knowledge, but should also be familiar with the history of collections, the material they are made of, and the contents of the documents - so as to be able to understand better the preservation problems. Librarians, library staff at all levels, and students of librarianship should be acquainted with the importance of preservation within a library's overall function and policy.

Part of the process of formulating a preservation policy is to define whether, and to what extent, the library will acquire and retain material. There can be no general guidance for libraries on what material should be selected for acquisition and future preservation; this will depend on each individual library and its policy. However, national and regional libraries should cooperate in sharing the responsibilities of what to preserve and retain. In order to be able to care for its holdings, a library must make a comprehensive and honest assessment of the physical state of the institution, the collections, and their preservation requirements.

Moreover, to care for collections with a limited budget and limited resources, it is important that decisions are made on a clear and rational basis. Such an assessment can be done internally, by the library itself, or by independent consultants, whose expertise is established - both have advantages and disadvantages. Consultants are expensive and take up a lot of staff time. However, the final assessment should reveal the stark truth of the facts.

An internal assessment will probably be cheaper but might be influenced by staff politics. Unfortunately, it is also usually easier to accept recommendations from a body outside than from within. Such an undertaking must be a cooperative effort of all the departments and be endorsed at the most senior level. An assessment without authority is likely to be ineffectual. Identifying major and immediate threats to the library's holdings or particular collections should be of primary concern. Such threats will vary for different institutions, from renewing a fire and smoke detection system, through setting up an integrated pest management programme, to moving an important collection of photographs to an area with a more stable environment.

Surveys are a fundamental tool for developing a library's preservation policy. However, while they should be comprehensive, they do not necessarily have to be too detailed. Surveys can often result in enormous amounts of information being accumulated which later become very difficult to put into order and analyse. Short questions and answers are the key to successful surveys.

Once a preservation needs assessment has been carried out, the next step is to prioritise the recommendations which have been made. Because of both limited resources and the potential scale of the problem it is necessary to be selective in deciding what is to be done in terms of securing the fabric of the buildings improving environmental control improving the storage and handling of the collections. Such selectivity needs to be an explicit part of a library's policy if its responsibilities towards future users are to be properly undertaken. It is important to understand that selectivity does not preclude adopting an holistic approach to caring for library collections. All library material may not warrant special attention in the way of boxing or being stored in specific environmental conditions, but all should be safeguarded against man-made and natural disasters, theft and mutilation, pest and mould attack, and poor handling practices. Generally, selecting material for specific preservation processes such as reformatting or boxing is based on common sense.

Boxing a collection which is in good condition and not used before attending to a collection which is in poor condition and heavily used is not common sense; neither is reformatting material which has been reformatted by an institution elsewhere. Almost always, the amount of information held in libraries is greater than the resources available for carrying out their objectives with total success. It is not, and never has been, possible to save everything.

A commitment to indefinite or permanent retention involves considerable financial expenditure on accommodation, special storage conditions, and possibly reformatting. Therefore, decisions have to be made as to what will be collected and preserved. Every library has a duty to ensure the welfare of its collections for present and future users. There is no avoiding the fact that the maintenance and retention of collections costs money. For too long, libraries have spent a large proportion of their budget on acquisitions.

Most libraries have no, or inadequate, funds set aside for preservation purposes. Spending time and resources on preventing damage to library material is almost always cheaper than repairing or replacing it. No library can afford not to take precautionary measures against fire, flood, theft, and mould and insect infestation, for salvaging material which has suffered from these disasters is extremely expensive in terms of human and financial resources. The consequences of such disruptions are manifold. Serious disasters are often caused by circumstances which could have been avoided at little cost. Prevention is not only better but, more often than not, cheaper than cure.

Caring for library material does not necessarily mean an excessive expenditure of library funds. There are many common-sense and economical solutions to preservation problems. However, all libraries must realise that preserving and maintaining their collections is as important as acquiring them, and that appropriate funds should be allocated accordingly. It is not simply sufficient for librarians to be aware of their responsibility for the preservation of their collections, although awareness is the first necessity. It is also important to raise awareness among the general public and those who are in a position to fund preservation programmes. Governments must play an active role in ensuring the welfare of a nation's heritage.

National preservation offices, financially supported either by government or private funding, are essential if a country's written heritage, in whatever format, is to survive. These establishments should be in a position to encourage all libraries and institutions to adopt sound preservation policies. Very useful services, such as supplying literature on disaster planning, photocopying, or security matters on request are not enough.

Active training and education should also be provided. Furthermore, national preservation offices can sometimes be appropriate bodies for coordinating retention policies on a national scale. There is also the potential for them to be the political mouthpiece for libraries on issues like the mandatory use of permanent paper in publishing. Enlightening the general public through poster campaigns in schools and public libraries about the respect for and care of library material is another useful responsibility that can be assumed by national preservation offices. If a nation's heritage is to survive, then the coordination of national, regional, consortial, and institutional preservation programmes is essential. It is unrealistic to expect libraries and archives to address individually and resolve successfully the technical and financial problems associated with preservation on a national level. For instance, in 1996 IFLA and ICA established the Joint IFLA - ICA Committee for Preservation in Africa (JICPA) to raise awareness of preservation issues and coordinate activities in the region. Libraries should cooperate not only with archives but also with museums and galleries.

Considerable savings can be made and duplication of effort avoided by institutions consulting with each other over areas such as environmental control, building and collection evaluation, and disaster preparedness and recovery plans.

Security Policy in Libraries

It is the responsibility of the library manager to intitiate, coordinate, and implement the development of a security policy within the library. When drafting such a policy other libraries, police, and staff should be consulted. Library perimeters and grounds should be kept tidy. Building exteriors should be assessed for ease of access by criminals. An alarm and closed-circuit television system should be seriously considered. All areas should be well-lit.Close attention should be paid to doors and windows in respect of locks, security glass, or film.

The interior of the building should be kept tidy. It will present an image of care and supervision which will deter the potential criminal. All entry/exit points and routes should be kept separate if possible and staffed at all times. Expensive equipment should be chained or bolted down and marked with security markings. All contractors should sign in and out of the library and wear passes at all times. The need for an alert attitude should be instilled in staff. All storage areas should be kept secure and clear policy guidelines provided on who has access to what areas. Criminal and antisocial behaviour ranges from the rowdy visitor to the determined thief. Staff, books, equipment, and personal property are all at risk.

Starting-points in deterring criminal and antisocial behaviour include: having a calm and ordered library creating an environment which the genuine reader regards as helpful and efficient, but in which the villain feels anxious and wary having prominent notices which clearly define what is unacceptable behaviour training staff in how to deal with an awkward or aggressive user or a suspected book thief. All library material should be stamped in a way that clearly identifies it as belonging to a particular institution. Library stamps should be fast-drying, non-fading, stable, and indelible.

Security tagging systems, if present, should be regularly inspected. It is useful for all staff to have easy access to an emergency information booklet which lists only the immediate steps to be taken, key personnel, and how they can be contacted in the event of: accidents to staff and visitors vandalism, theft, and assault incidents like power failures, lift failures, loss of security keys emergencies which threaten the welfare of people, the collections, and the fabric of the buildings - e.g. bomb threats hurricane, earthquake, and flood warnings. It is vital for any library, no matter what its size, to take every precaution possible to prevent the occurrence of an avoidable disaster.

Of equal importance is having measures in place to cope with the consequences of disasters, whether they be natural or man-made. Numerous resources have been published to aid institutions in implementing disaster avoidance measures and formulating a disaster response and salvage plan. Only the key points are listed here. It should be mandatory for every library to have a written plan in which all these elements are fully developed. A 'phased' approach can be used in disaster preparedness. That is, it is acceptable, as a first phase, to begin with a few sections, particularly if the institution focuses first on those issues that are of greatest concern.

In a subsequent phase, the planners can gradually add more detail and other sections as they become better educated, have time to pursue the plan, and are able to develop consensus on how the institution should organise its preparedness activities. Disaster planning usually involves five phases:

— Risk assessment ascertaining the dangers to the building and its collections

— Prevention implementing measures which will remove or reduce any danger

— Preparedness developing a written preparedness, response, and recovery plan

— Response procedures to follow when disaster strikes

— Recovery restoring the disaster site and damaged material to a stable and usable condition.

Once the risks have been assessed, take all the necessary precautions to make the library buildings and their holdings secure. Consult with the emergency services (fire, police, and hospital). All parts of the building should be provided with a fire and smoke detection system, which simultaneously alerts occupants and the local fire brigade. Smoke detection equipment can provide early warning of a developing fire, thereby giving an opportunity of manual suppression prior to the activation of a sprinkler system. Manually operated fire-alarm call points, which can be used by occupants to indicate the presence of fire or smoke, should also be present throughout the building. If an automatic fire extinguishing system is not present, the following should be installed:

— Hose reels or racks so as to ensure that all parts of the building are within 6 m of the nozzle of a fully extended hose.

— Hydrant systems or rising mains on all buildings more than 30 m in height or where a single floor exceeds 1000 m^2.

— The hydrant or rising mains should be located so as to permit the fire brigade to pressurise the pipework from outside the building.

— Portable fire extinguishers should always be available, even if an automatic fire suppression system has been installed. There should be a suitable number of hand-held extinguishers (CO_2, water, or foam according to the likely cause of fire, i.e., electrical or chemical) strategically placed.

— Consideration should be given to the benefits offered by an automatic fire extinguishing system.

A CO_2 gas system is only suitable for smaller compartments, i.e., spaces which can be made airtight and which are not normally occupied by people. Halon gas systems are no longer produced as they are environmentally damaging, particularly toward the earth's protective ozone layer.

Wet-pipe sprinkler systems are a reliable and safe extinguishing method and are relatively easy to maintain. Contrary to popular belief, the activation of one sprinkler does not cause all sprinklers to operate; and so danger of accidental discharge should not be overestimated. The average sprinkler discharges 15-20 gallons per minute while typical fire hoses release 120-250 gallons per minute. It is important to remember that the environmental and human safety aspects of water are known, unlike the possible impact from various chemical agents.

Furthermore, the recovery techniques for water-damaged material are also known. Dry-pipe sprinkler systems are essentially the same as wet-pipe systems except that the pipes in the protected area contain pressurised air. When the sprinkler is activated a valve opens allowing water to flow into the pipes. This lessens any threat of water leaking into collection areas. Micromist systems are being developed which discharge limited quantities of water at very high pressures, resulting in exceptionally efficient cooling and rapid fire control with significantly little water. Tests have proved that water saturation, often associated with standard firefighting procedures, is avoided.

Other anticipated benefits include: lower installation costs, minimal aesthetic impact, and known environmental safety. Fire alarms and suppression systems, the building fabric, plumbing, electric, and gas supplies and fittings, etc., should be maintained and routinely tested. The fire services may allow entry into a building for salvage purposes for a limited time, and it is essential to know what items are to be saved and where they are located. Selecting and training an emergency response team comprising voluntary members of staff who live near the library. Detailed, step-by-step instructions on all phases of salvage operation, covering a range of incidents that are possible and the various media included in the collections, such as books and journals, manuscripts/records, coated vs. uncoated stock, sound recordings, photographic media, computer/electronic media, etc. Instructions for long-term rehabilitation: procedures for activities including identification and labelling, smoke/soot removal, cleaning, sorting and rehousing, repair and rebinding, etc.

As part of the preparation for a disaster plan it is essential to be familiar with the various procedures for drying different types of library material. The following drying methods all have advantages and disadvantages:

— Air-drying

— Dehumidification

— Freeze-drying

— Vacuum thermal-drying

— Vacuum freeze-drying

If time must be taken to make critical decisions, books and records should be frozen to reduce physical distortion and biological contamination. Air-drying is the simplest technique for drying damp - not totally wet - material. A damp book can be stood on its end and its pages fanned out or interleaved with blotting paper. Although this is an effective technique which does not require expensive equipment or materials (fans and interleaving paper), it is labour-intensive, time-consuming, and generally results in some dimensional distortion. Environmental conditions in all areas should be adequately monitored and recorded with reliable and regularly maintained thermohygrographic or electronic recording equipment.

Monitoring is very important because it documents existing environmental conditions; supports requests to install environmental controls; and indicates whether any climate-control equipment present is operating properly and producing the desired conditions. When monitoring equipment indicates notable changes in environmental conditions, reports should be given to authorities so that appropriate measures are taken immediately. In general, library material should be stored and used in stable conditions which are not too hot, not too dry, and not too damp.

Many attempts have been made to provide 'ideal' figures for temperature and relative humidity levels. However, it is now recognised that it is probably impractical and unrealistic to maintain a building or stack temperature at one setting throughout the year, especially in areas with extreme temperature variations, without incurring huge costs.

In humid parts of the world, where relative humidity does not fall below 65% all year round and is much higher for long periods, it is unrealistic to expect a level much below 65%, unless the institution is air-conditioned day and night all the year round at great cost. In these regions good air circulation is imperative if mould is to be discouraged. Air pollution is to a large extent associated with towns and industry and is another cause of damage to paper and other organic materials. Air pollutants vary greatly in nature, from gases to particulates such as dirt and dust.

Gaseous pollution is caused overwhelmingly by the burning of fuels. Pollutants such as sulphur dioxide, hydrogen sulphide, and nitrogen dioxide combine with moisture in the air to form acids that attack and damage library material. Ozone is a powerful oxidant which severely damages all organic materials. It is a product of the combination of sunlight and nitrogen dioxide from automobile exhaust; it may also be produced by electrostatic filtering systems used in some air conditioners, as well as by electrostatic photocopy machines. Smoking, cooking, and off-gassing from unstable materials may also produce harmful gaseous pollutants. Wood, particularly oak, birch and beech, emit acetic and other acids, and vulcanised rubber releases volatile sulphides that are especially damaging to photographs.

The composition of all equipment, materials, and finishes used for the storage, transport, and display of objects should be tested by recognised methods to ascertain whether they are likely to produce harmful emissions. Particulate pollutants, such as soot, dirt, and dust abrade, soil, and disfigure materials. Dust and dirt that have absorbed gaseous pollutants from the air become sites for harmful chemical reactions when they settle on library material. Particulate pollutants can also aid mould growth.

Modern library material, such as magnetic and optical media, are very sensitive to dust and dirt. Dust is commonly a mixture of fragments of human skin, minute particles of mineral or plant material, textile fibres, industrial smoke, grease from fingerprints, and other organic and inorganic materials. There are often salts such as sodium chloride and sharp gritty silica crystals. In this chemical mixture are the spores of countless moulds, fungi, and microorganisms which live on the organic material in the dust (fingerprints, for example, serve as good culture media). Much of the dirt is hygroscopic (water-attracting), and this tendency can encourage the growth of moulds, as well as increase the corrosiveness of salts, hydrolysis, and the release of acids.

Light is energy and energy is required for chemical reactions to take place. All wavelengths of light - visible, infrared, and ultraviolet (UV) - promote the chemical decomposition of organic materials through oxidation. Higher-energy ultraviolet is the most harmful. However, light in all its forms, especially in the presence of atmospheric pollutants, leads to a weakening and embrittlement of cellulose, adhesives, cloth, and skin materials. Light can cause some papers to bleach and others to yellow or darken; it can also cause media and dyes to fade or change colour, altering the legibility and appearance of documents, photographs, art works, and bindings. The following factors concerning light should be known by all those responsible for preserving library material:

- Chemical reactions initiated by exposure to light continue even after the light source is removed and materials are put into dark storage.
- Light damage is irreversible.
- The effect of light is cumulative.

Incandescent lamps are the most familiar type of electric light source. Light is produced by passing an electric current through a thin tungsten wire filament. Incandescent lamps usually have less harmful UV radiation output than fluorescent lighting, but they generate more heat through infrared radiation. Tungsten incandescent lights also burn less efficiently and must be replaced more often than fluorescent lights. Tungsten-halogen lamps also produce light by passing an electric current through a thin tungsten wire filament but with the addition of a halogen gas in the bulb, which enables the filament to operate at higher temperatures yielding a 'whiter', more efficient light source. Halogen lamps have three to five times the life and UV output of tungsten incandescent lights.

Fluorescent lamps are low-pressure mercury discharge lamps which produce UV radiation which in turn excites a phosphor coating that emits visible light. The use of different phosphors is responsible for the various colour characteristics these lamps exhibit. Although fluorescent lighting is high in ultraviolet content, it is usually installed in libraries because it generates less heat and is more economical to operate. It is necessary to measure and record light and UV levels at different times of the year, as readings will change with the seasons.

A light meter or lux meter measures the intensity of visible light in lux. A camera with a built-in light meter can also be used to measure light levels indirectly. A UV meter measures the amount of UV radiation in units of microwatts of UV radiation per lumen. Lighting in museums, galleries, and exhibition rooms is usually left to specialists. This should also be the case for library reading rooms and storage areas. While 200-300 lux are acceptable levels for reading rooms, attaining such levels with a combination of natural and artificial light, which satisfy staff and researchers, is difficult.

In stack and storage areas 50-200 lux is sufficient. However, to achieve these levels it would be necessary to exclude all natural light and rely entirely on artificial lighting. Light sources with ultraviolet radiation emissions above 75 microwatts per lumen require filtering. In exhibition situations, the light level falling on the surface of objects on display must be kept low.

The spores of fungi that become mould are always present in the air and on objects and will grow wherever conditions are favourable. In general, moisture, darkness, and poor air circulation are ideal conditions. War mth is a factor, but certain moulds and bacteria will thrive in cold temperatures too. Mould can weaken, stain, and disfigure paper and photographic material. It is generaly recognised that 'foxing' may be attributable to mould reacting with trace elements in paper. Cloth, leather, vellum, and certain adhesives are also affected by mould. Mould can be checked to see whether it is active or inactive.

Generally, active mould is damp, slimy, and smears if touched. Inactive mould is dry and powdery and can be brushed off with a soft brush. If mould is discovered in large portions of a collection, isolate the area immediately and do not attempt to clean up without first consulting a mycologist to determine if toxic moulds are present. Certain moulds commonly found in libraries can pose serious health risks, causing headaches, nausea, eye and skin irritation, and respiratory problems.

A conservator may have to be employed or at least consulted on the treatment of infested items and on the return of the affected area to a suitable condition for housing material. If only a few items are affected, place them in a dry paper-based box until treatment. If possible, include a desiccant, such as conditioned silica gel packets. This enclosure will prevent spores from circulating, but will not encourage the growth potentially created by the tightly sealed microclimate of a plastic bag.

If immediate drying is not possible, or if many objects are wet, freeze them; later they can be thawed, dried, and cleaned in small batches. Material may also be freeze-dried and then cleaned. When dry, the items should be cleaned and stored under suitable environmental conditions. The storage environment is critical since even after cleaning, fungal residue will be present. If the outbreak is small, and equipment limited, take the items outside - well away from the building - on a calm, mild day and brush them off with a soft white brush, away from you and downwind.

Remove mould only with a vacuum cleaner that contains an HEPA (high efficiency particulate air) filter capable of retaining 99.97% of all particles down to 0.3 microns. Vacuum cleaners designed to filter air through water are unsuitable for capturing mould's small particles. Even if a fungicide is present in the water, this will not prevent particles of mould from being discharged back into the air. While certain treatments can kill mould that is active, they are far less effective with dormant spores, which are protected by relatively impervious cell walls. Proper conditions will insure that dormant fungi remain inactive and will prevent germination of accidentally introduced active spores.

If the environment is favourable to fungal activity, mould will grow. Even if complete eradication were possible, it would not be a permanent solution in storage spaces without climate controls. More spores are always being introduced and would sooner or later become a problem. If it is not possible to remove mould outdoors, work in front of a fan, with the fan blowing contaminated air out a window, or work in a ventilation hood. Make sure the ventilation hood uses a filter that traps mould. Be sure to remove the mould in an area well away from collection storage and other people. Small brushes and nozzles used for cleaning computers are useful for this purpose. Papers can be vacuum cleaned through a plastic screen held down with weights. A brush attachment should be used for books. Covering the nozzle or brush with cheesecloth or screening will guard against loss of detached pieces. Remember active mould is soft and subject to smearing, and is easily rubbed into porous materials such as paper or cloth.

Active mould is best removed from valuable artifacts with a small low-pressure vacuum cleaner. This delicate work is best done by a conservator. When fungal growth is visible on art objects or valuable items, it should be removed by a conservator. Staining caused by mould can often be removed or at least lightened. This is an expensive procedure and therefore most suitable for objects of significant value.It is important to find out what caused the mould outbreak in the first place.

The room where a mould outbreak occurs must be dried and thoroughly cleaned before the affected material can be returned to it. For moderate to large mould outbreaks contact a professional service that provides dehumidification or cleaning of the premises. Insects which most commonly cause damage in libraries and archives throughout the world are cockroaches, silverfish, book-lice, beetles and termites. They feed on organic substances such as paper, pastes, glues, gelatine sizing, leather, and bookcloth; birds nests are also a major source of food for insects, and bird droppings are corrosive. They prefer warm, dark, damp, dirty, and poorly ventilated conditions.

Their damage is usually irreversible - text and images lost by insects eating and boring through paper and photographs cannot be replaced. Termites can devastate buildings and collections. While some commercial freezers are adequate for pest control, others are not able to lower the temperature quickly enough. A slow reduction in the temperature allows some insects to go into a state resembling 'suspended animation' and survive the treatment.

Naturally, it is also important to ensure that the objects are not damaged by the low temperatures and that condensation is controlled. It is now accepted that an integrated pest management (IPM) approach should form part of every preservation programme. IPM involves: monitoring the building regularly for the presence of insects and pests ensuring all staff, from cleaners to librarians, are vigilant and report any signs of fresh damage and activity checking all material which is to be accessioned before it enters the library using sticky traps. Traps have the advantage of catching insects before they can be found visually; they catch a wide range of species; they can be placed in areas which are difficult to inspect; trapped insects can be identified and counted; traps are good indicators of an increase in insect numbers in one area; they also highlight any failure of control treatment understanding the biology and life cycles of insects and pests, which helps to know when and where they are likely to breed, what they are likely to eat, where they are likely to live eliminating or containing all sources of likely infestation - ideally food and drink should not be consumed on the premises; flowers and plants should not be allowed in the building maintaining an environment not conducive to pests and insects, which is clean, cool, dry, and well-ventilated preventing pests and insects from entering the building - making sure doors close properly, installing mesh screens for windows and doors, etc. using appropriate exterior lighting, such as sodium vapour, which is less attractive to insects implementing a cleaning and hygiene programme - rubbish should be safely and properly disposed of; attics and basements regularly checked and cleaned.

Library buildings should be designed as far as possible to meet preservation requirements. These requirements affect many aspects of planning: design and orientation of buildings; building materials (which can, under some circumstances, be used to produce satisfactory internal climatic conditions in preference to mechanical air control systems); internal building and furbishing materials; and materials used for furniture, including shelving as well as lighting, both natural and artificial.

Indigenous and traditional building methods and materials in subtropical and tropical areas often provide better storage conditions for library material than those that are imported. It is always worth considering constructing a sealed area within a building for material which needs tight temperature and relative humidity control. In many places heating, ventilating, and air conditioning systems (HVAC) may be too costly to install and maintain or may have to be restricted to specific collections.

Nevertheless, there are many rudimentary measures and precautions that can improve a library's environment and protect collections. A first step in all efforts to improve the environment should be sealing the structure. This step alone will improve the physical condition of the building by reducing air infiltration, pest access, heating loss or heat gain, and air and particulate pollution. Making the building watertight will also reduce the sources of moisture within the structure and may significantly reduce relative humidity levels. Use draft excluders and weatherstripping to make the building weathertight.

Preserving Photographic Media

Since the birth of photography in 1839, photographs have been made employing many different methods. Some of the materials used were extremely self-destructive, others were very sensitive to physical contact, and almost all photographic material is sensitive to the environment - not only temperature, relative humidity, and air pollution but also oxidising substances found from emissions in building materials, wall paints, wooden furnishing, cardboard, wall paints, and even the enclosures used to protect them. While the conservation of photographic material should be left to specialists, library staff can take certain precautions to safeguard the welfare of photographs within their collections. A typical photograph consists of three different parts:

— *Support* - the support layer may be of glass, plastic film, paper, or resin-coated paper.

— *Binder* - The emulsion or binder layer, most commonly gelatine, but also albumen or collodion, holds the final image material or image-forming substance to the support.

— *Final image material* - The final image material, made of silver, colour dyes, or pigment particles, is usually suspended in the emulsion or binder layer. Many different final image materials and binders have been used over the years.

Today, however, almost all black-and-white photographs are composed of silver suspended in gelatine. Photographic media are extremely susceptible to damage from careless handling; staff and users should therefore: provide copies rather than originals whenever possible wear clean, lint-free cotton gloves when handling photographic media and never touch the emulsion side of any photographic image prepare a clean work surface use two hands to hold a photograph, or support it with a piece of stiff card not use adhesive tapes, staples, pins, paper clips, or rubber bands on photographic material consult a photographic conservator on issues of storage and handling.

Many manufacturers and suppliers of housing materials now conduct this test on their products. If at all possible, purchase products that have passed the PAT, or specify that any housing purchased must pass the PAT. Enclosure materials for photographs fall essentially into two groups: paper/ board and plastic. Paper and board should conform to the following criteria: high cellulose content neutral pH undetectable reducible sulphur content free of lignin, pH buffers, metal particles, acid, peroxides, for maldehydes, and harmful sizing agents.

Photographic media are exceptionally sensitive to environmental factors. Generally, storage temperatures should be kept as low as possible and measures should be taken to reduce exposure to light, UV radiation, atmospheric, and particulate pollution. Black and white prints and negatives should be kept below 18 °C and 30-40% RH. Colour material should be placed in cold storage and 30-40% RH if its longevity is to be ensured. Place material in cold storage only after consulting a specialist. Photographs - it is best for each item to have its own enclosure. This reduces damage to the photograph by giving it protection and physical support.

Because paper enclosures are opaque, the photograph must be removed from the enclosure when it is viewed; clear plastic 'L' sleeves (two sheets of polyester placed on top of one another and joined along two adjacent edges), with a piece of board behind the print for added support, have the advantage of allowing researchers to view the image without handling it, thus reducing the possibility of scratching or abrasion. Special care must be given to the storage of oversize photographic prints mounted on cardboard.

This board is often acidic and extremely brittle. Embrittlement of the support can endanger the image itself because the cardboard may break in storage or during handling, damaging the photograph. Such prints must be carefully stored, sometimes in specially made enclosures. They should be handled with great care.

Once photographs have been properly housed in folders, sleeves, or envelopes, they may be stored upright or flat in drop-front boxes of archival quality. Horizontal storage of photographs is usually preferable to vertical storage, since it provides overall support and avoids mechanical damage such as bending. Vertical storage, however, may make access to the collection easier and decrease handling. With vertical storage, photographs should be placed in acid-free file folders or envelopes that are themselves housed in hanging file folders or document storage boxes. Overcrowding should be avoided. The use of hanging file folders will prevent photographs from sliding down under each other and will facilitate their handling. In either case, care should be taken not to pack the photographs too tightly. Prints in albums - may be interleaved with a photographic conservation paper if they appear to be suffering damage from adjacent prints or album pages.

This should not be done if the binding will be stressed by the extra volume of paper. Modern albums of the type that have adhesive coated pages and plastic cover sheets should not be used.

Photographic albums - should be stored flat, preferably in boxes lined with acid-free tissue paper padding.

Glass-plate negatives - should be kept in individual paper enclosures and stored vertically in suitably padded cabinets or strong boxes with a board separator after every fifth plate.

Film negatives - can be stored in paper or polyester sleeves. They can then be placed in boxes or in a hanging file system in a cabinet.

Cased photographs - such as Daguerreotypes and Ambrotypes should be kept horizontally in their cases and these stored in cabinet drawers and/or boxes. Boxes containing photographic material should be housed on metal shelves. Where possible, items of similar size should be stored together; the mixing of different sizes can cause abrasion and breakage, and can increase the risk of misplacing smaller items. Regardless of the size of the photograph, all enclosures within a box should be the same size and should be the size of the box. Boxes should not be overfilled.

Film-based Media

There are three main types of film-based photographic materials: cellulose nitrate, cellulose acetate, and polyester. These materials have been used as a support for negatives, positive transparencies, motion pictures, microfilms, and other photographic products. Cellulose nitrate and cellulose acetate are unstable.

The by-products of their degradation can severely harm and even destroy photographic collections. In particular, institutions should isolate and properly store cellulose nitrate material because of its extreme flammability, especially when in a deteriorated condition. It was manufactured 1889-1951 and in use 1900-1939. It is unstable and highly flammable.

At room temperature and lower, it slowly and continuously deteriorates, emitting gases in the process. If these gases cannot escape from the container in which the film is kept, then decomposition accelerates - the base turns yellow, then brown, becomes sticky and then brittle, until it disintegrates into ashy-brown powder, resulting in the complete destruction of the picture/sound records.The reaction can lead to spontaneous combustion of the film with disastrous consequences for other adjacent material, people, and buildings. It was introduced in 1935, and from 1939 onwards almost totally replaced cellulose nitrate.

It slowly decomposes at room temperature, giving off gases that resemble the smell of vinegar - hence the process is known as 'vinegar syndrome'. It eventually breaks down altogether. Until recently, cellulose triacetate films had been considered suitable for archival records; however, stability problems have become evident with this film as well. Commonly known as 'safety film'.

Film-based media can be damaged easily, even when in good condition. All three film types, and the gelatine binder on them, can be scratched, abraded, and creased. Oils and dirt from hands can also damage the support and binder, as well as the final image material. Once deterioration has begun, film-based media are even more prone to handling damage. Deteriorated media can become quite brittle; in this state, repeated removal from a housing can cause considerable harm.

Digitising

Digitising is a way of capturing and storing images using computer technology. A digital camera or a scanning device takes an electronic photograph, which is converted into binary digital code (essentially a string of zeros and ones), and can be viewed on a computer screen or printed out on paper. The data are stored within magnetic and optical media.

The information content of digital images is not converted to alphanumeric form at the time of scanning and thus is not text-searchable. OCR software enables a scanned printed document to be converted into text which can be edited using word processing programmes. Unfortunately, the process is not completely accurate and time has to be spent rectifying misread letters.

Moreover, OCR programmes are not capable of saving the original document's typography or page layout. Digitising offers quick access to multiple users worldwide. Images can be electronically restored and enhanced. High-quality user copies can be provided. Automated retrieval aids facilitate the finding of information.

Digitising provides an image which can be reproduced many times with no loss of quality. Digital images do not decay with use. It requires an expensive commitment to supporting technologies used to convert and retrieve records. A digital image, displayed or printed, may not yet be acceptable as a legal substitute for the original. Standards are lacking in many areas.

Digital storage is not yet accepted as truly archival - it requires continuous monitoring and eventual or periodic refreshing and transfer. The drive systems will become obsolete. There are relatively high but rapidly declining storage and production costs. The time needed to capture and store high-resolution archival images, and the costs of doing so increase as the quality increases. It is expensive to reproduce colour images.

The technological life span of any optical or electronic medium and its associated hardware and software is a major issue that does not exist when considering microfilming as a reformatting process. Computer hardware and software both change rapidly, with new versions of each coming out on a regular basis. In addition, technologies come and go. Libraries will probably not be able to use many of the technologies of today in the future. Certainly, parts for the hardware will no longer be manufactured, and old software will eventually not work on new machines. What this means is that libraries may not be able to retrieve information stored on optical media in 25 years, and this will almost certainly be a problem in 100 years.

Management of Library Resources

In recent years, a great deal has been written on standards, codes of practice and general guidelines for the management of libraries and archives, and this has come about for a number of reasons. The political shift towards restrictions on public spending gave rise to a need for organisations of all kinds to demonstrate efficiency, value for money and user satisfaction; this stimulated the development of service charters, codes of conduct and performance indicators within the sector.

Collections held by libraries and archives continued to grow, both in volume and range, as traditional holdings of books, documents and photographs were supplemented by audio and visual recordings, microforms and digital records of all kinds. This created a need for more effective collection management, whilst the relative fragility and impermanence of some modern media stimulated study of their deterioration mechanisms and methods of enhancing their stability. Advances in the study of energy efficiency and preventive conservation led to more holistic approaches to the design of buildings, control of the environment within, and improved techniques for the handling, storage and conservation of a range of archival materials.

Various well-publicised library and archive disasters prompted increased awareness of the necessity for disaster prevention, emergency planning, and appropriate methods for the retrieval and conservation of damaged items. The rapid development of information technology changed the expectations of both providers and users of libraries and archives, and necessitated fresh guidance on the management of, and access to, digital information. This leaflet is aimed at personnel in libraries and archives wishing to be sure that their institution is performing according to currently accepted best practice; those considering an expansion, refurbishment or relocation of their service; or those wishing to build upon past achievements to improve their performance.

In UK, standards and codes of practice are also developed by professional bodies and other organisations, such as the Society of Archivists, the Library Association, and the Royal Commission on Historical Manuscripts. The international lead body on standards is the International Standards Organisation (ISO), of which BSI is a member. The ISO is a global federation of national standards organisations from more than 90 countries, dedicated to developing and maintaining international standards, with a view to facilitating the international exchange of goods and services.

Standards may be mandatory or voluntary. Mandatory standards include those pertaining to building regulations, Health and Safety, and fire precautions; failure to adhere to these can result in fines or prosecution. In the case of voluntary standards, the onus is placed on the organisation, practitioner or consumer to be aware of the standard and insist on conformance with it. Mandatory standards are essential to ensure the safety and wellbeing of staff and members of the public in libraries and archives, and the long-term preservation of their collections.

Voluntary standards demonstrate the best practice which can be aspired to across a wide range of activities (preservation, conservation, security, access, training and so on). The application of standards enables libraries and archives to carry out their functions consistently, and to an agreed level of quality. Having a benchmark against which performance can be measured helps to demonstrate professionalism, accountability and efficiency to staff, user groups and funding bodies. Adherence to standards builds confidence in the professions, helps to ensure customer satisfaction, and facilitates co-operative working with other organisations both in the United Kingdom and abroad. Furthermore, the holdings of libraries and archives are, by their nature, fragile and susceptible to damage from a variety of sources. These include human intervention, environmental factors, disasters and other external events.

Standards and codes of practice specify the action which libraries and archives can take to safeguard their (often valuable and sometimes irreplaceable) holdings against risks such as these. Thus adherence to standards is of great benefit in terms of preserving the nation's documentary heritage, and also in terms of continuity of service to the public.

Archive Building

The building is the first line of defence between a library or archive collection and potentially damaging environmental and human factors. Its design and.4 construction have profound implications for access and security, energy-efficiency and running costs, environmental stability and disaster prevention. New buildings can be designed to very high specifications to take these factors into account; however, it is possible to make modifications to existing structures to improve their performance.

The main standard relating to archive buildings, environment, security and storage is BS 5454; many of the recommendations made in this document are equally applicable to libraries. A substantial amount of additional information, case studies of new and converted buildings, and an extensive bibliography, can be found in a Royal Commission on Historic Manuscripts survey of archive buildings.

The Museums and Galleries Commission (MGC) have produced a useful publication on the selection and conversion of industrial buildings; and whilst this is aimed primarily at the museum sector, it contains many recommendations relevant to libraries and archives using, or considering using, buildings of this nature. Investing in improvements to a building's energy-efficiency can lead to significant long-term revenue savings in addition to improved environmental stability. The Energy Efficiency Office (EEO) produces guidelines on all aspects of energy management in public buildings, including one aimed specifically at libraries.

Archival conservators are expected to have completed a recognised course of training offered by one of several conservation training schools, or a Society of Archivists apprenticeship scheme. The British standard pertaining to repair and conservation is BS 4971. Best practice guidelines for archives and record offices have been published by the Society of Archivists, and the British Library Research and Innovation Centre. The first of these documents covers the role of conservators, their training and employment, funding for archival conservation and many practical issues, and includes a valuable bibliography; the British Library publication summarises recent research in the field, and makes recommendations for further research and national cooperative strategies. Emergency planning and disaster mitigation is an essential component of any preservation strategy.

In recognition of this, the British Library Research and Innovation Centre produced a project report and guidelines on disaster management. These guidelines are to assist library and archive staff in preventing disasters, and producing effective plans to minimise their effects should they occur. Again, the document contains an excellent bibliography, including reference to the RAMP study on disaster planning for UNESCO. Libraries and archives may hold extensive collections of photographic material, ranging from early glass plate negatives to modern colour prints. BSI have produced a range of standards relating to the care of photographic materials, including BS ISO 10214:1991, on filing enclosures for the storage of processed photographic materials.

The MGC standard on the care of photographs also contains much relevant information. Wear and tear on many other types of original archival material can be minimised by preservation microfilming. BSI has also issued a range of standards giving recommendations and specifications for microcopying various materials; details of these, and other British Standards, can be found on their web site.

Almost forty years ago the International Federation of Library Associations and Institutions (IFLA) initiated a fundamental re-examination of cataloguing theory and practice on an international level. The first important outcome of that effort was a set of cataloguing principles agreed to at an international conference held in Paris in 1961 that have subsequently come to be known as the Paris Principles. A second key undertaking was initiated at the International Meeting of Cataloguing Experts held in Copenhagen in 1969 with the adoption of a resolution to establish international standards for the form and content of bibliographic descriptions.

The first of the standards developed under that resolution, the International Standard Bibliographic Description for Monographic Publications, was published in 1971. In the years that have followed those initial undertakings the Paris Principles and the ISBDs have served as the bibliographic foundation for a variety of new and revised national and international cataloguing codes.

During that same period, however, the environment within which cataloguing principles and standards operate has changed dramatically.

Key factors contributing to the change have been the introduction and ongoing development of automated systems for the creation and processing of bibliographic data, and the growth of large-scale databases, both national and international in scope, that contain records contributed and used by thousands of libraries participating in shared cataloguing programs. The growth of shared cataloguing has been spurred not only by the opportunities that new technologies bring with them but also by an increasing need to reduce cataloguing costs by minimising duplicate cataloguing effort.

Economic pressures have also prompted libraries to try to simplify the cataloguing process and to do more and more "minimal level" cataloguing in order to keep pace with the continued growth of publishing output. On the other side of the coin, there has been an increasing need to adapt cataloguing codes and practices to accommodate change resulting from the emergence of new forms of electronic publishing, and the advent of networked access to information resources.

Equally important has been a recognised need to respond more effectively to an increasingly broad range of user expectations and needs. Included in that aggregate of data are descriptive data elements such as those defined in the International Standard Bibliographic Descriptions (ISBDs); data elements used in headings for persons, corporate bodies, titles, and subjects that function as filing devices or index entries; other data elements used to organise a file of records, such as classification numbers; annotations such as abstracts or summaries; and data specific to the copies in library collections, such as accession numbers and call numbers.

Data associated with persons, corporate bodies, titles, and subjects are analysed only to the extent that they function as headings or index entries for the records describing bibliographic entities. A study assumes that the data included in bibliographic records produced for national bibliographies and library catalogues are used by a wide range of users: readers, students, researchers, library staff, publishers, distribution agents, retailers, information brokers, administrators of intellectual property rights, etc.

The study takes into account the wide variety of applications, both within and outside a library setting, in which the data in bibliographic records are used: collections development, acquisitions, cataloguing, the production of finding aids and bibliographies, inventory management, preservation, circulation, interlibrary loan, reference, and information retrieval.

The functional requirements for bibliographic records are defined in relation to the following generic tasks that are performed by users when searching and making use of national bibliographies and library catalogues:

— using the data to find materials that correspond to the user's stated search criteria (e.g., in the context of a search for all documents on a given subject, or a search for a recording issued under a particular title);

— using the data retrieved to identify an entity (e.g., to confirm that the document described in a record corresponds to the document sought by the user, or to distinguish between two texts or recordings that have the same title);

— using the data to select an entity that is appropriate to the user's needs (e.g., to select a text in a language the user understands, or to choose a version of a computer program that is compatible with the hardware and operating system available to the user);

— using the data in order to acquire or obtain access to the entity described (e.g., to place a purchase order for a publication, to submit a request for the loan of a copy of a book in a library's collection, or to access online an electronic document stored on a remote computer).

The first step in the entity analysis technique is to isolate the key objects that are of interest to users of information in a particular domain. These objects of interest or entities are defined at as high a level as possible. The entities that have been defined and represent the key objects of interest to users of bibliographic data. The entities have been divided into three groups.

The first group comprises the products of intellectual or artistic endeavour that are named or described in bibliographic records: work, expression, manifestation, and item. The second group comprises those entities responsible for the intellectual or artistic content, the physical production and dissemination, or the custodianship of such products: person and corporate body. The third group comprises an additional set of entities that serve as the subjects of intellectual or artistic endeavour: concept, object, event, and place.

The entities in the first group represent the different aspects of user interests in the products of intellectual or artistic endeavour. The entities defined as work (a distinct intellectual or artistic creation) and expression (the intellectual or artistic realisation of a work) reflect intellectual or artistic content. The entities defined as manifestation (the physical embodiment of an expression of a work) and item (a single exemplar of a manifestation), on the other hand, reflect physical form.

The entities in the second group represent those responsible for the intellectual or artistic content, the physical production and dissemination, or the custodianship of the entities in the first group. The entities in the second group include person (an individual) and corporate body.

The entities in the third group represent an additional set of entities that serve as the subjects of works. The group includes concept (an abstract notion or idea), object (a material thing), event (an action or occurrence), and place (a location). The entity defined as manifestation encompasses a wide range of materials, including manuscripts, books, periodicals, maps, posters, sound recordings, films, video recordings, CD-ROMs, multimedia kits, etc. As an entity, manifestation represents all the physical objects that bear the same characteristics, in respect to both intellectual content and physical form.

When a work is realised, the resulting expression of the work may be physically embodied on or in a medium such as paper, audio tape, video tape, canvas, plaster, etc. That physical embodiment constitutes a manifestation of the work. In some cases there may be only a single physical exemplar produced of that manifestation of the work (e.g., an author's manuscript, a tape recorded for an oral history archive, an original oil painting, etc.). In other cases there are multiple copies produced in order to facilitate public dissemination or distribution. In those cases there is normally a more formal production process involved, and a publisher, producer, or distributor takes responsibility for the process.

In other cases there may be only a limited number of copies made of an original exemplar for purposes such as private study (e.g., a dubbing of an original recording of a piece of music), or preservation (e.g., a photocopy produced on permanent paper of an author's original typescript). Whether the scope of production is broad (e.g., in the case of publication, etc.) or limited (e.g., in the case of copies made for private study, etc.), the set of copies produced in each case constitutes a manifestation.

All copies produced that form part of the same set are considered to be copies of the same manifestation. The boundaries between one manifestation and another are drawn on the basis of both intellectual content and physical form. When the production process involves changes in physical form the resulting product is considered a new manifestation. Changes in physical form include changes affecting display characteristics (e.g., a change in typeface, size of font, page layout, etc.), changes in physical medium (e.g., a change from paper to microfilm as the medium of conveyance), and changes in the container (e.g., a change from cassette to cartridge as the container for a tape). Where the production process involves a publisher, producer, distributor, etc., and there are changes signaled in the product that are related to publication, marketing, etc. (e.g., a change in publisher, repackaging, etc.), the resulting product may be considered a new manifestation. Whenever the production process involves modifications, additions, deletions, etc. that affect the intellectual or artistic content, the result is a new manifestation embodying a new expression of the work.

Changes that occur deliberately or even inadvertently in the production process that affect the copies result, strictly speaking, in a new manifestation. A manifestation resulting from such a change may be identified as a particular "state" or "issue" of the publication. Changes that occur to an individual copy after the production process is complete (e.g., the loss of a page, rebinding, etc.) are not considered to result in a new manifestation. That copy is simply considered to be an exemplar (or item) of the manifestation that deviates from the copy as produced.

Defining manifestation as an entity enables us to name and describe the complete set of items that result from a single act of physical embodiment or production. The entity manifestation serves to describe the shared characteristics of copies of a particular publication, edition, release, etc., as well as to describe unique productions such as manuscripts, original oil paintings, etc. With the entity defined as manifestation we can describe the physical characteristics of a set of items and the characteristics associated with the production and distribution of that set of items that may be important factors in enabling users to choose a manifestation appropriate to their physical needs and constraints, and to identify and acquire a copy of that manifestation.

Defining manifestation as an entity also enables us to draw relationships between specific manifestations of a work. We can use the relationships between manifestations to identify, for example, the specific publication that was used to create a microreproduction.

The entity defined as item is a concrete entity. It is in many instances a single physical object (e.g., a copy of a one-volume monograph, a single audio cassette, etc.). There are instances, however, where the entity defined as item comprises more than one physical object (e.g., a monograph issued as two separately bound volumes, a recording issued on three separate compact discs, etc.). In terms of intellectual content and physical form, an item exemplifying a manifestation is normally the same as the manifestation itself.

However, variations may occur from one item to another, even when the items exemplify the same manifestation, where those variations are the result of actions external to the intent of the producer of the manifestation (e.g., damage occurring after the item was produced, binding performed by a library, etc.). Defining item as an entity enables us to separately identify individual copies of a manifestation, and to describe those characteristics that are unique to that particular copy and that pertain to transactions such as circulation, etc. involving that copy. Defining the entity called item also enables us to draw relationships between individual copies of manifestations.

Manifestation

The title of the manifestation is the word, phrase, or group of characters naming the manifestation. There may be one or more titles associated with a manifestation. Titles associated with a manifestation include all those that appear in the manifestation itself (e.g., the title on the title page, title frame, etc., a cover title, added title-page title, caption title, running title, spine title, etc., the title in a colophon, explicit, etc., the title on a container, on a microfiche header, etc.), as well as those that have been assigned to the manifestation for purposes of bibliographic control (e.g., key title, expanded title, translated title, supplied title, etc.).A statement of responsibility is a statement appearing in the manifestation (normally in conjunction with the title) that names one or more individuals or groups responsible for the creation or realisation of the intellectual or artistic content embodied in the manifestation. An individual or group named may be directly responsible for the work embodied in the manifestation (e.g., the author, composer, etc.), or indirectly responsible (e.g., the author of a novel on which a film script is based).

Other individuals or groups named in the statement may include those responsible for the expression of the work contained in the manifestation (e.g., translators, performers, etc.), or those responsible for the compilation of works contained in the manifestation (e.g., the editor, compiler, etc.). A statement of responsibility may name an organisation responsible for sponsoring or issuing the work contained in the manifestation. The statement may also indicate the role or function performed by each of the individuals, groups, or organisations responsible.

The names appearing in the statement of responsibility in the manifestation may or may not be those of the persons and corporate bodies actually responsible for the creation or realisation of the intellectual or artistic content embodied in the manifestation. Similarly, the stated functions may or may not reflect the actual relationship that exists between the individuals and groups named and the intellectual or artistic content.

The edition or issue designation of the manifestation is a word or phrase appearing in the manifestation that normally indicates a difference in either content or form between the manifestation and a related manifestation previously issued by the same publisher/distributor, or simultaneously issued by either the same publisher/distributor or another publisher/distributor (e.g., large print edition, British edition, etc.). The edition/issue designation pertains to all copies of a manifestation produced from substantially the same master and issued by the same publisher/distributor or group of publishers/distributors.

The place of publication/distribution of the manifestation is the city, town, or other locality associated in the manifestation with the name of the publisher/distributor. The place of publication may comprise the name of the state, province, territory, and/or country as well as the local place name. A manifestation may be associated with one or more places of publication/distribution. The publisher/distributor of the manifestation is the individual, group, or organisation named in the manifestation as being responsible for the publication, distribution, issuing, or release of the manifestation.

A manifestation may be associated with one or more publishers or distributors.The date of publication/distribution of the manifestation is the date (normally a year) of public release of the manifestation. The date may be a single date of publication or release, or a range of dates (e.g., in the case of a serial publication). In the absence of a date designated as the date of publication or release, a copyright date or a date of printing or manufacture may serve as a substitute.The fabricator/manufacturer of the manifestation is the individual, group, or organisation named in the manifestation as being responsible for the fabrication or manufacture of the manifestation.

A manifestation may be associated with one or more fabricators or manufacturers. A series statement is the word, phrase, or group of characters appearing in the manifestation naming the series to which the manifestation belongs. A series statement may also include a number designating the sequential position of the manifestation within the series. There may be one or more series and/or subseries named in the manifestation.The form of carrier is the specific class of material to which the physical carrier of the manifestation belongs (e.g., sound cassette, videodisc, microfilm cartridge, transparency, etc.).

The carrier for a manifestation comprising multiple physical components may include more than one form (e.g., a filmstrip with an accompanying booklet, a separate sound disc carrying the sound track for a film, etc.). The extent of the carrier is a quantification of the number of physical units making up the carrier (e.g., number of sheets, discs, reels, etc.). Physical medium is the type of material from which the carrier is produced (e.g., paper, wood, plastic, metal, etc.).

The physical medium may include in addition to the base material any material that is applied to the base (e.g., oil paint applied to canvas, a chemical emulsion applied to a film base, etc.). Each component of a manifestation comprising multiple physical components may be produced from a different type of material. Capture mode is the means used to record notation, sound, or images in the production of a manifestation (e.g., analogue, acoustic, electric, digital, optical etc.). The dimensions of the carrier are the measurements of the physical components and/or the container of the manifestation.

The manifestation identifier is a number or code uniquely associated with the manifestation that serves to differentiate that manifestation from any other manifestation. A manifestation may have one or more identifiers associated with it. The identifier may be assigned as part of an international numbering or coding system (e.g., ISBN, etc.), as part of a national system (e.g., legal deposit number), or it may be assigned independently by the publisher or distributor of the manifestation (e.g., government publication number, music publisher's number, clearinghouse inventory number, etc.).

A manifestation identifier may also be assigned by a bibliographer, musicologist, etc. The manifestation identifier may comprise both a numeric component and a textual or coded component identifying the system under which it was assigned and/or the agency or individual that assigned the number, so as to render the identifier unique to the manifestation.

11

Digital Heritage and Preservation

The media we use to carry and store it are unstable, and the technology needed for access is quickly superseded by newer technologies, wave after wave. As technologies lose support, access to the digital heritage that they fostered is also lost. These challenges are not only technical in nature; they have organisational and societal dimensions as we struggle with the responsibility of keeping access lines open over extended periods of time, often with insufficient resources and uncertain strategies. The interest of UNESCO in this situation comes as no surprise. UNESCO exists in part to encourage and enable the preservation and enjoyment of the cultural, scientific and information heritage of the world's peoples. The growth of digital heritage and its vulnerability could hardly go unnoticed.

The UNESCO Draft Charter on the Preservation of the Digital Heritage

Introduction

The UNESCO Draft Charter on the Preservation of the Digital Heritage presents a compelling case for digital preservation. It is included in the Guidelines to provide a clear link between the two documents, and to present those advocacy and public policy issues that are outside the scope of technical and practical guidelines.

Preamble

The General Conference,

Considering that the disappearance of heritage in whatever form constitutes an impoverishment of the heritage of all nations,

Recalling that the Constitution of UNESCO provides that the Organization will maintain, increase and diffuse knowledge, by assuring the conservation and protection of the world's inheritance of books, works of art and monuments of history and science, that its "Information for All" Programme provides a platform for discussions and action on information policies and the safeguarding of recorded knowledge, and that its "Memory of the World" Programme aims to ensure the preservation and universal accessibility of the world's documentary heritage,

Recognizing that such resources of information and creative expression are increasingly produced, distributed, accessed and maintained in digital form, creating a new legacy - the digital heritage,

Aware that permanent access to this heritage will offer broadened opportunities for creation, communication and sharing of knowledge among all peoples, as well as protection of rights and entitlements and support of accountability,

Understanding that this digital heritage is at risk of being lost and that its preservation for the benefit of present and future generations is an urgent issue of worldwide concern,

Bearing in mind the UNESCO Universal Declaration on Cultural Diversity,

Proclaims the following principles and adopts the present Charter.

The Digital Heritage as a Common Heritage

Article 1 - Digital heritage

Resources of human knowledge or expression, whether cultural, educational, scientific and administrative, or embracing technical, legal, medical and other kinds of information, are increasingly created digitally, or converted into digital form from existing analogue resources. Where resources are "born digital", there is no other format but the digital original.

Digital materials include texts, databases, still and moving images, audio, graphics, software, and web pages, among a wide and growing range of formats. They are frequently ephemeral, and require purposeful production, maintenance and management to be retained. Many of these resources have lasting value and significance, and therefore constitute a heritage that should be protected and preserved for current and future generations. This heritage may exist in any language, in any part of the world, and in any area of human knowledge or expression.

Article 2 - Access to the digital heritage

The purpose of preserving the digital heritage is to ensure that it remains permanently accessible. Accordingly, access to digital heritage materials, especially those in the public domain, should be equitable and free of unreasonable restrictions. At the same time, the security of sensitive and personal information should be protected from any form of intrusion. It is for each Member State to cooperate with relevant organizations and institutions in encouraging a legal and practical environment which would maximise accessibility of the digital heritage.

A fair balance between the legitimate rights of creators and other rights holders and those of the public to access digital heritage materials should be reaffirmed and promoted.

Guarding Against Loss of Heritage

Article 3 - The threat of loss

The world's digital heritage is at risk of being lost to posterity. Contributing factors include the rapid obsolescence of the hardware and software which brings it to life, uncertainties about resources, responsibility and methods for maintenance and preservation, and the lack of supportive legislation.

Attitudinal change has fallen behind technological change. Digital evolution has been too rapid and costly for governments and institutions to develop timely and informed preservation strategies. The threat to the economic, social, intellectual and cultural potential of the heritage - the building blocks of the future - has not been fully grasped.

Article 4 - Need for Action

Unless the prevailing threats are addressed, the loss of the digital heritage will be rapid and inevitable. Awareness-raising and advocacy is urgent, alerting policy makers and sensitizing the general public to both the potential of the digital media and the practicalities of preservation. Member States will benefit by encouraging legal, economic and technical measures to safeguard the heritage.

Article 5 - Continuity of digital information

The digital heritage is part of the wider continuum of digital information. To preserve digital heritage, measures will need to be taken throughout the information's life cycle. Preservation of digital heritage begins with the design of reliable systems which will produce authentic and stable digital objects.

Measures Required

Article 6 - Developing strategies and policies

Strategies and policies to preserve the digital heritage can be developed, taking into account the level of urgency, local circumstances, available means and future projections. The cooperation of creators, holders of copyright and related rights, and relevant institutions in setting common standards and compatibilities, and resource sharing, will facilitate this.

Article 7 - Defining what should be kept

As with all documentary heritage, selection principles may vary between countries, although the main criteria for deciding what digital materials to keep would be their significance and lasting cultural, scientific, evidential or other value. Selection decisions and any subsequent reviews need to be carried out in an accountable manner, and be based on defined principles, policies, procedures and standards.

Article 8 - Protecting the digital heritage

Member States need appropriate frameworks to secure the protection of their digital heritage. Market forces alone will not achieve this. As a key element of national preservation policy, archive legislation and legal or voluntary deposit in libraries, archives, museums and other public repositories should embrace the digital heritage. Copyright and related rights legislation should allow preservation processes to be undertaken legally by such institutions.

The right to permanent access to legally deposited digital heritage materials, within reasonable restrictions, should be guaranteed without causing prejudice to their normal exploitation.

Legal and practical frameworks for authenticity are crucial to prevent manipulation or intentional alteration of digital heritage. Both require that the content, functionality of files and documentation be maintained to the extent necessary to secure an authentic record.

Article 9 - Promoting cultural diversity

The digital heritage is inherently unlimited by time, geography, culture or format. It is culture-specific, but potentially accessible to every person in the world. Minorities may speak to majorities, the individual to a global audience.

The digital heritage of all regions, countries and communities should be preserved and made accessible, creating over time a balanced and equitable representation of all peoples, nations, cultures and languages.

Responsibilities

Article 10 - Roles and responsibilities

It is for each Member State to designate one or more agencies to take coordinating responsibility for the preservation of digital heritage, and to provide the necessary staff and resources. The sharing of tasks and responsibilities may be based on existing roles and expertise.

Measures should be taken to:

(a) urge hardware and software developers, creators, publishers, producers, and distributors of digital materials as well as other private sector partners to cooperate with national libraries, archives, museums and other public heritage organizations in preserving the digital heritage;

(b) develop training and research, and share experience and knowledge among the institutions and professional associations concerned;

(c) encourage universities and other research organizations to ensure preservation of research data.

Article 11 - Partnerships and cooperation

Preservation of the digital heritage requires sustained efforts on the part of governments, creators, publishers, relevant industries and heritage institutions. In the face of the current digital divide, it is necessary to reinforce international cooperation and solidarity to enable all countries to ensure creation, dissemination, preservation and continued accessibility of their digital heritage.

Industries, publishers and mass communication media are urged to promote and share knowledge and technical expertise.

The stimulation of education and training Programmes, resource-sharing arrangements, and dissemination of research results and best practices will democratize access to digital preservation techniques.

Article 12 - The role of UNESCO

UNESCO, by virtue of its mandate and functions, has the responsibility to:

(a) take the principles set forth in this Charter into account in the functioning of its Programmes and promote their implementation within the United Nations system and by intergovernmental and international non-governmental organizations concerned with the preservation of the digital heritage;

(b) serve as a reference point and a forum where Member States, intergovernmental and international non-governmental organizations, civil society and the private sector may join together in elaborating objectives, policies and projects in favour of the preservation of the digital heritage;

(c) foster cooperation, awareness-raising and capacity-building, and establish standard ethical, legal and technical guidelines, as a companion sourcebook to this Charter;

(d) determine, on the basis of the experience gained over the next six years in implementing the present Charter and the Guidelines, the need for further standard-setting instruments for the promotion and preservation of the digital heritage.

Digital preservation is used to describe the processes involved in maintaining information and other kinds of heritage that exist in a digital form. In these Guidelines, it does not refer to the use of digital imaging or capture techniques to make copies of non-digital items, even if that is done for preservation purposes. Of course, digital copying, may well produce digital heritage materials needing to be preserved.

Digital materials is generally used here as a preferred term covering items of digital heritage at a general level. In some places, digital object or digital resource have also been used. The terms have been used interchangeably and generically: they do not imply a particular kind of item unless that is clearly stated. Preservation programme is used to refer to any set of coherent arrangements aimed at preserving digital materials.

More commonly used terms such as digital archive and digital repository have been avoided because of their potential ambiguities: archive has different meanings for the records management community and the ICT community, whereas both archive and repository may imply a single storage site - not an appropriate implication where very distributed arrangements may be in place.

Of course, the term programme also comes with some baggage. It should be understood to cover all the aspects of preservation responsibility, including policy and strategy as well as implementation. Presentation, re-presentation are used to describe the processes of providing access to digital materials. The second term has been consistently (and idiosyncratically) hyphenised to emphasise the understanding that digital preservation seeks to re-present what was previously presented.

Not all digital materials need to be kept, only those that are judged to have ongoing value: these form the digital heritage. For those materials that warrant keeping, continuity of survival and accessibility is critical. The chances of recovering lost access to large amounts of data are very slim. Continuity requires sustained, direct action (called digital preservation) rather than passive 'benign neglect.'

Digital materials cannot be said to be preserved if access is lost. The purpose of preservation is to maintain the ability to present the essential elements of authentic digital materials. Digital preservation must address threats to all layers of the digital object: physical, logical, conceptual and essential.

Digital preservation will only happen if organisations and individuals accept responsibility for it. The starting point for action is a decision about responsibility. Everyone does not have to do everything; everything does not have to be done all at once. Comprehensive and reliable preservation programmes are highly desirable, but they may not be achievable in all circumstances of need. Where necessary, it is usually better for non-comprehensive and non-reliable action to be taken than for no action at all. Small steps are usually better than no steps.

Currently, preservation efforts have to work against the prevailing trend of digital technology and how it is developed and used. Digital materials are very often created without long-term preservation intentions in mind. Working with producers to influence the standards and practices they use, and to increase their awareness of preservation needs, are important investments.

Preservation programmes must clarify their legal right to collect, copy, name, modify, preserve and provide access to the digital materials for which they take responsibility. Digital heritage materials must be moved to a safe place where they can be controlled, protected and managed for preservation.

Digital heritage materials must be uniquely identified, and described using appropriate metadata for resource discovery, management and preservation. 18. Taking the right action later depends on adequate documentation. It is easier to document the characteristics of digital resources close to their source than it is to build that documentation later. Preservation programmes should use standardised metadata schemas as they become available, for interoperability between programmes.

The links between digital objects and their metadata must be securely maintained, and the metadata must be preserved. Authenticity is a critical issue where digital objects are used as evidence. It may also be important for other kinds of digital heritage. Data that underlies digital objects must be safely stored and managed if there is to be any chance of re-presenting authentic objects to users.

Digital preservation programmes are subjected to increased authenticity concerns because they so frequently have to use processes that involve change. Authenticity is best protected by measures that ensure the integrity of data is not compromised, and by documentation that maintains the clear identity of the material. Data protection is built on the principles of system security and redundancy.

For preservation programmes, redundancy must include securely stored backups designed around the long-term maintenance of data rather than a cycle of overwriting old data with new. The goal of maintaining accessibility is to find cost-effective ways of guaranteeing access whenever it is needed, both in the short-term and the long-term. Standards are an important foundation for digital preservation, but many programmes must find ways to preserve access to poorly standardised materials, in an environment of changing standards.

Preservation action should not be delayed until a single 'digital preservation standard' appears. Digital data is always dependent on some combination of software and hardware tools for access, but the degree of dependency on specific tools determines the range of preservation options. It is reasonable for programmes to choose multiple strategies for preserving access, especially to diverse collections.

They should consider the potential benefits of maintaining the original data streams of materials as well as any modified versions, as an insurance against the failure of still uncertain strategies. Strategies for preserving accessibility do not stand alone: they are supported by other responsibilities, and many strategies can be combined to good effect. Preservation programmes are often required to judge acceptable and unacceptable levels of loss, in terms of items, elements, and user needs.

Preservation programmes require good management that consists largely of generic management skills combined with enough knowledge of digital preservation issues to make good decisions at the right time. Digital preservation incorporates the assessment and management of risks programmes are usually faced with more material and more issues than they can cope with, so they must set priorities.

The costs of preservation programmes are hard to estimate because they encompass so much uncertainty, including evolving techniques, changing technologies and very long timeframes. Costs may well be lower per unit of information than for non-digital materials, but the amount of information to be managed in digital form is very large so total costs are also likely to remain high, including set-up costs and significant recurrent costs.

Preservation programmes may start as pilot projects but they eventually need to establish sustainable business models. While suitable service providers may be found to carry out some functions, ultimately responsible for achieving preservation objectives rests with preservation programmes, and with those who oversee and resource them. Working collaboratively is often a cost effective way to build preservation programmes with wide coverage, mutual support and the required expertise.

Digital Heritage and Digital Continuity

Digital heritage is made up of computer-based materials of enduring value that should be kept for future generations. Digital heritage emanates from different communities, industries, sectors and regions. Not all digital materials are of enduring value, but those that are require active preservation approaches if continuity of digital heritage is to be maintained.

Heritage is explained in UNESCO documents as "our legacy from the past, what we live with today, and what we pass on to future generations." A heritage is something that is, or should be, passed from generation to generation because it is valued. The idea of cultural heritage is a familiar one: those sites, objects and intangible things that have cultural, historical, aesthetic, archaeological, scientific, ethnological or anthropological value to groups and individuals. According to the Draft Charter for the Preservation of Digital Heritage: Resources of human knowledge or expression, whether cultural, educational, scientific and administrative, or embracing technical, legal, medical and other kinds of information, are increasingly created digitally, or converted into digital form from existing analogue resources.

Where resources are "born digital", there is no other format but the digital original. Digital materials include texts, databases, still and moving images, audio, graphics, software, and web pages, among a wide and growing range of formats. They are frequently ephemeral, and require purposeful production, maintenance and management to be retained. Many of these resources have lasting value and significance, and therefore constitute a heritage that should be protected and preserved for current and future generations. This heritage may exist in any language, in any part of the world, and in any area of human knowledge or expression.

Using computers and related tools, humans are creating and sharing digital resources - information, creative expression, ideas, and knowledge encoded for computer processing - that they value and want to share with others over time as well as across space. This is evidence of a digital heritage. It is a heritage made of many parts, sharing many common characteristics, and subject to many common threats. UNESCO defines a world heritage made up of globally outstanding sites of cultural and natural value that should be preserved; many national and state legislatures also define their own national, regional or state heritage.

However, heritage value may also be based on what is important at a group or community level. Heritage materials can exist well beyond the limits suggested by national legislation or international conventions. Anything that is considered important enough to be passed to the future can be considered to have heritage value of some kind. This digital heritage is likely to become more important and more widespread over time. Increasingly, individuals, organisations and communities are using digital technologies to document and express what they value and what they want to pass on to future generations.

New forms of expression and communication have emerged that did not exist previously. The Internet is one vast example of this phenomenon.It is also likely that the development of tools to support greater multi-lingual and multi-script use of the Internet will lead to further rapid growth in digital heritage in parts of the world that are currently disadvantaged by the predominant use of English on the Internet. Making sure this burgeoning digital heritage remains available is thus a global issue relevant to all countries and communities.

Types of Digital Heritage

Over time, new types of digital heritage can be expected to emerge: we have already seen the enabling power of the technology in forms as diverse as word processing, email, websites, relational databases, computer models and simulations, digital audio and video, space imagery and computer games. Electronic publications, being information that is made available for wide readership. Publications are distributed in various ways including online via the World Wide Web, or on portable carriers such as CDs, DVDs, floppy disks and various electronic book devices. Some publications manage to combine both online and portable carrier access to different parts of the publication.

As well as their means of distribution, digital publications may be classified by genres, some familiar from traditional publishing formats like monographs and serials, and others less easily defined like websites and e-zines. Some publications are released as complete items, but others evolve over time, their creators taking advantage of the interactive potential of the Internet. Print publishing continues to grow, but increasingly publications are appearing in digital versions, increasingly in digital-only versions. Both commercial and non-commercial publishers produce digital publications, as do millions of other people who would not see themselves as publishers at all. 'Semi-published' materials such as pre-print papers and theses held in e-print and other archives available for restricted use within specific communities such as universities and scholarly societies. Organisational and personal records of activity, transactions, correspondence, etc. A very large part of the world's business and government records now exist in electronic record keeping systems. Email, messages to discussion lists and bulletin boards, web diaries, 'blogs' and 'cams' - dynamic, informal interactions enabled by digital technology - may also include important digital records amongst a tidal wave of data.

Datasets collected to record and analyse scientific, geospatial, spatial, sociological, demographic, educational, health, environmental and other phenomena · Learning objects used in technology-assisted education · Software tools such as databases, models, simulations, and software applications · Unique unpublished materials that may include research reports, oral history and folklore recordings. Electronic 'manuscripts' such as drafts of works and personal correspondence. Entertainment products from the film, music, broadcasting and games industries, both commercial and non-commercial.

Digitally generated artworks and documentary photographs. Digital copies of images, sound, text and three-dimensional objects from non-digital originals. Many of these materials exist only in a digital form. With no equivalent non-digital version, their content is especially vulnerable to the influences that threaten digital materials. There are also rapidly growing collections of digital copies. Having originally been generated from non-digital sources, these might appear to be less vulnerable, but many of them are the only surviving version of originals that have since been damaged, lost or dispersed.

Continuity of the digital heritage is profoundly important. Increasingly this is a heritage that documents the actions of governments, the results of scientific research, the debate of ideas, the aspirations and imagination of communities, the histories of the current and coming world. If these are not to be lost or distorted, continuity is required: continuity of production, continuity of survival, and continuity of access. This must be achieved in the face of many threats:

— The carriers used to store these digital materials are usually unstable and deteriorate within a few years or decades at most

— Use of digital materials depends on means of access that work in particular ways

The Internet is an interesting scenario in which many of these threats are played out. In assessing the risks associated with the Internet, it is necessary to distinguish between two overlapping but different concerns. One concern is to look at the Internet as a whole. There is no central agency that can decide what happens to material made available through the Internet. Typically, users connect with a kaleidoscope of information for which no single creator, publisher, or any other agency is responsible. A different viewpoint is to look at individual resources published through the Internet.

These may also be quite unstable, but their instability reflects the decisions and actions of their owners in deleting, changing, moving, or renaming them. The loss of materials in this environment is attributable to how they are managed at a local level, exposed to many of the same threats that other kinds of digital materials experience. While it is largely beyond the power of Internet users to control whether information remains available, it is very much within the power of those owning and managing digital objects and sites. If they are committed to maintaining access, it is generally within their power to do so. However, the Internet does present some special risks. For example:

— There is a strong novelty factor, so some publishers choose to change things frequently - sometimes the way information looks, sometimes also the content

— Many Internet resources are a virtual composite drawn from a number of sources, which may not be stored together anywhere.

Digital Preservation

Digital preservation consists of the processes aimed at ensuring the continued accessibility of digital materials. To do this involves finding ways to re-present what was originally presented to users by a combination of software and hardware tools acting on data. To achieve this requires digital objects to be understood and managed at four levels: as physical phenomena; as logical encodings; as conceptual objects that have meaning to humans; and as sets of essential elements that must be preserved in order to offer future users the essence of the object. Digital preservation can be seen as all those processes aimed at ensuring the continuity of digital heritage materials for as long as they are needed. The most significant threats to digital continuity concern loss of the means of access.

Digital materials cannot be said to be preserved if the means of access have been lost and access becomes impossible. The purpose of preserving digital materials is to maintain accessibility: the ability to access their essential, authentic message or purpose. There is an underlying similarity in the way digital objects are accessed in the present, and how they will be accessed in any future use. In both cases, access can be seen as a performance.

Digital objects are made accessible by applying software and hardware tools to data in order to create a presentation or performance that has meaning to a user. It may be the presentation of a word processing document, or a piece of recorded audio, or a Web page, or results from a database query, or any other kind of digital object depending on the way the data is encoded and on the actions the tools are programmed to perform. Digital preservation must work in the same way, somehow re-presenting what are judged to be the essential elements of the original performance when required at some later time.

Conceptualised in this way, digital preservation can be seen as straightforward. Indeed, copying data from carrier to carrier, and providing the right tools to recreate the intended performance will preserve continuity of access to most digital objects. However, this simple model encompasses great complexities: it may be hard to define the performance that must be re-presented; it is usually difficult to work out what tools are needed once the original ones have been lost; the tools themselves typically rely on other tools that also may have been superseded; and it may be difficult to find tools that will create the required performance in a reliable, cost-effective and timely way, especially in the context of many thousands, millions or more of digital objects.

Despite such underlying complexities, the performance model helps in recognising what digital preservation programmes must aim for: the best means of re-presenting what users needs to access. Preservation programmes must deal with digital objects in four guises:

— As physical objects, consisting of 'inscriptions' (usually binary states of 'on-ness' or 'off-ness') on carrier media such as computer disks or tapes.

— As logical objects consisting of computer readable code, whose existence at any particular time depends on the physical inscriptions but is not tied to any particular carrier

— As conceptual objects that have meaning to humans, unlike the logical or physical objects that encode them at any particular time.

— As bundles of essential elements that embody the message, purpose, or features for which the material was chosen for preservation.

This multi-layered nature of digital objects has profound implications for digital preservation. Preservation means different things for each layer. Preservation programmes for non-digital heritage have traditionally worried about preserving the physical object as the embodiment of the object's meaning. However, individual physical manifestations of a digital object are almost inevitably lost, one after another, because the media used for physical storage are typically unstable and liable to short-term deterioration. Preservation requires a succession of data transfers from one physical carrier to another.

Despite this shift in focus from the physical object to a conceptual object inherent in digital preservation, it must never be forgotten that digital objects cannot survive without some kind of appropriate physical form. The logical encoding normally has a much longer life than any particular physical inscription, but it is by no means sacrosanct. As the layers of technology used for access - hardware such as computer processors, disk drives and peripheral equipment, and many layers of software such as operating systems, specific applications, and presentation tools - become obsolete, it may be necessary to change the logical encoding so that it can present the same conceptual object using different technology.

The conceptual object is the ultimate focus of preservation concern; as noted above, it is at this level that digital objects convey meaning to human users. However, for most digital objects there is a further layer that must be considered. Many objects consist of several elements, some of which are more important than others in carrying the object's essential message. Preservation programmes have to decide which sub-set of elements should be preserved for re-presentation to users.

Preserving Digital Materials

Digital preservation involves choosing and implementing an evolving range of strategies to achieve the kind of accessibility discussed above, addressing the preservation needs of the different layers of digital objects. The strategies include:

— Working with producers (creators and distributors) to apply standards that will prolong the effective life of the available means of access and reduce the range of unknown problems that must be managed

— Recognising that it is not practical to try to preserve everything, selecting what material should be preserved

— Placing the material in a safe place

— Controlling material, using structured metadata and other documentation to facilitate access and to support all preservation process

— Protecting the integrity and identity of data

— Choosing appropriate means of providing access in the face of technological change

— Managing preservation programmes to achieve their goals in cost-effective, timely, holistic, proactive and accountable ways.

Preservation programmes have certain responsibilities and functions that have been defined, at least at a conceptual level. Comprehensive programmes must take control of appropriate digital materials and ensure they remain understandable and usable as authentic copies.

This generally involves taking the materials, properly prepared, along with associated documentation or metadata, into an archival digital storage system of some kind, where they can be managed to deal with the threats of data loss an technological change. The characteristics or attributes of programmes that can be relied upon to deliver ongoing digital preservation have also been described, in terms of responsibility, viability, sustainability, technical suitability, security, and accountability. Digital information objects are generally not understandable or re-presentable by themselves: users need help to use them.

Preservation depends on maintaining digital objects and any information and tools that would be needed in order to access and understand them. Together, these can be considered to form an information package that must be managed either as a single object or as a virtual package. Preservation programmes must identify a safe place where digital materials can be stored and managed. Because the concept of the preservation programme allows for distributed arrangements and shared responsibilities, it is quite conceivable that while some programmes will create their own repositories, others may decide to look for a suitable 'safe place' operated and managed by someone else.

The processes of receiving, preparing and transferring digital materials into the archival system are usually referred to as ingest. Preparing material for entry into the archival information system is critical to the way the whole system is managed. It involves a number of important steps that may determine how easy or difficult it is to maintain the archived information packages in the system. These steps include:

— Applying collection policies and selection criteria to assess whether material is in scope so that it can be sought, or accepted if submitted

— Clarifying or negotiating rights issues with rights owners

— Checking the quality of the submitted information package, including its completeness, the functionality of its component parts, its authenticity, and whether it contains unwanted material such as viruses

— Labelling the material with unique identifiers

— Assessing the elements that must be maintained, and assigning preservation objectives

— Setting retention and review periods for the material, if appropriate

— Checking and if necessary upgrading the documentation that describes the material, including the technical and preservation metadata

— Assessing the file format(s) and deciding if they need to be changed to comply with the Programme's policy on what formats it will manage

— If necessary, changing the file formats to comply with the policy

— Adjusting the documentation to reflect any changes.

Once the digital object and its metadata have been prepared and associated with each other to form an information package, they are saved to the archival storage system. A preservation programme must provide archival storage that maintains, protects and verifies the integrity of the stored information packages, both the digital object and the metadata, whether stored as a single data stream or as separate but linked data streams. To achieve this, the storage function must include practices that protect the data stream from unintended change, damage or loss: this will usually require regular copying of the data stream to fresh media, and when necessary copying to new media types.

Storage practices must also include checking that the data stream has not been corrupted; system security; backup regimes that place copies at remote sites; and disaster recovery plans that address contingencies such as complete loss of the system's operating infrastructure. Obviously, this requires technical capabilities to provide a suitably secure and reliable storage service. Such a capability can be achieved with modest equipment so long as the equipment and the whole system are well managed. The more material there is, and the more diverse and complex it is, the more sophisticated the storage system needs to be. For most digital materials, preserving accessibility requires more than the data protection offered in the Archival Storage function. Only material being kept for very short periods could be stored without further attention to the means of providing access.

The purpose of the Preservation Planning function is to monitor threats to accessibility, and to specify action to pre-empt or respond to them. The relevant threats mostly relate to changes in the technology that underlies access, so this function looks for such changes and takes action to maintain accessibility despite these changes.

Data Management

Managing information packages in the archive generates its own data about what material is stored, what can be accessed, and about the management of the archive. This data must be managed to support use of the archive, and to support its effective administration. This function provides a user interface to the archive, allowing users to discover what is held, to request material and if appropriate to receive copies. For many archives, access will be subject to restrictions for some or all potential users.

The Access function may well require mechanisms to control access. The preservation programme must find ways to advocate good practices among producers, aimed at facilitating preservation of the material for which the programme will be responsible. There is also a need to understand who the likely users of the material will be, so that preservation and access arrangements can be tailored to their needs and expectations. The overall operation of the programme must be managed. In part this responsibility involves the development of policy frameworks and standards covering all areas of operations; in part it involves the ongoing supply of appropriate resources and infrastructure including suitable technical systems; and in part management processes such as monitoring and reporting on the programme's operations. Reference Model for Open Archival Information Systems (OAIS), released in 2002 as a draft international standard by the International Standards Organisation.

The OAIS Reference Model is the most successful attempt to define both a conceptual model for managing digital materials of enduring value, and a vocabulary with which to discuss it. Anyone contemplating a responsibility for managing digital materials should seek to understand the concepts articulated in the Reference Model itself. The Reference Model is a high level conceptual framework that can be used as a reference point for those designing, using and evaluating real implementations.

It is important to realise that it is not an implementation specification: it does not provide a set of instructions on how to preserve digital information. Its value lies in explaining what is required at a highly conceptual level, regardless of the means chosen to achieve it. The reliability and trustworthiness of digital preservation programmes are very important issues to many stakeholders. Producers, users, investors and the broad community have a strong interest in ensuring that digital heritage materials are managed by arrangements that can be trusted. Those potentially responsible for the programmes also have an interest in assessing what they can offer and the risks of accepting responsibility.

Preservation programmes offering long-term reliability are expected to have the following characteristics:

— *Responsibility*: a fundamental commitment to preservation of the digital materials in question · Organisational viability, including the prospect of an ongoing mandate; a legal status as an organisation that would support an ongoing preservation role; and a demonstrated ability to put together the resources, infrastructure and work teams that could manage the complexity of digital preservation

— *Financial sustainability*: a likely prospect of the organisation being able to continue to provide the required resources well into the future, with a sustainable business model to support its digital preservation mandate

— *Technological and procedural suitability*: the use of appropriate systems and procedures to do what is required to manage and preserve digital resources

— *System security of a very high order:* Procedural accountability, with clear allocation of responsibilities and mechanisms for reporting and assessing performance.

Arrangements that are able to demonstrate these attributes should be trustworthy. Development of trust may be a matter of demonstrating these characteristics over time. In the long term, certification programmes will probably be needed but at the time of writing no certification programmes for digital preservation arrangements have appeared. It remains very much the responsibility of those proposing digital preservation programmes to show why their arrangements should be trusted, and very much the responsibility of other stakeholders to determine that any arrangements on offer can provide an acceptable level of reliability.

Responsibility in Digital Preservation

Responsibility is a crucial issue in the preservation of digital heritage. The starting point for action is a decision about responsibility. Because the cost implications for an organisation can be significant, and because the requirements may be complex and uncertain, it is no small thing to accept a responsible role. The purpose of such arrangements is to provide a good prospect of preservation continuing beyond their own involvement, should that become necessary.

Fail-safe arrangements extend along a continuum, from a commitment to find someone else to take over responsibility before discarding digital materials, through to legally mandated arrangements for one agency to take over the management of data held by another agency if it fails to meet its preservation responsibilities. Responsibility for initiating and maintaining succession plans obviously lies with whomever is managing the material, but there may be other players who should accept some responsibility. In facing the daunting challenges of preservation responsibility, it may help to consider some pragmatic principles:

— *Someone has to take responsibility*: if no one does, the chances of any particular materials surviving are very small

— *Everyone does not have to do everything*: responsibility can be shared. As these guidelines indicate, there are more than enough responsibilities for one preservation Programme. Many tasks, such as deciding what should be preserved, are best managed in partnership with others. If there is no one suitable to share responsibilities, preservation programmes should make realistic judgments about the responsibilities they can carry alone

— *Everything does not have to be done at once*: developing all the components of a large-scale, comprehensive preservation programme takes time. It is good to approach the task with a sense of urgency, but it may also be necessary to look for ways of buying time. This might require prioritising the issues that need to be addressed, or the material that needs attention. It may involve looking for easily managed materials ('low hanging fruit'). Some problems must be addressed without delay; some can be addressed in stages; and some can wait

— *Responsibility does not have to be forever*: there is definitely a place for time-limited contributions to an overall preservation programme, so long as the time limits are explicitly understood

— *Limited responsibility should not mean causing harm*: preservation programmes may need to take steps before all problems are solved and all techniques settled, but they must also try to minimise the harm of making later preservation efforts more difficult

— *Someone must take a leading role*: even when responsibility is shared, progress usually depends on at least one partner accepting the responsibility to lead.

Some people believe that new institutions will be needed to take on the task of preserving digital heritage. Presumably these agencies would offer specialist expertise and facilities dedicated to digital materials, and possibly dedicated to preservation rather than a wider range of functions which existing collecting institutions perform, like arranging and interpreting materials and promoting their use. Many data archives fit into such a field already, as they exist solely to manage and preserve digital materials.

They often have the paradoxical advantages of being able to focus on a limited range of materials and management tasks, while being able to offer services to a wider range of data-producing communities. Just as it is too early to judge the long-term role of libraries, archives and museums, it is too early to attempt a definitive list of others who may play an important role. Universities and other institutes of research and learning have a natural interest in ensuring ongoing access to certain kinds of digital materials, and may have both the long-term viability and the technical infrastructure to play a preservation role · Publishers and creators of digital content have a range of interests in ongoing management and accessibility.

In many cases this extends beyond immediate commercial considerations to a longer-term investment in the exchange of ideas and the intellectual and cultural capital that ongoing accessibility encourages. Some publishers and creators may be willing and able to provide the infrastructure needed to maintain digital heritage materials in which they have an interest. When preservation programmes have decided what kind of responsibility they will take, it is very important that they declare their intentions. This makes it easier for others to work with them, reduces the likelihood of effort being unnecessarily duplicated, and provides a clearer picture of what material is likely to survive and what is not.

Managing Digital Preservation Programmes

Preservation programmes require good management, often drawing on generic management skills such as tailoring programmes to the priorities and circumstances of the case, and making the right decisions at the right time. Digital preservation programmes present some particular management issues associated with their developing nature, the range of stakeholders, and the long-term impacts of current decisions. Like all programmes, preservation programmes need to be managed in a coherent way. Digital preservation management should not be seen as a mysterious art: it draws on good general management skills, allied with enough subject knowledge and understanding of technical issues to see realistic possibilities and to make good decisions. The discussion that follows focuses on those issues specifically relevant to digital preservation.

Good management often comes down to knowing what decisions have to be made and making them at the right time. The important decisions do not have to be made all at once, but eventually they will be required on issues including:

— Whether to get involved in preserving digital materials at all

— The mission of the programme

Preservation programmes must seek to understand and respond to threats that would jeopardise ongoing accessibility and other aspects of the programme's mission. A risk management approach provides an appropriate basis for deciding what risks warrant attention, and for planning action that will lower the level of risk. There are many suitable risk management models available. Risk analysis, even undertaken informally, helps in a number of ways:

Recognising:

— The most pressing threats (such as web publications disappearing; media failure of magnetic carriers; impending replacement of equipment or software; a change in government agency arrangements that will threaten record keeping systems)

— Threats that may not require immediate action (such as the eventual obsolescence of a standardised, ubiquitous file format such as TIFF, the impact of which should be manageable when a replacement standard appears) - Threats over which the programme may have no influence (such as the business imperatives of producers)

— Threats that are so pressing but so intractable that the programme may decide to withdraw from responsibility (such as a refusal by rights owners to allow any form of access or preservation copying at any future time).

Deciding:

— Where to allocate resources

— What steps to take as a priority

— When action may be needed

— What supporting action is needed to address priority risks.

— Planning ahead

— Justifying decisions.

Risk assessment is especially helpful if it is extended beyond the immediately apparent risks to include:

— The risks associated with the action that is proposed to deal with the threat. For example, the programme may not have the required skills, resources, permissions, etc. This in turn might lead to action that is a prerequisite for dealing with the priority threat

— The causes of the original threat. For example, web publishers may not be aware of steps they could take; producers may be using standards incorrectly; or producers may be at risk of business failure. This analysis might lead to action that addresses the causes, such as education campaigns, the development of standards in conjunction with producers, or development of indicators of impending business failure including signs that web sits are not being maintained or personal knowledge that projects are coming to a close.

A broad range of stakeholders have an interest in digital heritage materials and how they are managed. They may include those creating or distributing the materials, those who need to use them now or in the future, and those who cite the materials, assuming that they will remain available. Some stakeholders may be hidden but play a very influential role behind the scenes, such as hardware and software manufacturers, providers of funds, and bodies authorised to control access to certain materials.

Some stakeholders may be of direct interest to the preservation programme itself, such as potential collaborative partners, standards bodies, and researchers developing new digital preservation methods. Preservation programmes must recognise those who have an interest in their objectives or who could exert an influence on them. Risk assessment is likely to indicate which stakeholders will be most important, as well as suggesting the kind of relationship the programme needs to develop with them.

Because the windows of opportunity for preservation are much narrower than for non-digital heritage, preservation programmes may have to be much more active in pursuing relationships with producers of heritage materials. They may also have to look for ways of influencing the 'hidden' stakeholders whose decisions may have a critical impact. Reliable preservation programmes must be sustained over long periods, so they require business models that guarantee adequate resources will continue to be available. Unfortunately, such guarantees are rare in the real world.

Most programmes have to survive with less certainty. Especially in the initial stages, sustainability presents a dilemma: programmes must eventually have it, but they often cannot tell what resources will be needed to fulfil their responsibilities, nor what resources may become available once a successful programme has been established. Programme managers have the challenge of finding long-term business models, but they may also have to find short-term funding arrangements, and recognise the appropriate time to switch from one to the other. Some of the business models commonly considered for preservation programmes include:

— General community funding, often through taxes or the allocation of grants from special sources such as lottery funds

— Funding by a specific community with an interest in the programme, such as a local community project, or an industry peak body levying members

— Central funding by a parent organisation as a normal cost of business, such as a university library or a business archive

— Payments by users of the material
— Payments by producers who deposit material with the programme.
— Sponsorship or philanthropic assistance
— Cross subsidisation by other activities within an organisation

Standards and practices in digital preservation are evolving rapidly (though perhaps not as rapidly as they are needed), and programme managers must find ways to keep their knowledge up to date. There are a number of international initiatives dedicated to just such a purpose, including the journals, websites and subject gateways included in the Reading List.

Despite some overlap, these initiatives complement each other; they offer excellent ways of keeping abreast of developments. There also appears to be an opportunity to explore solidarity relationships between programmes with different levels of experience and expertise. Most existing programmes are willing to share information and ideas but often find themselves overwhelmed with requests.

Formal information sharing arrangements may ease that burden while offering real benefits to those developing new programmes. Digital preservation programmes often start as experiments and projects with a speculative mission and an uncertain future. They can be easily dismissed as important but bothersome add-ons to already overstretched organisations. It often takes some time for a definite set of workflows to emerge and for the programme to take shape.

Availability of resources is always a critical constraint. It is important to tailor the ambitions of the programme to a reasonably realistic idea of what can be achieved: it may not be possible to do everything! It is difficult to estimate the long-term costs of digital preservation. While unsatisfactory from a planning point of view, it may be necessary to estimate expected costs over a short- to medium-term period, such as five years, and to use the knowledge gained in that timeframe to inform more accurate estimates of long-term costs. However, there is always likely to be a problem in estimating the costs of long-term actions that are still unclear, such as migration costs. Some costs do become much easier to predict following a few years' experience in collecting material, preparing it for storage, and protecting it. Some cost assumptions can be reasonably made:

— Development costs are likely to be high, depending on how ambitious the programme is from the start. Systems design is a necessary investment in the long run but it can be a significant set up cost

— There are obvious recurrent costs associated with staff, accommodation, energy supplies, network use, telecommunications costs, storage media such as disks and tapes, and consumables. Although often funded as capital expenditure, equipment and software should be seen as recurrent costs because they will have to be replaced on a regular basis

— The staff costs of working with producers can be high because of the need to address new issues with each change in technology. The costs of negotiating rights may vary depending on the complexity of rights ownership and on whether or not rights need to be purchased

— The costs of identifying and selecting materials for preservation are likely to be low per unit, but there may be many units. A nonselective approach may reduce costs, although adding to long-term preservation costs overall, as more material must be stored, processed, preserved and organised for access. Human judgments about selection are expensive where labour costs are high; automating decisions may reduce costs if the high set-up costs can be spread over a large amount of material, and if it is feasible to automate what are often complex human judgments

— The costs of collecting or transferring materials are likely to be low per unit but large programmes may generate significant transfer costs overall. This may incorporate high transmission costs where automated gathering searches and downloads large amounts of data. The cost of quality control checking is likely to be high unless it can be automated

— Converting material to a restricted range of standard formats may be inexpensive if the conversion is easy, but expensive if individual handcrafting or correction is needed. However, there may be considerable long-term cost benefits in being able to deal with a restricted range of formats

— The costs of describing material and adding metadata are likely to be high because of the amount of information to be recorded, and the difficulty of finding it in some cases. Costs could be greatly reduced by producers using more standardised structures and creating good metadata and documentation themselves. For heavily standardised formats such as those widely used for archival versions of images and audio, costs will be reduced by automated gathering of metadata from files and during production processes

— Costs associated with storage are theoretically low and decreasing, but in total they reflect the amount of data to be stored, which may be large. Estimates of storage and processing costs should take account of backups and multiple versions of material. The cost of regularly copying data to new media is generally discounted by regular increases in storage densities

— The costs of providing means of access - such as analysing data structures, writing new code for migration, writing or finding emulators, quality checking, and so on -may be high or low, depending on how difficult the process turns out to be. For example, if a conversion software tool can be developed that works automatically for millions of similar files, the unit costs may be extremely low, although the total cost of computer time could still be significant. On the other hand, strategies that must be managed item by item will be very expensive

— Computer costs to store and serve large numbers of access copies, or to generate them on request, should not be ignored. These would generally not be counted as preservation costs, but preservation programmes may still have to bear them as part of their business function.

Where the material is very similar and well organised, and where the preservation tasks are straightforward, it may be possible to automate most processes and reduce staffing requirements to a minimum. On the other hand, where repeated human intervention is needed, the programme will need staff who are adequately equipped to provide it. It is very hard to automate processes that require subjective judgments, although not impossible. Even highly automated programmes, however, will eventually need staff to deal with changes in the operating environment and with the need to replace systems.

Programme managers need to have:

— Good problem solving skills, and an ability to deal with complex problems for which there may be no current long-term answers

— A pro-active approach that considers short-term, medium-term and long-term issues

— Adequate awareness of the relevant technical, preservation, corporate, legal and political aspects

— An ability to think critically, but also to receive new ideas and to adapt to change

— Collaborative abilities and in interest in sharing information and looking for ways to work with others.

Preservation programmes require sophisticated systems and tools, although small programmes dealing with largely un-automated processes and with carriers that can be stored on shelves may be able to get by using quite modest computer equipment that is already available. Where services have been contracted from an outside supplier, the programme itself may not need to provide much of the technological infrastructure.

The systems and tools likely to be required include those for:

- Storing and managing the collection material
- Storing and managing metadata
- Managing the transfer of material to the collection, possibly including gathering
- Managing information about rights and managing access in accord with rights
- Storing and managing accessibility tools such as original software, plug-ins, conversion and emulation programmes
- Searching by users
- Making appropriate copies available for users
- Managing many of the processes described in these guidelines, especially those that generate management information, copy material from one place or format to another, or require automated process checking.

Procurement of appropriate systems is a significant task, requiring special attention to specifications and the evaluation of options. Some existing programmes are willing to share information on the specifications they have used and their experience in procuring suitable systems.

Tools for Preservation Programmes

Standards lie behind almost everything that computers do, so they form a crucial foundation to the creation and use of digital materials. However, they have not yet been great enablers of preservation. They can be expected to make several important contributions if they are well chosen and well used. Those contributions can be seen in:

— The creation of digital materials that should be relatively straightforward to preserve. Some file formats (themselves standardised) have proven to be so widely useful that they have been adopted by creator communities as a best practice, raising the prospect that they will continue to be used for a long time. Examples include the Tagged Interchange File Format (TIFF) for images, and the Structured General Markup Language (SGML) family of formats including HTML and XML, for structured documents

— Where such widely adopted formats are based on open source, non-proprietary specifications (as is the case with TIFF and SGML); it should be relatively easy to find or develop tools when they are needed to provide ongoing access across changes in technologies

— Agreed approaches to a number of preservation processes, including the recording of metadata, migration processes, data protection and item identification. Standards are still evolving in these areas

— Defining the responsibilities and functions of certain kinds of preservation programmes. The outstanding example of this to date is the Reference Model for an Open Archival Information System (OAIS), accepted by the International Standards Organisation in 2002.

Standards should not be seen as a preservation panacea. Even where they exist, they are subject to change, versioning and non-standard use by producers. Many format standards are in fact proprietary specifications that may not be publicly available, so it may be impossible to know whether tools for future access will be available. While increased standardisation of processes can only help preservation programmes, it is important not to wait for a single 'digital preservation standard' to emerge before taking sensible preservation action.

There are many different models that have been used as organisational structures to manage digital preservation. Some possibilities include:

— Setting up a single separate digital preservation unit to look after all aspects

— A series of specialist units looking after different aspects

— A matrix of people working in different areas, responsible to an overall programme manager

— Mainstreaming of the work through existing work areas so that it becomes part of the normal work integrated with other operations

— Embedding the programme in a particular existing work area such as IT, preservation, collection development, or collection management sections.

These different models tend to produce different emphases, reflecting various levels of comfort with IT tools, collecting objectives, preservation thinking, etc. Any model can be made to work effectively, so long as it draws on the perspectives and skills that are needed and has strong management support.

Preservation programmes should be guided by a policy framework that says what the programme is trying to do and how it will try to achieve it. In a field of such complexity and evolving understandings, a policy document needs to provide clear, long-term direction as well as regularly reviewed guidance. In implementing policy and developing action plans, it is almost always necessary to decide what issues, actions and materials should be given priority for attention, and to understand what work is critical before other work can be attempted. There may be alternative paths for achieving the preservation commitments of the programme.

Organisations should consider whether they will get a better result from doing the work in-house, or by contracting with someone else to do it, or by a combination of approaches. Many processes such as storage and documentation may be amenable to contracting, which may offer access to specialised expertise and facilities that would not be available otherwise. In many cases, programmes may not be able to afford the initial investments involved in setting up and maintaining infrastructure, so paying for someone else to provide services may be attractive. Contracting may present some potential risks, including:

— Creating a distance between programme objectives and service provision

— The possibility of being locked into the service provider's services because the cost of seeking alternatives is greater than the cost of continuing

— Less control over what happens on a day-to-day basis

— Higher costs (they may also be lower) than in-house arrangements over the long term

— Fewer learning opportunities that might suggest better ways of doing things.

The success of contracting may depend on the programme manager's ability to define what is needed; finding a reliable supplier who can offer the services required at a suitable price; being able to negotiate a suitable contract with adequate safeguards; and skills in managing the contract. In working with service providers, preservation managers must ensure they:

— Understand their business and what they need to achieve

— Communicate their needs

— Rigorously assess the capabilities, motivations, and understandings of potential suppliers

— Prepare and negotiate an appropriate contract

— Ensure communication channels are open so that any problems that be reported early

— Monitor performance closely and evaluate arrangements regularly. Ensure there are responsible exit strategies and succession plans in place for when arrangements come to an end.

There are good technological, economic and political reasons for preservation programmes to cooperate. Decisions about collaboration should be based on assessment of the benefits expected and the costs involved. There are a number of possibilities regarding where to look for partners, what the focus of the relationship should be, and structural frameworks that would be suitable. Successful cooperation is usually the result of careful attention to these choices, and to putting in the effort required to manage the collaboration in practice.

Perspectives of Management

Digital heritage and collaboration go together very well. The technology of digital materials supports collaboration: such materials are easy to duplicate, and many are designed for networked access, so remote management is not difficult. It is also expensive - often too expensive - to set up the whole infrastructure of digital preservation for every preservation programme, so there is a strong incentive to look for ways of sharing facilities.

There may even be a political imperative to work cooperatively: the community may reasonably expect that programmes will collaborate to ensure as much digital heritage as possible can be preserved, as coherently as possible.

Organisational priorities can be sidetracked by problems in the collaborative relationship itself, taking attention away from the real mission of preserving digital materials. In the face of such potential costs and difficulties, it is important to identify the benefits that any collaboration is meant to deliver. Benefits driving a cooperative effort could include:

— Access to a wider range of expertise
— Shared development costs
— Access to tools and systems that might otherwise be unavailable
— Shared learning opportunities
— Increased coverage of preserved materials
— Better planning to reduce wasted effort
— Encouragement for other influential stakeholders to take preservation seriously
— Shared influence on agreements with producers
— Shared influence on research and development of standards and practices
— Attraction of resources and other support for well-coordinated programmes at a regional, national or sectoral level.

The benefits of collaboration usually do not happen by accident, but result from careful attention to choices. Programmes need to consider their potential partners, ways of working together, structural models, and the steps involved in making the proposed collaboration work. Potential partners are likely to be others working in the same sector. Examples could include a consortium of university libraries, or networks of data archives, or government agencies agreeing to use the same application software, or a group of recording studios sharing storage facilities for masters.

It may be possible to join an existing collaboration, or to form new partnerships. However, there may also be benefits to be gained from looking beyond sectoral boundaries, especially as digital technologies and users expectations are increasingly blurring the edges between sectors. For example, a number of libraries, archives, research institutes, data archives and producers in a regional area may consider joining forces to develop a local programme that meets all their needs.

There may also be opportunities for formal cooperative arrangements between preservation programmes and interested stakeholders including groups of producers, industry peak bodies, user groups, IT industry groups, or government bodies interested in fostering good practice. There are many ways that preservation programmes can work together, depending on the benefits they want to achieve and what each partner has to offer. They include:

— *Shared standards*: agreements to do things in the same ways, either with a view to interoperability between programmes, or simply based on a shared understanding of what practices will best support preservation objectives

— *Information sharing*: agreements to share information either at a general level or on specific issues, such as procurement specifications or research results

— *Speaking with a common voice*: agreements to develop and present a common message in advocacy campaigns, or in publicity aimed at raising the profile of digital heritage preservation

— *Division of labour*: agreements to work together at an operational level, taking preservation steps in a coordinated way, with responsibilities either carried out in parallel or divided between programmes

— *Shared resources*: agreements to share resources such as systems, staff or funds to work on a common programme.

Technical and Practical Perspectives

It is usually necessary to decide what digital materials are worth keeping, as has been the case with non-digital materials. Many of the same approaches - selection based on criteria embodied in collection development policies, and good knowledge of the materials and their context - are fundamental for digital heritage selection. Preservation programmes also need to define the elements or characteristics of the materials they select that give them value, so that those elements can be maintained.

Deciding what should be preserved, by whom, and for how long, have been fundamental decisions in managing all kinds of tangible heritage. Such decisions are necessary because there are usually more things - more information, more records, more publications, more data than we have the means to keep. Every choice to preserve is at the expense of something else.

The selection of digital heritage is conceptually the same as selection of non-digital materials. Any existing programme with well-established procedures for assessing and selecting material for preservation will already have policies, skills and tools that can help in selecting digital materials, even though they may need some adjustment. However, digital materials do present some new challenges that programme managers must take into account in making the best selection decisions they can.

— There is often a large amount of material to be assessed

— The means of producing and disseminating digital materials are widely available, so their quality is often inconsistent

— At the same time, there may be pressure to preserve the entire traffic carried by new communication channels such as the World Wide Web, regardless of quality

— Timing of selection is usually critical, as digital materials quickly de-select themselves by becoming unusable. It may not be possible to wait for evidence of enduring value to emerge before making selection decisions

— Some digital objects may be hard to pin down. New genres may not fit into existing classifications; some digital resources consist of linked or overlapping parts; many also exist in parallel versions.

— Even when external boundaries have been defined, it may be hard to tell which elements need to be maintained if the digital object is to fulfil its essential purpose

— It may even be difficult to tell where digital materials come from, making it hard to decide who is responsible for their preservation and with whom to negotiate the rights required by preservation programmes.

There are dangers in assuming that current value assessments are a completely reliable guide to future values. For example, remote sensing data collected in previous decades has become unexpectedly important for assessing environmental change. This experience suggests it is probably better to err on the side of collecting more material rather than less, if the preservation programme can manage it.

Where digital materials can only be understood by reference to a set of rules such as a record keeping system, database or data generation system, or other contextual information, selection processes must identify the documentation that will also need to be preserved. Producers of digital materials may have a significant role to play in selecting what should be preserved. They are often well placed to understand why digital objects were brought into being, their essential 'message', and the relationships between objects and their context. If that information is not captured from the producer it may be too difficult to reconstruct it later. Both comprehensive and selective approaches are supported by strong arguments. Advocates of a comprehensive approach argue that any information may turn out to have long-term value, and that the costs of detailed selection are greater than the costs of collecting and storing everything.

Advocates of a more selective approach argue that it allows them to create collections of high value resources, with some assurance of technical quality and an opportunity to negotiate access rights with producers. There may well be a place for both approaches, as they are likely to produce quite different collections of digital heritage that are valued for different purposes.

To minimise the risk of important materials being missed, and to avoid unnecessary duplication of effort, it may be necessary to seek agreements with other potential collecting and preservation agencies about respective roles and responsibilities. Selection policies may have to decide whether to select whole items and whole collections, or samples only. It is generally preferable to preserve whole items to retain their integrity, but it may be necessary to restrict collecting to representative samples as a way of at least evidencing the existence of some kinds of materials. Selection policy may also have to consider whether the re-use of material constitutes a new item that should also be preserved.

Rights issues may influence selection decisions. Preservation programmes often select materials that are still subject to rights, but generally would not select material if rights were so restrictive that arrangements for giving access at some future stage cannot be negotiated. If the material can never be made available for use, or if necessary preservation steps cannot be taken, there is little point in selecting it as heritage material. Managing selection also requires the development of criteria for appraisal. Where the amount of material is so large that it is not feasible to assess items individually, it may be necessary to establish classes of material that can be assessed on the basis of representative samples. Preservation programmes often act as agents for other stakeholders: they take preservation action on behalf of someone who wants material kept for a reason. The 'someone else' may be as broad and many-faceted as 'the nation' or 'the general community', who may mandate a programme to collect and preserve a very broad range of materials; or it may be as narrow as the members of an organisation or researchers working in a particular discipline who want their own research output preserved for later use. The needs of the 'community' - however defined - for whom the material is being kept will drive many decisions, from what material is selected, to the kind and level of documentation that is recorded, to the level of concern with authenticity, to the strategies that are used. For example, some programmes must offer users the option of interrogating old data to produce new results, whereas others have a brief to present material in a read-only form to that it cannot be changed or manipulated.

Some programmes may even have to ensure users can run old simulations, play old computer games, or view digital art in ways that reproduce the original experience rather than a speeded up experience that later technologies may provide. Defining the essential elements or characteristics is not conceptually difficult, as the examples above illustrate. In some circumstances - such as clearly defined and constrained user expectations, and easily characterised materials that are all similar - defining and encoding the essential elements should be straightforward.

For instance, a programme may decide that users of a large collection of electronic mail messages only need to see elements that can be characterised as 'content information', such as the name and address of the sender, subject, date and time, recipients, and the message, in a standardised structure with only the most simple of formatting. A government archive with this approach could expect to apply this essential elements template to very large numbers of email records. On the other hand, some materials are much more difficult to characterise, and expectations about how they will be re-presented for use, especially to an open-ended community of potential users, may be so hard to define in advance that it becomes almost impossible.

Approaches to this issue are developing as more people encounter the problems of describing, storing and planning to re-present digital objects in growing collections over long periods of time. Preservation programmes with few resources must still make decisions about the materials for which they accept responsibility. Because the costs of preservation are related to the amount of material to be managed, such programmes may need to be highly selective, limiting their ambitions to a small amount of highly valued material. Preservation costs are also related to the range of problems and formats that need to be managed, so it may also make sense to severely limit the kinds of materials selected to a very few formats. Collecting agreements with other programmes may shift some of the burden of selecting materials.

While these would normally be negotiated with other preservation programmes, there may be potential for agreements with producers that would lead them to make decisions about what should be collected and preserved. The preservation programme would still need to take some responsibility for quality control, as well as articulating the criteria by which material should be chosen. Digital heritage is often created without consideration of ongoing use and accessibility. However, there are definitely standards and practices that producers can use that either help or hinder preservation. Programme managers need to look for ways of exerting a positive influence from as early in the digital heritage life cycle as possible. This often requires a willingness to work with producers. Digital materials are created by producers who are not necessarily concerned with long-term availability: creation of 'digital heritage' may not be part of their intention.

Even those hoping to make something of enduring value may not have the knowledge or the means to do so, or be constrained by other impediments in their working environment. Without some kind of intervention, it is unlikely that digital heritage materials will automatically be made in ways that will minimise costs and remove barriers to preservation. Many practices in fact make preservation much harder. Preservation efforts that wait until problems start to appear are likely to be more costly, more difficult, and less effective than efforts that start early.

Organisations that have both heritage-creating and heritage-preserving functions have learnt from experience that care invested from the start in the use of standards, documentation, good file management and other practices, pays dividends later in lower preservation and maintenance costs, as well as more easily accessed, re-used and managed collections. While all preservation programmes do not have the same opportunities to influence production practices, all programmes should seek to influence the way materials are created, and managed, from as early in their life cycle as possible. It is important to recognise that creators of digital materials work in different environments and are likely to be quite diverse in many ways: how they approach their work, their size of operations, the organisational and technical support at their disposal, and their interest in long-term access issues.

For example, scientists collecting data are likely to have an overriding interest in how accurately and securely their data is protected; how well any proposed formats and standards fit with their working needs; the convenience of transfer arrangements; and maintenance of moral rights and access controls over their data. On the other hand, commercial publishers of CD-ROM packages are likely to be more interested in controls on unauthorised copying; the costs and risks associated with providing 'unprotected' versions to a preservation programme; the potential re-use of their content; and their licence obligations to software owners whose products they have used. There are many ways in which those responsible for preserving digital heritage may approach working with those who create and disseminate it. Preservation programmes should proactively promote awareness of their own role.

It may be advantageous to identify particular groups of producers and work with them, addressing specific issues, rather than trying to resolve everyone's concerns at a generic level. At a broader industry level, it may be helpful to develop a code of practice that sets out agreed understandings about roles and responsibilities, and defines the scope and terms of ongoing cooperation. Many sectors have active industry groups that provide forums for discussing issues.

As well as offering opportunities for dialogue with industry leaders, such forums may help in establishing new norms of thinking that incorporate a longer term perspective. It is important for preservation programmes to offer positive encouragement and feedback for the steps producers are willing to take, and to provide a level of accountability for the way preservation programmes deal with their materials. In many situations, working with producers means a real input by the preservation programme, not just the producer. Possible areas of input may include:

— Providing written guidelines and specifications
— Providing training for staff
— Help in designing systems and workflows
— Exchange of information and working tips
— Succession arrangements for material in a producer-managed preservation programme.

Digital preservation programmes with few resources may find they are unable to spare any resources to work with producers. However, it may be possible to make a worthwhile investment in reducing future costs by taking limited, targeted actions aimed at influencing the material they have to manage.

Bibliography

Abid, A., *Memory of the World: preserving our documentary heritage*. Paris: UNESCO, Information and Informatics Division, July 1997.

Bearman, D., Archival data management to achieve organizational accountability for electronic records. *Archives and Manuscripts*, 21, 1993, 14-28. Reprinted in: Bearman, D., Electronic *evidence*. Pittsburgh, Pa.: Archives and Museum Informatics, 1994, 12-33.

______________ ., Record-keeping systems. *Archivaria*, 36, 1993, 16-36. Reprinted in: Bearman, D., Electronic *evidence*. Pittsburgh, Pa.: Archives and Museum Informatics, 1994, 34-70.

______________ ., The implications of Armstrong v. Executive Office of the President for the archival management of electronic records. *American Archivist*, 56, 1993, 674-689. Reprinted in: Bearman, D., Electronic *evidence*. Pittsburgh, Pa.: Archives and Museum Informatics, 1994, 118-144.

______________ ., "Electronic evidence: strategies for managing records in contemporary organizations". Pittsburgh, Pa.: *Archives and Museum Informatics*, 1994.

Cook, T., The impact of David Bearman on modern archival thinking: an essay of personal reflection and critique. Archives and Museum Informatics, 11, 1997.

Cox, R.J., Electronic information technology and the archivist: bright lights, lingering concerns. *American Archivist*, 55, 1992.

______________ , Readings in archives and electronic records: annotated bibliography and analysis of the literature. In: Hedstrom, M. (ed.) Electronic *records management program strategies*. Archives and Museum Informatics Technical Report, No. 18. Pittsburgh, Pa.: Archives and Museum Informatics, 1993, 97-152.

______________ ., *The first generation of* electronic *records archivists in the United States: a study in professionalization*. Binghamton, N.Y.: Haworth Press, 1994.

Gertz, J., Selection for preservation: a digital solution for illustrated texts. *Library Resources & Technical Services*, 40 (1), 1997, 380-401.

Graham, P.S., Intellectual preservation and the electronic environment. In: Hirshon, A. (ed.) *After the* electronic *revolution, will you be the first to go? Proceedings of the 1992 Association for Library Collections and Technical Services President's Program*. Chicago: American Library Association, 18-38.

Kenney, A.R. and Personius, L.K., *The Cornell/Xerox/Commission on* Preservation *and Access joint study in digital* preservation. Report: Phase 1, Digital capture, paper facsimiles and network access. Washington, D.C.: Commission on Preservation and Access, 1992.

McInnes, S., Electronic records: the new archival frontier? *Journal of the Society of Archivists*, 19 (2), 1998, 211-220.

_______________ ., Optical disk vs. magnetic storage. Westport, Conn.: Meckler, 1990.

Saffady, W., Optical storage technology, 1990-91: a state of the art review. Westport, Conn.: Meckler, 1990.

Index